The Military and Domestic Politics

By creatively applying concordance theory to five unique settings, Rebecca Schiff has made an invaluable contribution to civil–military studies. This is a most timely reference for social scientists, military leaders, and concerned citizens.

The late Charles C. Moskos
Professor Emeritus of Sociology
Northwestern University

Rebecca Schiff's work on concordance theory brings an important perspective to the study of civil–military relations. Her sophisticated and well written analysis deserves a wide audience of military professionals, academicians, and interested civilians. It is highly recommended for graduate and advanced undergraduate classes in national security policy and military professionalism.

John Allen Williams
Professor of Political Science, Loyola University Chicago
Chair and President, Inter-University Seminar on Armed Forces and Society

The intervention of the military in national politics and the everyday lives of citizens is a key issue in civil–military relations. This book explains how concordance theory can provide a model for predicting such domestic intervention.

Models dealing with the relationship between the military and society are usually based on Western nations with power and influence, and therefore may not be appropriate for the circumstances of non-Western countries. By contrast, concordance theory considers national contexts where the balance of military involvement in civilian life depends greatly on historical circumstances, institutional nuances, and cultural realities. Using five case studies – India, Pakistan, Israel, Argentina, and post-revolutionary United States – this book challenges traditional views on the role of the military in society and offers convincing examples for the continued application of concordance theory. It also explores the evolution of the theory from the field of military studies to one of "corporate concordance."

This book will be of much interest to advanced students of civil–military relations, military sociology, political science, and US politics.

Rebecca L. Schiff is currently the Associate Director of Corporate and Foundation Relations at Harvard Law School. She is also an adjunct professor at the U.S. Naval War College in Newport, Rhode Island. She has a Ph.D. in Political Science from the University of Chicago.

Cass military studies

Intelligence Activities in Ancient Rome
Trust in the gods, but verify
Rose Mary Sheldon

Clausewitz and African War
Politics and strategy in Liberia and Somalia
Isabelle Duyvesteyn

Strategy and Politics in the Middle East, 1954–60
Defending the northern tier
Michael Cohen

The Cuban Intervention in Angola, 1965–1991
From Che Guevara to Cuito Cuanavale
Edward George

Military Leadership in the British Civil Wars, 1642–1651
'The genius of this age'
Stanley Carpenter

Israel's Reprisal Policy, 1953–1956
The dynamics of military retaliation
Ze'ev Drory

Bosnia and Herzegovina in the Second World War
Enver Redzic

Leaders in War
West Point Remembers the 1991 Gulf War
Edited by Frederick Kagan and Christian Kubik

Khedive Ismail's Army
John Dunn

Yugoslav Military Industry 1918–1991
Amadeo Watkins

Corporal Hitler and the Great War 1914–1918
The list regiment
John Williams

Rostóv in the Russian Civil War, 1917–1920
The key to victory
Brian Murphy

The Tet Effect, Intelligence and the Public Perception of War
Jake Blood

The US Military Profession into the 21st Century
War, peace and politics
Edited by Sam C. Sarkesian and Robert E. Connor, Jr.

Civil–Military Relations in Europe
Learning from crisis and institutional
change
Edited by Hans Born,
Marina Caparini, Karl Haltiner and
Jürgen Kuhlmann

Strategic Culture and Ways of War
Lawrence Sondhaus

**Military Unionism in the Post-Cold
War Era**
A future reality?
Edited by Richard Bartle and
Lindy Heinecken

Warriors and Politicians
U.S. civil–military relations under
stress
Charles A. Stevenson

**Military Honour and the Conduct
of War**
From Ancient Greece to Iraq
Paul Robinson

**Military Industry and Regional
Defense Policy**
India, Iraq and Israel
Timothy D. Hoyt

Managing Defence in a Democracy
Edited by Laura R. Cleary and
Teri McConville

Gender and the Military
Women in the armed forces of western
democracies
Helena Carreiras

Social Sciences and the Military
An interdisciplinary overview
Edited by Giuseppe Caforio

**Cultural Diversity in the Armed
Forces**
An international comparison
Edited by Joseph Soeters and
Jan van der Meulen

**Railways and the Russo-Japanese
War**
Transporting war
Felix Patrikeeff and Harold Shukman

War and Media Operations
The US military and the press from
Vietnam to Iraq
Thomas Rid

Ancient China on Postmodern War
Enduring ideas from the Chinese
strategic tradition
Thomas Kane

**Special Forces, Terrorism and
Strategy**
Warfare by other means
Alasdair Finlan

Imperial Defence, 1856–1956
The old world order
Greg Kennedy

**Civil–Military Cooperation in
Post-Conflict Operations**
Emerging theory and practice
Christopher Ankersen

Military Advising and Assistance
From mercenaries to privatization,
1815–2007
Donald Stoker

Private Military and Security Companies
Ethics, policies and civil–military relations
Edited by Andrew Alexandra, Deane-Peter Baker and Marina Caparini

Military Cooperation in Multinational Peace Operations
Managing cultural diversity and crisis response
Edited by Joseph Soeters and Philippe Manigart

The Military and Domestic Politics
A concordance theory of civil–military relations
Rebecca L. Schiff

The Military and Domestic Politics

A concordance theory of
civil–military relations

Rebecca L. Schiff

Routledge
Taylor & Francis Group

LONDON AND NEW YORK

First published 2009
by Routledge
2 Park Square, Milton Park, Abingdon, Oxon OX14 4RN

Simultaneously published in the USA and Canada
by Routledge
270 Madison Ave, New York, NY 10016

Routledge is an imprint of the Taylor & Francis Group, an informa business

Typeset in Times by Wearset Ltd, Boldon, Tyne and Wear
Printed and bound in Great Britain by TJI Digital, Padstow, Cornwall

British Library Cataloguing in Publication Data
A catalogue record for this book is available from the British Library

Library of Congress Cataloging in Publication Data
The military and domestic politics : a concordance theory of civil-military
relations / Rebecca L. Schiff.
p. cm. – (Cass military studies)
"Simultaneously published in the USA and Canada by Routledge."
Includes bibliographical references.
1. Civil-military relations. 2. Civil-military relations–Case studies. I. Title.
JF195.S26 2008
322'.501–dc22   2008007522

ISBN10: 0-415-77340-7 (hbk)
ISBN10: 0-203-89230-5 (ebk)

ISBN13: 978-0-415-77340-9 (hbk)
ISBN13: 978-0-203-89230-5 (ebk)

Contents

Acknowledgments

This book is dedicated to the memory of my father, Elias Schiff, and to my mother, Gloria Schiff. My parents were both immigrants who came to the United States and worked very hard to provide a warm and supportive family environment. My father's Eastern European heritage and my mother's Hispanic origins created a unique combination of wisdom, cultural awareness, and motivation to inspire me to never give up or settle for anything but the best. My persistence in writing this book, at the right time, during my professional and personal odyssey is a testament to their creativity, sensitivity, and trust in my pursuits. In addition to my academic work, I have spent many years in philanthropy, including corporate philanthropy, individual major gifts, and raising scholarship funds for students to study and pursue their dreams. My parents simply assumed I would have dreams, and they never questioned their active support in helping me make them come true. My father, whom I lost while completing my doctorate at the University of Chicago, is sorely missed. He was an extraordinary father whose insight and advice for the first 25 years of my life gave me the confidence and the freedom to embrace challenge and opportunity. My mother continues to provide moral support and constant encouragement. I am grateful to both of my parents for their kindness, generosity, and unconditional love.

I would also like to thank colleagues and friends who watched the layers of this project unfold over the years and provided valuable guidance, advice, and important experiences along the way. My interdisciplinary dissertation committee at the University of Chicago encouraged the development of concordance theory: Susanne Rudolph, Marvin Zonis, Moshe Lissak, and John Mearsheimer. I particularly thank Moshe Lissak from the Hebrew University for taking me on as his student during my dissertation fieldwork and post-doctoral year in Jerusalem; he also graciously agreed to serve on my dissertation committee. His expertise in sociology and Israeli and Jewish history were pivotal in applying concordance theory to the original Israeli case study. Susanne and Lloyd Rudolph introduced me to the importance of cultural studies in political science and its profound impact on India and Pakistan.

Randy Billings from Harvard University provided me with the opportunity to learn the development profession from world-class fundraising professionals.

Randy is a wonderful mentor and role model, and I thank him for his support and wisdom.

As the Director of Alumni Giving at the Harvard School of Public Health, I learned how philanthropy truly affects the lives and generations of individuals and entire populations. My early Harvard development career had a profound impact on my work in civil–military relations. I learned that academic and theoretical training were simply not enough to gain the institutional and cultural perspective that is required for an uncommon understanding of this field. My professional development experience deepened my appreciation of academic theory and its benefits to the world. Development and philanthropy enhance and borrow from the social sciences by embracing skills found in fields such as anthropology and sociology. My years of building relationships with Harvard alumni and scholars, connecting their individual interests to far-reaching domestic and global enterprises, have enriched my perspective on civil–military relations. An effective fundraiser simply cannot think dichotomously – too many life-altering interests are at stake and must be stewarded with the utmost care and sophistication. Development became the professional linchpin in deepening my political science expertise and helped me to understand the broader global relationships and subtle connections between the military, the political elites, and the citizens.

I thank Nancy Winship, Robert Silk, and Marty Krauss at Brandeis University for providing me with a unique professional opportunity in Corporate and Foundation Relations. This development experience, in particular, had a strong influence on Chapter 8 which offers my perspective on the military–industrial complex as it relates to corporate philanthropy.

I thank Betty Smith for my very first development position in higher education at the University of Michigan and her amazing encouragement throughout the years. She has been a wonderful and important source of moral support throughout much of this odyssey.

I am also indebted to the following role models, colleagues, friends, and organizations: John Allen Williams, Robert Vitas, the late Charles C. Moskos, Stephen P. Cohen, James Burk, David Mares, Patricia Shields, Gabi Scheffer, Richard S. Wells, Oren Barak, Anit Mukherjee, Dafna Shaked, Alex Roland, Ronald Krebs, David Woodruff, Bryan Rogers, Patty Shea, Margaret Loret, Anne Hubbard, Nadine Lambert, Julie Brown, Margaret Trevor, Catherine D'Amato, Barbara Ackley, Sarita Bhalotra, Robert "Uncle Bob" Myers, Sandra Myers, Karin Kiewra, Ricky Fine, Jane Jaquette, Megan Casey, Kathryn Graves, Colleen Capodilupo, Richard Jacobson, Marie Gaines, Lisa Ginex, Becky Robert, Kelly Wesley, Emily Giske, Bayla Spiegel, Julie O'Brien, Richard Babson, Allison Sulke, Andrew Humphries, Colleen Sexton, Michelle Miles, Nancy Davis, Lynne Sherr, Megan Tabor, Elizabeth Birch, Hilary Rosen, Patrick Guerriero, and my girlfriend Chantal Birdsong.

I thank the United States Army for their role in my concluding chapter, particularly Captain Dana C. Rood, First Sergeant Antonio Correa, and Sergeant First Class Justine M. Beaulieu.

Special thanks to Sarah Seewoester.

Finally there is Princess, my feline companion since my Chicago graduate school years, who was close to 100 years old and feisty as ever before she passed away just days after I finished my final book chapter. She is missed.

The Inter-University Seminar on Armed Forces and Society

The Inter-University Seminar on Armed Forces and Society (IUS) is an important combination of scholars, policy makers, and practitioners who have profound interests in the field of civil–military relations. The organization was founded by the father of civil–military relations, Morris Janowitz, perhaps the most renowned military sociologist of this field. Moshe Lissak, one of my dissertation committee members, was a student of Morris Janowitz during the inception of IUS in the early 1960s. I have met a broad array of academics, policy makers, military officers, and researchers who continue to contribute to the diversity and intellectual camaraderie of this organization.

The IUS also has an important journal, *Armed Forces and Society*. Concordance theory was first published by *AF&S*, and the journal continued to be a source of inspiration for my book. For example, James Burk's outstanding treatment of the Federalists which appeared in *AF&S* inspired my book chapter on concordance theory in the post-revolutionary United States. I serve on the editorial board of *AF&S*. But the real driving force behind the journal is Patricia Shields who has steered the direction and international influence of the publication. Pat is also a terrific colleague and friend. Overall, IUS is an organization that provides a critical reservoir for academic integrity and intellectual inclusiveness.

1 Introduction

I have always admired the Kennedys and the stories of their politically successful yet paradoxically tragic lives. And living in Boston has made it almost too
easy to feed my fascination with the Kennedy family. I easily could attend a
Kennedy fundraiser in Hyannis or Washington, DC, or visit JFK's birthplace in
Brookline. At Harvard I could tap into the Kennedy–Harvard mystique. I even
had the opportunity to hear Ted Kennedy speak at a luncheon for the Greater
Boston Food Bank. But despite my fascination with the Kennedy family as a
whole, it was the brother I knew least about who sparked my continued interest
in the family and their ongoing complexity and drama.

I went to see the movie *Bobby* – the story of US Senator Robert F. Kennedy's
1968 assassination – after much anticipation and personal desire to learn more
about him and his life. Much to my surprise, the movie was less about Bobby
Kennedy and more about the people at the Ambassador Hotel who had been
affected by Bobby's run for the presidency and subsequent assassination. I was
disappointed at first to see the great Anthony Hopkins, who played a brilliant
Nixon ten years earlier, perform a rather obscure and secondary role as an
Ambassador Hotel doorman in the movie. I remember my girlfriend turning to
me halfway through the film and remarking, "This should have been called
Everything But *Bobby*."

And then it happened ... Bobby entered the Ambassador Hotel, gave his stun-
ning victory speech that electrified the post-primary election crowd, was ushered
into the hotel kitchen, and was shot in front of his wife, his closest supporters,
the hotel staff, and the entire world. All of the vignettes portraying common
people who were going through their own personal crises and epiphanies, that
seemed so unimportant and distracting throughout the movie, came together in a
fascinating weave of history and popular culture. It was as though I had witnessed the assassination again but this time with a richer understanding of the
complexity, interconnectedness, and relational aspects of the event itself and the
numerous lives affected by Bobby Kennedy's untimely and unanticipated death.
All of a sudden, Hopkins' obscure and undefined character became more
poignant, and it was then that I had my own epiphany about this project on
civil–military relations.

The purpose of this book is to present a topic (the relationship between military and society), a unique theoretical approach (concordance theory), and several case studies, in that order. This book will explain what causes or prevents domestic military intervention in a particular nation from a unique perspective. It is intended for the eyes of policy makers and scholars. And although political science and sociological terminology abound throughout the book, the relationship between the military and society really progresses more like the film *Bobby* – people with unique stories who are part of a drama that will continue to unfold.

Civil–military relations involves the drama between the armed forces of a particular nation, political elites, society at large, and institutions, with the importance of their interconnectedness often not fully realized until a dramatic climax. Scholars and policy makers are so eager to superimpose trained perspectives on political and social situations that they often lose sight of the fact that it is the individual citizens and their unique culture that comprise the expected and the unexpected. This book attempts to cut through the obscure and often unnecessary academic terminology, so that citizens who witnessed the assassination of Bobby Kennedy, citizens who are concerned about current civil–military conflicts in Afghanistan and Iraq, and citizens who wonder about their own military gain a thoughtful perspective on the topic and their relationship to it.

Bobby Kennedy was expected to win the California primary; his assassination was unexpected. But this event, though tragic in itself, should not be isolated from or dwarf the cultural reality of the time that somehow fostered great heroism and great tragedy. It should not ignore the people existing in that cultural space who witnessed and experienced the gruesome killing. It is from this perspective that I approach the topic of civil–military relations, exposing the particular elements of history and individual experience that are often ignored in favor of grand propositions.

Concordance theory is not a grand proposition, but does a good job of explaining both institutionally and culturally why some nations fall prey to domestic military intervention and why others do not. Domestic military intervention may include forcible actions like *coups d'état*, palace revolts, or other forms of takeover by a nation's armed forces.

Concordance theory and civil–military relations are also topical because they are part of the larger themes of nation building and foreign policy making. Civil–military relations is a vital part of the long nation-building continuum: the process of creating the political and social infrastructure that delineates the role of the military. Effects of the nation building or rebuilding process are intertwined with civil–military relations and are continuous; the civil–military relationship continues during the life of a nation, although at some point nation building appears to end as a mature nation emerges. Most recently, the world has witnessed this nation-building continuum in Iraq and parts of Africa as it also witnessed previously in post-World War II Japan and Western Europe.

But a fully established nation does not emerge in a linear pattern with similar, predictable outcomes. Political maturity is culturally and socially distinct for each country. For example, if a nation has a stable government with a delineated military institution but is not considered a Western democracy, it still has achieved successful nation building. Many may not agree with China's form of government, but few would argue its status as a mature nation with an indigenous political and social infrastructure. The father of realist international theory, Hans Morgenthau, understood the domestic role of the military in the nation-building and foreign policy process.

> What gives the factors of geography, natural resources, and industrial capacity their actual importance for the power of a nation is military preparedness ... [it] requires a military establishment capable of supporting the foreign policies pursued. Such ability derives from a number of factors of which the most significant ... are technological innovations, leadership, and the quantity and quality of the armed forces.
>
> (Morgenthau 1973: 121)

Prominent scholars, however, believed that if nations did not achieve a Western-style democracy, then, regardless of military strength, modern nation building was not complete (Shils 1962). It will be argued later in this book that mature nations may not necessarily include countries significantly influenced by Western models. Moreover, emerging nations may achieve concordance among the military, political elites, and citizenry regarding the role and function of the armed forces within indigenous governments while not conforming to Western governmental standards. In other words, governments often shift in levels of representation and institutional involvement within society.

In addition, the concept of "modernity" is far more fluid than Western scholars often propose. The chapters on India, Pakistan, and Israel, for example, reflect nations that possess an amalgam of traditional and modern attributes, sometimes borrowed from the West yet frequently derived from their non-Western social customs and cultural norms. But this amalgam of modern and traditional attributes with indigenous political and social institutions does not necessarily preclude successful concordance or agreement among the military, political elites, and citizenry over the role of the armed forces.

Today, the United States' nation-building process has reached maturity; yet, the country's political and social dynamic continues to evolve, and the relationship between political elites and the citizenry develops within a healthy democracy in partnership with the armed forces. In 1790, as Chapter 4 will demonstrate, the United States began this process of nation building. President Washington, the citizen militias, and local political elites were trying to bring order to the young nation with a new constitution, new political structures, and ongoing internal and external threat conditions posed by countries such as Britain and France. The United States' nation-building process lasted almost 100 years – it achieved early eighteenth-century success, fell into civil war, and evolved into a unified democracy. Its emergence as a nation involved "evolution" and "process" – key words to consider in the lengthy route to a mature nation.

Presently, however, nation building often appears out of sync with US political and social culture. We do not have the patience for century-long infrastructural transitions – not with e-mail, podcasts, and the most sophisticated military and computer technology at our fingertips. But nation building, even in this high-tech era, cannot be rushed. There exist political legacies, cultural and religious traditions, and entire populations inexperienced in participatory politics. In many ways our superconductor world is at odds with centuries of native tribal and religious conflict. Consequently, when the pressure is on to "make it happen"– get that infrastructure up and running, stop the tribal infighting, hold free elections, and join our United Nations – the emerging nations are like high school football teams playing against the New England Patriots in the Super Bowl. It is not that nations can't make it happen; it is that their nation-building process has yet to evolve and may not evolve for 100 years, as was the case for the United States.

Indeed, some US policy makers understand the complexity of the process and often prefer not to lend our military support and become entangled in another country's nation-building efforts. During recent presidential campaigns, both Republican and Democratic candidates were careful to delineate the role of the US military as fighters and winners of wars, not as nation builders. Having the military bogged down in institutional development and foreign cultural entanglements, it is argued, only diminishes the army's ability to protect the United States. Nevertheless, the United States experienced the evolution of its own military during the eighteenth and nineteenth centuries while in the process of creating a US political and social infrastructure.

The relationship between the military and society is critical during the earliest stages of building or rebuilding a nation. As the United States experienced its own era of citizen militias in the 1790s, India and Pakistan (see Chapter 5) had very different early nation-building experiences and contrasting civil–military relations outcomes. After a nation matures politically, the civil–military relationship continues as long as there are political institutions, armed forces, and a citizenry willing to take part in this evolutionary process.

Today in Iraq, we are conflicted and discouraged about the nation-building process. American generations (and their children) who experienced the Kennedy legacy, the Vietnam War, and the protests that followed are uncomfortable with having US troops fight in Iraq and elsewhere for a prolonged period of time. The discomfort appears both generational and pressing. Vietnam seared our memories with an anti-war perspective that was briefly overcome by more recent generations, parents in particular, who witnessed the horror of September 11 and supported foreign policies that would protect their children and country. But the belief in this vote for increased national security was that the security response and protection would come quickly – get in and out of Afghanistan, topple Saddam Hussein, and punish the al-Qaeda terrorists who dared to penetrate US territory.

During World War II, the response to Japan's attack on United States soil was quick, devastating, and precise. After a few years of avoiding overt involvement in the conflict, the United States declared war on Japan and mobilized forces on the Pacific front. By 1943 Japan's advance began to falter and the tides of war started to turn, ensuring the Allied victory in 1945. Certainly with our cutting-edge warfare technology we could end the current War on Terror more rapidly and with less collateral damage to civilian populations than we did in Japan. But today's enemies have become more insidious and less prone to "Western" reform. Moreover, US military institutions are at risk because the military objectives lack the clarity of World War II. Multidimensional cultural features often confuse military objectives and create a spectrum of conflict not seen in previous wars. US citizens' perspectives on national security and foreign policy are stuck in the Cold War mentality of a clearly defined enemy and are focused on good versus evil.

The United States' separation of civil and military institutions, while preventing US domestic military intervention, has also created a cultural alienation between American citizens and the US military. Citizen respect of US military institutions "from a distance" and lack of participation in them creates a dilemma that greatly impacts our foreign policy, especially during periods of external threat. Sarkesian *et al.* (2002: 149) understand this dilemma:

> Yet for most people, lack of personal military experience makes it more difficult to evaluate military-related issues, especially those concerning the internal dynamics of the military itself. Such personal disassociation from the military weakens the ability of civilian society to make informed judgments about military issues, let alone influence military decision-making.

These authors further add: "The gap between US perceptions and realities of the security environment poses a challenging and often dangerous dilemma for US national security policy" (Sarkesian *et al.* 2002: 149, 42).

Concordance theory encourages the discussion and incorporation of the multidimensional institutional and cultural qualities that all nations possess. While US policy makers and military officers understand the estrangement that often occurs between the military and civilian realms, they also are wary of tampering with the civil–military institutional separation that has been the US status quo since World War II. That status quo has effectively prevented domestic military intervention in the United States and has for the most part kept US citizens at a comfort level in their daily lives that is uninvolved with the rigors and unpleasant realities of military business. "You can't handle the truth!" – the famous line uttered by Jack Nicholson as a Marine Corps general in the movie *A Few Good Men* – illustrates that we as civilians really don't want to handle the truths of military and war. But as the War on Terror hits closer to home, we are forced to think about the grizzlier side of foreign policy involvement, the impact it has on civilians at home and abroad, and its affect on indigenous cultures both out there in Fallujah and close by in the suburbs of Detroit, Los Angeles, and El Paso.

Indigenous cultures have been a part of our US and Western landscape for centuries: in the 1700s they were called "American colonists" by the British

Crown; in the 1800s they were called "Indians" by the newly independent Americans; and in the 1900s they were called "Jews and Italians" by the Protestant US majority. The African-American culture, throughout this entire nation-building process, was forcibly placed into the melting pot that from time to time resembled a scalding cauldron of ethnic and religious turmoil.

One of the critical factors that made many indigenous US conflicts less pronounced than, for example, similar British or Israeli experiences is US geography. If acts of domestic unrest or terror happen in New York City, an entire family could move to the opposite coast or to the beauty and isolation of Montana, Wyoming, or Vermont within a short period of time. This historical geographic luxury, however, is now diminished when we go to airports across the country and wish to travel abroad with the security and peace of mind of previous years. We are now being forced to come to terms with "the Other," their culture, and their motives for harming innocent people. We are also required to understand that "the Other" takes on many historical forms and characteristics. The black civil rights struggle of the 1960s was very different from the gay civil rights movement for legal and political equality, although both movements highlight critical social differences distinct from the ruling majority. Both of these domestic civil rights issues are in stark contrast to the latest "Other"– international terrorists who have infiltrated our domestic reality and the implications that has on minority and majority citizens in this and other countries. The current situation requires us to think less dichotomously about our US civil–military relationship, when airport employees and travelers walk the same airport terminals as uniformed soldiers fully armed and prepared to respond to any potential incident of terror.

Unlike separation theory in its latest form, concordance theory takes culture seriously. Purely institutional or rational choice models based on sanitized or measurable views of the world no longer seem useful or relevant. They do not help policy makers, scholars, the media, or the average citizen understand the full context of military, political, and citizen relationships in Fallujah, Islamabad, or Buenos Aires. Concordance theory does not insist that civilian and military boundaries which currently exist separately (as in the United States) should co-mingle or become integrated; although, this could be an acceptable scenario especially under conditions of high external threat, such as the United States during World War II. But concordance theory does embrace the concept of partnership. In fact, the partnering of political elites, the military, and the citizenry is the hallmark of concordance theory as well as the institutional and cultural perspective the theory offers to the field. Arriving at agreement over the role and function of the armed forces, rather than superimposing an often culturally inappropriate post-World War II separation model on all nations, is what this theoretical perspective offers to our multicultural world.

Concordance theory therefore has significant foreign policy and national security consequences. The worldwide policy issues at stake are entrenched in culture, which is why an alternative to the culturally deficient separation and agency theories is greatly needed. The "new world order," since the end of the Cold War, has actually become more of an "international disorder" with the

advent of a multi-polar world that exerts a myriad of ethnic, religious, and tribal issues and conflicts. While each region exhibits distinct indigenous tensions, US foreign policy has prided itself on asserting its dominant culture on other nations in order to maintain US foreign policy legitimacy and prevalence of the United States as the global superpower. On the civil–military relations front, superimposing separation theory tenets upon nations is extreme, especially in those countries where there is no inherent history of what Westerners consider "civilian life" or where separate institutions seem inappropriate.

For the United States, successful foreign policy demands an intricate marshaling of domestic partners and foreign alliances. It also involves debate and disagreement among the security establishment, government agencies, and the public – a process that both is domestically entrenched and often involves the role and function of the armed forces. If US citizens, politicians, and the military were on the same page with respect to national security interests and engaged in partnership, the alienation between military and citizens as encountered today in the United States and other nations would likely diminish. The result would be a more informed and coordinated civil–military relationship and security policy. A partnership in tune with world militaries and indigenous civilian conditions would also result in US civil–military relations policies that are more sensitive to foreign cultures. Similar to the academic community, which sorely yearns for theory that incorporates a cultural perspective, the US military is now looking to incorporate culture specialists who can assist in negotiating support for the local military leadership in Afghanistan and Iraq.

I recently came across a civilian job description within a US Army program called The Human Terrain System. The program is

> designed to improve the military's ability to understand the local socio–cultural environment in Iraq and Afghanistan. Knowledge of the local population provides a departure point for a military staff's ability to plan and execute its mission more effectively using less kinetic force.
>
> (National Association for the Practice of Anthropology 2007)

The military's first preference for this team that integrates Army Brigade Combat Teams and USMC Regimental Combat Teams is to hire a "cultural anthropologist" to assist in decision making that reduces support for the insurgency and increases support for the host nation's armed forces. Additionally, a recent US Army article stated the following regarding the importance of understanding indigenous cultures on the ground:

> Many of the principal challenges we face in Operation Iraqi Freedom and Enduring Freedom (OIF and OEF) stem from just such initial institutional disregard for the necessity to understand the people among whom our forces operate as well as the cultural characteristics and propensities of the enemies we now fight.
>
> (Kipp *et al.* 2006: 8)

The institutional disregard for understanding culture is not simply a military institutional deafness; it perpetuates civilian institutions, too. The US military takes orders from the civilian institutions, and both have been conditioned to think and act institutionally and separately (as separation and agency theories reinforce). The policy goal should be partnership among the civilian elites, the military, and the citizenry on critical issues of how domestic and foreign culture affects military tactics, foreign policy, US institutions, and nations abroad.

The U.S. military is beginning to understand the importance of culture. US Major General Benjamin C. Freakley, commanding general in Afghanistan, was quoted as follows:

> Cultural awareness will not necessarily always enable us to predict what the enemy and noncombatants will do, but it will help us better understand what motivates them, what is important to the host nation in which we serve, and how we can either elicit the support of the population or at least diminish their support and aid to the enemy.
>
> (Freakley 2005: 2)

It is now becoming clear that foreign policy could become more effective if US politicians, the academics who advise them, and the military would take foreign cultures into greater consideration. These leaders need to make a strategic commitment to understanding cultures and their indigenous political and military development. Right now we continue to pay homage to scholars who treat nations as abstract unitary actors or subjects of rational choice models. What the future of civil–military relations needs is a more realistic approach led by sociologists and anthropologists, as well as political scientists who embrace sociology and anthropology. This level of strategic cultural sensitivity would not sacrifice US global power but would enhance respect for the United States among developed and developing nations. Concordance theory, with a clear focus on culture and institutions, would improve the US civil–military relationship, national security, and foreign policy as it influences civil–military relations abroad. But before discussing concordance theory in detail, it is important to describe how this theory came about and the context for its theoretical development.

The Chicago theoretical approach

I was schooled at the University of Chicago where creating new theory or at least challenging prevailing theories was critical to one's success as a graduate student. For those unfamiliar with the character of the University of Chicago, *Chicago Tribune* columnist Mike Royko's description was probably the most astute – a medieval village, insulated from the glamour and polish of fashionable downtown Chicago. The university was indeed filled with brilliant scholars and Nobel Prize laureates who were often divorced from the world of popular culture. They walked around the gothic-styled landscape and gargoyled buildings thinking about other thinkers, like Heidegger and Kant, or contemplating game theory and mathematical equations. Many would walk around for years and years, truly experiencing what Hannah Arendt called "The Life of the Mind."

University of Chicago graduate students were known for their immersion in a quasi-monastic life inside the Joseph Regenstein Library, myself being no exception. I spent what seemed a lifetime in "the Reg." I was neither brilliant nor completely monastic; but I was smart enough to be accepted on the University of Chicago's program, to reflect on important intellectual questions, and to set realistic and challenging educational goals. The doctoral program was extremely rigorous, and I was competing with colleagues who had come from Yale, Harvard, Princeton, and other distinguished universities. Sometimes during the day-to-day rigor of the Chicago program, I looked back on my southern California undergraduate years at Occidental College with wistful memories … there, throwing a Frisbee around the quad on a spring day was acceptable and even encouraged after a long day of classes.

At the University of Chicago, by contrast, we learned how to become theoretical sharks, and we worked around-the-clock to hone those theoretical skills. The method appeared simple: find an important question to answer, present the current and competing theories of your field, explain the weaknesses of those theories point by point, supplant the most prominent theory with a new one, and discover case studies to support your new theory. There were courses, seminars, and roundtables where this occurred continuously. Graduate students would swim around the Reg hoping to discover another argument that would weaken the most current theoretical proposition – fish food for the mind. We would talk about it, think about it, read about it, and write papers about it. Our papers were then critiqued and criticized to strengthen our argument, and somehow a new theory would emerge. We would hang out together at various Hyde Park Greek diners, local pizza joints, and the famed Tiki Room where spiked blowfish hung from the ceiling – perhaps a metaphor for failed arguments and floundering theories. As graduate students we were sometimes humiliated in front of our colleagues (but only temporarily because we were all swimming in the same murky intellectual waters), or we would bring scholars in from different schools and challenge their theories. It was beyond rigor … it was a complete immersion in theoretical training without the charm of other college towns or the glamour of the Chicago Gold Coast. Although many of us did experience some of the best blues music in the world, often not far from the University of Chicago campus; those were indeed highly cherished weekend breaks from the Reg.

I was initially drawn to the topic of civil–military relations – the domestic study of militaries and a subfield of political science – because of my interest in international relations and comparative politics. I wanted to study an area of politics that was not completely dependent on an abstract conception of states. I enjoyed learning about real people and their communities, and how their unique situations affected the political realm. The political thinker Hannah Arendt and her conception of "political action" influenced me profoundly. I spent most of my master's program studying Arendt's work with one of her former students and previous dean of the University of Chicago Divinity School, Franklin Gamwell.

I was also interested in militaries and had been taught by a protégé of political science comparativist Leonard Binder. He enjoyed discussing anthropology as much as political science theory and how they both applied to Middle Eastern countries like Egypt and Syria. Moreover, my dissertation adviser and her husband, Susanne and Lloyd Rudolph, had spent a lifetime conducting fieldwork in India. Finally, Morris Janowitz, the father of military sociology, was a University of Chicago legend. I never met Professor Janowitz because he was ill during my tenure as a graduate student. But I later relayed to his daughter Rebecca how important her father's work was to my research. I was also given the honor of presenting the Morris Janowitz Lifetime Achievement Award to one of my mentors and Janowitz's student Moshe Lissak. Civil–military relations, the field Janowitz sought to develop from a sociological perspective, somehow fit my seemingly diverse yet crucially interconnected interests of people, politics, and armed forces. I soon learned that it was a field that also was theoretically very weak ... fish food at last.

It was made very clear to us that without a theory or without at least challenging the prevailing theory of our chosen fields, we had not met our university's challenge. Later, my degrees from the University of Chicago (MA and PhD) would open up several very practical and professional doors for me, both in academic and non-academic fields. I am proud to have those degrees on my résumé; but I also needed to feel I had accomplished some semblance of intellectual and theoretical achievement upon leaving my alma mater.

Following graduate school, I continued my academic work on civil–military relations and entered into the philanthropic world of higher education. I honed my fundraising and development credentials at institutions such as the University of Michigan, Harvard University, and Brandeis University. My development jobs usually required accomplishing specific financial objectives and goals ... goals that often affected thousands of alumni and the programs they would fund each fiscal year. At Brandeis University, I marshaled resources among corporations and foundations for specific academic and policy-related programs. At all three institutions, my efforts contributed to multimillion-dollar university goals that needed to be met and exceeded. What I came to realize during my philanthropic career was that the civil–military relations dialogue had changed very little in the decade since I left graduate school. My colleagues who were part of academic "mafias" and "realist" schools of thought had done little to further the theoretical architecture that explained why domestic military intervention occurred in some nations and not others. Separation theory was still dominant, and the subsequent agency theory became the rational choice model offered to a field that was desperate for cultural, sociological, and anthropological perspectives of militaries and their society.

Civil–military scholars and policy makers were seeking a new perspective that would help explain important questions such as the one I chose to address: *Under what conditions will a military intervene in its own nation?* This question was initially important during the 1950s and 1960s because of the development of new nations and political regimes. Countries like India, Pakistan, and Chile did not pose a viable threat to the West in the way Germany, Japan, and Russia had during World Wars I and II. Those nations were militaristic and totalitarian forms of government with dominant and repressive military values, and they forced their populations to impose aggressive military designs on other nations. By contrast, policy makers in the West were optimistic regarding the role of the military in the smaller evolving countries of Latin America, South Asia, Africa, and the Middle East. Perhaps these nations could utilize their military as agents of modernization, i.e. to build industry, create economic reform, and work in partnership with civilian political leaders. These countries did not have the grand designs of previous militaristic conquerors. They were young nations trying to reinvent and reform themselves politically.

The field of civil–military relations evolved out of Western policy makers' belief that there really could be a healthy relationship between the military and civilian populations, as nations like India and Israel were demonstrating. By the 1970s, however, that optimism began to wane as reality showed in nation after nation that soldiers were often "not agents of modernization … but were more or less an autonomous state within a state without a constituency to which they are responsible" (Nordlinger 1970: 1131). Civil–military relations soon became a sub-field addressing how to curb armies, if not militaristic nations, that were often terrorizing or taking control of their own governments and transforming them into domestic weapons of politicization and abuse.

One theory emerged during this time to explain why these nations had gone astray. The theory was actually a restatement of the US model of civil–military relations – civilian institutional dominance over a separate and professionalized military (Huntington 1957). The full argument of this separation theory will be discussed in Chapter 3. It is enough to mention here that the greatest weakness of separation theory, or objective civilian control, is in the civil–military dichotomy – civil versus military. This theoretical approach pays little attention to a nation's unique and indigenous culture, or any culture at all, since it is a theory that focuses on replicating US civil and military institutions. The latest version of separation theory is agency theory, which preserves the civil–military dichotomy and looks at civil–military relations as a game of rational actors. Again cultural analysis and interpretation are absent from this model.

Scholars who study countries facing nation-building efforts and/or domestic military intervention, such as those in Eastern Europe and the Middle East, are hungry for a theoretical explanation that incorporates the indigenous qualities of a nation – qualities that are often not objective nor rational as we are finding in Iraq and Afghanistan. Scholars, policy makers, and military leaders are searching for a theoretical architecture that can also predict important questions such as how does a nation prevent domestic military intervention or what causes militaries to intervene? Concordance theory provides this much needed and innovative approach that incorporates cultural uniqueness with predictive value.

When concordance theory was first published in 1995, Richard S. Wells offered several critical comments, which will be addressed in Chapter 3. One observation he made, however, is appropriate to mention here: "Schiff is essentially correct in her apparent belief that a reconsideration of civil–military relations theory is needed.... Her problems lie in an apparent need to destroy or discredit the old theory, and in developing a unifying concept – concordance" (Wells 1996: 18–19). Here was my response to that point:

> I am rather offended by Wells' assertion that my piece is meant to "destroy or discredit" the old theory. Unlike some scholars in the academy, whose sole purpose is to undermine the thoughts and writings of others, my intention is to provide a positive contribution to the field of civil–military relations. Anyone who has had even a limited exposure to this field knows that it is in sore need of new theory. As I have stated before, there is no "crisis" in American civil–military relations. The United States still has one of the most professional militaries in the world. The crisis, rather, lies with the field itself, in its dearth of appropriate theoretical frameworks. It is Wells who amply asserts that separation theory no long applies to the institutional realities of American civil–military relations.
>
> (Schiff 1996: 282)

I look back on that response now and think – wow ... a university development officer would have never written commentary like that. The response would have been diplomatic, muted, and carefully crafted so as not to offend. Of course the context of my response was quite different than that of my current day-to-day reality as a fundraiser. I did not see Professor Wells as a prospective donor but as a critic of my theory. And we learned early on in graduate school that criticism, no matter how constructive, must be dealt with aggressively. We were taught to take on the critics, stand up to them, and let them know that an important theoretical point was being made. While I stand by the content of my response, these days I am far more appreciative of the time and effort Professor Wells took to comment on my article.

An interdisciplinary methodology: culture matters

The University of Chicago approach calls for challenging current theory and offering alternative theories. And finding an interesting and relevant question to answer from a new theoretical perspective is a critical accomplishment. However, alternative approaches require a methodology that allows us to determine their strengths and weaknesses.

Concordance theory utilizes deductive causation or generalizations about the world that can be tested empirically while incorporating the values and culture of a particular society. In the following chapters, concordance theory is applied to several case studies thereby fulfilling the test of deductive causation.

Concordance theory does not presume that civilian institutions must control the military, since partnership and dialogue among the major sectors of society is more relevant to this theoretical approach. Rather, the underlying premise of concordance theory is that domestic military intervention can be avoided if there is agreement among the military, the political leadership, and the citizens regarding four indicators:

- social composition of the officer corps
- political decision-making process
- recruitment method
- military style.

The theory postulates that if concordance is achieved among several indicators of analysis, domestic military intervention is less likely to occur. But the causal statement that concordance prevents domestic military intervention does not explain why it is that some nations can or have achieved concordance while others have not. Alan Ryan suggests that this type of explanation remains causally sound:

> causal laws have often been described as telling us which lever to pull in order to bring about what event in the world; it is on this analogy surely plausible to say that we can have an idea of what lever we need to pull even if we cannot so fully describe the machinery connecting cause and effect as we should like.
>
> (Ryan 1970: 57)

The theory postulates that if concordance is achieved among several indicators of analysis, domestic military intervention is less likely to occur. The major reason for the theory's causal limitation results from the cultural aspect of the methodology, which is discussed in greater detail below. Why one nation maintains concordance between the military, political elites, and society and another nation does not is also a valid and interesting empirical question; however, it is not one addressed by this book.

This study considers the context under which the military and society are found. Some of the indicators of analysis deal with the norms, customs, and values of a particular society, how they affect the military, and how the military in turn impacts the society. Concordance theory can explain what major aspects of a nation should be in agreement. How a particular society arrives at such agreement is, however, largely dependent upon the nature of that society. For example, there is concordance over the social and ethnic composition of the officer corps in both India and Israel. The military, the political leadership, and the citizens in both countries agree on the makeup of the corps; however, why and how concordance over the officer corps is achieved differs mainly because of the political, social, and cultural variances between the two nations. These differences cannot be explained by a causal and universal theory; they can only be accounted for by understanding and explaining each country on its own merit.

The power of concordance theory is that it can causally show, without super-imposing foreign values and standards, which institutional and cultural attributes are important in order to prevent domestic military intervention. Thus, the US model of professional officer separated from civilian institutions is not the only possible pattern for studying civil–military relations. Rather, the most relevant model for any particular society will arise out of the dialogue between the mili-tary, the political leadership, and the citizens. This approach requires both a spe-cific set of indicators that illustrate concordance, such as the officer corps composition and recruitment method, and an understanding of a nation's indigenous political and cultural conditions, such as religious and tribal influ-ences.

One of the most prominent scholars of civil–military relations, Stephen P. Cohen, summarized the need for a theoretical approach that captures the inter-disciplinary quality of military–society relations – an approach that integrates the fields of political science, sociology, and anthropology:

> the study of armies – and armed forces in general transcends any single dis-ciplinary perspective. Besides the obvious importance of the historical evo-lution of armies as institutions, the study of the military draws the skills of the anthropologist and sociologist (for the relationship of an army to the society and culture that support it), the political scientist (for the compara-tive domestic political role of the military), and the student of international relations (since the size, quality, and performance of a military establish-ment will affect a state's foreign and security policies).
>
> (Cohen 1992: 3)

It is possible to determine what causal conditions are more or less likely to miti-gate domestic intervention; but those conditions cannot be predetermined without reference to the social structures, culture, and values of a particular nation.

Concordance theory pays homage to culture while separation theory argues that civil–military relations is bound to the United States and Western European historical experience. Yet the term "civil" in the context of civil–military rela-tions theory is defined through the Western European and US experiences and may not be applicable to other countries. Moreover, one specific indicator of concordance "military style" reflects the importance of military symbols such as uniforms, rituals such as parades and saluting, and traditions such as the officer and the gentleman. These aspects of the military focus on style and appearance. They help define the role of the military in society. They help mark specific boundaries or elide them. They shed light on the meaning, structure, and compo-sition of the military and its relation to society. Most importantly, they highlight the indigenous character of a nation's military and facilitate comparison with other militaries.

This work does not pretend to be an anthropological piece, but neither does it shy away from important forms of understanding which cultural interpretation supplies. It is interested in what Clifford Geertz calls the "symbolic forms of authority" (1983: 5). Uniforms, religious symbols, and daily public comportment are forms of authority that go beyond the traditional investigations of political science. Realms of authority reside not only in the institutions of politics but also in the inner mental states and daily constructions of human beings.

Embracing indigenous culture also means either being immersed in that culture or finding the works of experts who have conducted significant observational fieldwork. I have therefore relied on experts who have conducted fieldwork or cultural research in each case study. For example, while I have never traveled to India or Pakistan, I consulted sources written by scholars who value anthropology, sociology, and political science and have studied those countries for decades. Those experts understand why the Indian caste system in relation to the armed forces cannot be reduced to a rational actor model. The merits of the caste system must be viewed through the lens of the Indian people. Similarly, my discussion of the overlap between the militia army and the citizenry during the US post-revolutionary period is influenced by historians who are immersed in official documents, personal letters, and public essays written during that period. Finally, my own personal experiences and research, such as witnessing reenactments of life during the post-revolutionary United States, provide up-close encounters with cultures and artifacts long since past.

I became aware of the importance of culture and fieldwork during my graduate school years at the University of Chicago ... one of the great schools of political science and anthropology. I also spent close to three years in Israel during the 1990s studying the military and Israeli society. I learned Hebrew and traversed the country interviewing hundreds of Israeli officers, soldiers, politicians, and citizens. I sat in a sealed room in Jerusalem during the first Gulf War waiting for instructions from the Israeli military on when it would be safe to take off my gas mask and leave the room. I watched Israeli children go to school with gas mask boxes decorated with pictures and symbols to commemorate the Purim holiday. I had stones thrown at my car by Palestinian youth while passing though the West Bank town of Jericho. I had coffee with scholars and shopkeepers in the Muslim and Christian quarters of the Old City of Jerusalem. I interviewed an Israeli Defense Forces (IDF) colonel who was in charge of military education for religious soldiers. At the Hebrew University, I studied with renowned Israeli sociologist Moshe Lissak. I taught a course on civil–military relations in Hebrew to students who had served in the Israeli military. I knew that the only way to express the civil–military relations experience in Israel was to experience the civil–military situation myself or find researchers who had.

The trend in political science since the 1980s, however, has moved toward quantitative approaches such as rational choice models and game theory. There have been huge "perestroika" debates going on in the political science field over the benefits of quantitative methods versus comparative and area studies methods that often rely on historical and cultural analysis. I believe quantitative methods benefit studies that measure topics such as the voting patterns of groups or populations. For example, the University of Michigan election studies measure the behaviors and attitudes of voters in specific elections and enable us to better understand the electoral process. At the Harvard School of Public Health, I gained great appreciation for the work of Lemuel Shattuck who inspired the American Statistical Society, undertook comprehensive sanitation surveys, and set the foundation for the Massachusetts Department of Health. I also worked closely with a donor and Harvard alum who served as a biostatistician for the Centers for Disease Control and Prevention (CDC). And great statistical pioneers, such as Frederick Mosteller, have exemplified the appropriateness of quantitative methodologies in evaluating medical and public health practices. Clearly, the mathematical side of the social sciences plays an important role in political, social, and health fields when the outcome is truly to assist in comprehending problems, delineating processes, and shaping practical solutions.

But quantitative methods are less useful to this study of civil–military relations that requires an empirical and ethnographic understanding of politics, history, and culture. Moreover, the perestroika debate (similar to the civil–military relations theory debate) is a dichotomous one – mathematical versus non-mathematical interpretations, quantitative versus qualitative approaches.

It appears that the international relations theorists who view states as unitary actors, who do not utilize math to prove their arguments, but who shun cultural studies, are lumped in with the comparative politics and area studies specialists. The unitary actor model makes the state (not the political actors associated with a state such as the president or cabinet) the primary unit of analysis in an international system among other states. I believe, however, that international relations theorists who deem states abstractly as "unitary actors" and refuse to study domestic politics and the ethnography of nations have reinforced the dichotomous civil–military theory that is inapplicable to so many nations around the world. International relations is useful to the study of military and society since the composition of a specific military establishment will influence a state's foreign and security policies. Nevertheless, in the realm of real policy making and on-the-ground organization of military and political institutions, fieldwork and cultural interpretation provide critical skills and methods. The process for partnership between the military, the political elites, and the citizenry cannot be reduced to a mathematical formula or a unitary actor model. When the US military, as mentioned above, is looking to hire cultural anthropologists to help navigate through complex social and political involvement in Iraq and Afghanistan, it is not difficult to surmise that rational choice and unitary actor models are simply inappropriate (Miller 2001; Monroe 2005; Stuart 2003).

Long after graduate school and well into my development career, I presented an academic conference paper on the Federalist Papers and their influence on early US civil–military relations. It was a way to immerse myself more fully in my academic field without aggressively asserting my belief that I still had an important theoretical contribution to make to the field. As a University of Chicago-trained scholar, I knew the difference between good theory and the rest. And I knew that the latest rational choice model of civil–military relations was a variation and reification of the old institutional separation theory. But as a development professional, I had learned the art of diplomacy, cultivation, and patience. In contrast to the Hyde Park Tiki Room, Harvard University development suggested the fine dining of the Ambassador Pump Room to cultivate major gift prospects. I was a Chicago-theory shark dressed in a Harvard development suit, and after years of fundraising training I was careful, congenial, and wanted to address my field smoothly and with finesse. I had to demonstrate that the latest theory of civil–military relations, agency theory, was simply old wine in a new bottle, but I was going to do it gradually. So I spent time studying the Federalist Papers and the US post-revolutionary period, which led me to the conference presentation I now speak of. After presenting to the conference crowd Madison's and Hamilton's views on standing armies and personal liberties, one very renowned scholar in the civil–military relations field approached me and stated rather bluntly: "I came to your panel to hear about concordance theory, not the Federalist Papers. My students like your theory the best. When are we going to get a presentation on that?" It was at that moment that I knew I had to complete the concordance project.

2 Domestic military intervention and civil–military relations

This book is really about those nations where the fear of the military prevails or the military is uniquely present in daily life yet may not be feared. In chapters 5 and 6, I will explain how nations such as Pakistan and Argentina have not achieved concordance and suffer from *coups d'état*. I will explore why other nations like India and Israel have succeeded in creating a partnership or concordance between the military, the political elites, and the citizenry. In addition to offering an alternative concordance theory, this book moves beyond the traditional academic vernacular, "civil" and "military," and takes a closer look at the people, the culture, and the important drama that unfolds in a sampling of nations.

Western citizens often are caught unprepared in matters of military and war because of the disconnect between our daily dialogue and the military realities overseas – babies and children being harmed in Fallujah; soldiers coming home maimed or not coming home at all; rogue militias trying to undermine political processes. Military relationships are conspicuously absent from our daily lives, and these unexpected themes, photos, and stories seem incongruent with Western conceptions of being. Through the lens of concordance theory, those living in Western nations might learn more about how other communities live, not knowing if their governments are stable, if the military is protective, sequestered, or positively integrated into society, or if their children could be killed by a roadside bomb. Westerners might learn more about the average Pakistani citizen and soldier, so that when we are called upon by a nation to negotiate, serve, protect, or use military force, we are less surprised and more psychologically prepared to address situations with unique historical and cultural underpinnings. Concordance theory aims to help transform society's views of civil–military relations by respecting and recognizing that the historical, cultural, and political context is different in each country.

The field of civil–military relations – the relationship between the military and society – has become more prominent during the wars in Iraq and Afghanistan. Thousands of troops are in harm's way, and, at this writing, a military and political solution to the problems in Iraq appears problematic. Coupled with the War on Terror, the conflicts in Iraq and Afghanistan have brought the military to a level of awareness within US culture not seen since the Vietnam

War. In addition, we have domestic military recruitment issues that include increasing the number of rank-and-file military personnel and deciding how socially inclusive our military should be.

By and large, Americans prefer the military's lack of prominence in daily life. Since World War II, Americans prefer to know that the military is here to protect, but we are happy when it is not a part of our common dialogue or a topic of daily discussion. Yet here we are with soldiers abroad, airports that often feel like Cold War security checkpoints, an overall deficit of troops, and an officer corps that still pays allegiance to civilian authority. This is the current condition of civil–military relations in the United States.

US civil–military relations, though not perfect, is considered healthy unlike many nations around the world. Few Americans wake up in the morning wondering if the military top brass or rogue soldiers will take over the government. Citizens in Thailand, Argentina, and Pakistan, on the other hand, think about that scenario quite often. In the aftermath of the September 2006 Thai coup, for example, citizens were forbidden to protest or even discuss politics:

> The 19 September group, describing themselves as "social activists, students and regular citizens," rallied on Friday (September 22) at a Bangkok shopping mall, and wore black to symbolize the "death of democracy in Thailand."
>
> Their banners said: "No to Thaksin. No to coup," "Don't call it reform, it's a coup," and "No to martial law."
>
> About a dozen people showed up, recorded by police video.
>
> The military junta earlier banned political activity, and forbid people discussing politics on talk-show radios, Web sites, and TV.
>
> (Mokkarawut 2007)

More recently in Pakistan, prior to the assassination of Benazir Bhutto, *The Economist* reported on the plight of Pakistani politics and the status of General Musharraf after the army's showdown at the Red Mosque to curb religious extremism:

> The result of the military operation has been alienation among moderates across the country and outrage among the mullahs.... Some analysts argue that the PML [Pakistan Muslim League] is a drag on General Musharraf's agenda for "enlightened moderation" because it constantly seeks to ally with the mullahs.... Unfortunately the tide of political and religious extremism can probably not be stemmed by the weak, ill-disciplined political parties without the army's active help.
>
> (*The Economist* 2007a: 43)

Americans value their military and freely criticize the elected officials who direct the armed forces. They do not even consider, much less fathom, a day when tanks take to the streets and fire upon churches, synagogues, or mosques, soldiers pull innocent people from their homes, or troops simply stand on patrol because an unelected general commanded them to do so.

Much of the literature on civil–military relations is a spin-off from the US model of "objective civilian control," and Morris Janowitz's understanding of "subjective control" where the US military remains aloof from society, but should reflect the core values of the society it serves. Janowitz understood that the military had a separate recruitment and training system in place, distinctive uniforms, and rituals, but complete separation from the fundamental principles of society should not be encouraged. John Allen Williams (1995) elaborates:

> From Morris Janowitz ... comes the idea that the military and society are closely linked, and that the military can never be completely separate from society. It will reflect society in some important ways, and intellectual and other currents present in the society will find their way into the military sooner or later.... At the same time, the military must also remain somewhat aloof from society, as noted by Huntington. The military has a responsibility to defend the state, not to mirror it. Even in a democratic society the military cannot be completely democratic, and some of the privileges open to civilians are not applicable to it.

Chapter 4 will portray in great detail how the post-revolutionary US citizens militia almost completely reflected the values of the early United States and was characterized by an overlap between civilian and military boundaries. This tethering between citizen and military reappeared during World War II when all citizens were called to join the war effort. Since World War II, the US military is far more separate institutionally and culturally from the society it serves, and for the most part, US citizens prefer it that way.

As the United States began to take its place as a leader during the Cold War, it also wanted to assist other nations with both international and domestic threats to their survival. Given the success of the US model, it seemed appropriate that scholars and policy makers tried to apply the same model to other nations around the world. But the assistance was not void of foreign policy implications. Democratic ideals were esteemed over the less desirable tenets of communism, and this stance became the hallmark of the Cold War agenda. The United States exported its own successful formula of democratic government as a tactic to contain the communist threat.

During the 1960s and 1970s many countries in Latin American, Africa, Asia, and the Middle East suffered from military overthrow of their government. Domestic military intervention, such as military coup, became commonplace. In terms of the US model, success seemed dependent on the ability to separate and professionalize the armed forces, thereby preventing domestic military intervention. But despite efforts to apply this model abroad, domestic intervention by armed forces often continued in these regions and elsewhere.

In this post-Cold War era, foreign policy has changed dramatically. Communism has receded, but the nuclear threat has not. In many ways the collapse of the superpower rivalry has made the world more dangerous. Religious and ethnic factions threaten domestic stability in developing regions, and these factions encourage the unregulated procurement of dangerous weapons. In present-day Iraq, for example, Sunnis, Kurds and Shiites are grappling with democracy, religion, political participation, and the issue of how to build a legitimate military. These issues are being addressed in a very different way than the United States did during the 1930s (when its twentieth-century military was recreated) or the 1790s (when the citizen militias were slowly incorporated into a more federalized military reserve system). The current state of the international community has nations and foreign-policy makers clamoring for a better civil–military relations model – a model that incorporates both institutional and cultural differences that may be indigenous to unique nations.

Civil–military relations: anatomy of a coup

There are many forms of military intervention in domestic politics. The most dramatic and newsworthy is the *coup d'état*. The coup is "the infiltration of a small but critical segment of the state apparatus which is then used to displace the government" (Luttwak 1979: 26–7). A coup does not involve the takeover of government by a sizable army. A coup is also distinguished from a revolution or a mass attempt to overthrow the government, although it can have violent moments perpetrated by segments of the military. A coup is a plan executed to "seize power within the present system" (Luttwak 1979: 58–9). While political and social changes may occur afterward, the coup itself is an exchange of power by elites through military force without significant national transformations. Bruce Farcau (1994: 171) describes the aftermath of the 1955 coup against Argentina's Juan Perón noting that the military was unable to deliver improved political reformation:

> As an epilogue to the Argentine coup of 1955, it should be noted that, as this was very much a "minority coup," favored by only a portion of the officer corps, it did not produce a stable regime. The military quickly divided along the lines of the "reds" and the "blues," the former being those who wanted to continue a populist policy of Perónism without Perón, while their opponents, sometimes referred to as the "gorillas," were a far more repressive group opposed to any vestige of popular participation in government. They would go on trading coups right through the 1960s, Perón's return to power in the 1970s, and up to the return of Argentina to democracy in the 1980s.

Praetorianism is another form of domestic military intervention. On the basis of praetorian society – a politicized society where exclusive social and political groups are in collusion with the military – Huntington distinguishes "oligarchical praetorianism" coups and "middle class praetorianism" coups. Oligarchical praetorianism suggests that the dominant rulers are those who come from elite and wealthy segments of society. As the military becomes the more dominant oligarchical group, it seeks to take power through a coup, which is comparable to a "palace revolution." This is a non-violent coup where one elite group replaces another, and the population at large is uninvolved in the process (Huntington 1968: 195, 199, 201).

The 1932 overthrow of the monarchy in Thailand and the subsequent coup in 1933 are examples of oligarchic and non-violent coups. The 1932 coup reflects a group of civilians and soldiers who "were Western educated and both were resentful of the royal court monopoly of supreme power" (Finer 1988: 122–3). They simply seized power, imprisoned the royal family, and persuaded the king to accept limited powers. Pridi Phanomyong, a civilian intellectual who led the coup, assumed control of the government until his economic plans became unacceptable to the military leader, Colonel Phibun. The latter orchestrated the subsequent 1933 coup, also bloodless, and placed the military in full control (Huntington 1968: 205; Finer 1988: 1223).

The transition from oligarchical praetorianism to middle-class praetorianism involves a more broadly based army operating within a centralized state. In particular, the officer corps ally with various social groups that have become dissatisfied with the ruling oligarchy. At some point, a conspiracy against the state develops resulting in a coup. This type of overthrow is not simply a "palace revolt" but involves a more violent attempt to secure the reigns of power. Again, the overthrow of Juan Perón in 1955 exemplifies this violent middle-class praetorianism in contrast to a non-violent exchange of power or palace coup:

> General Lucero, proclaiming himself chief of the "forces of repression," quickly took measures to secure the capital and stamp out the rebellion. Infantry units marched on Córdoba from Tucumán and Santa Fé. Another regiment lay siege to Bahia Blanca. Antiaircraft batteries were set up around Buenos Aires; public buildings were placed under heavy guard; and the Plaza de Mayo was closed to the public. Movie houses, theaters, and bars were shut down. The police were ordered to break up gatherings of more than two people on the streets. Radio programs were severely censored. Despite this, *porteños* with shortwave sets were able to pick up "the Voice of Liberty," broadcast from Córdoba, which carried Lonardi's proclamation that his "liberating revolution" favored no party, class, or creed but was aimed simply at freeing Argentina from tyranny.
>
> (Lewis 1990: 212)

Apart from the bloodless (oligarchical praetorianism) and more violent coups, other forms of domestic military intervention can involve "supplantment" or "displacement" of a civilian regime by threatening or blackmailing the government. For example, if civil revolt is on the horizon or in process, the military or its elite recruits may threaten the government by refusing to defend it. Or the military may be politicized to such an extent that it becomes an integral part of the political system; hence, the army may threaten or blackmail the regime using "legitimate" procedures. Similar to oligarchical praetorianism, such scenarios may bring down governments without the use of troops or guns.

Japan during the 1930s depicts a military well entrenched in the political affairs of the state, that used "legitimate" means to maintain their power in the political realm. The army was officially included in the cabinet and could withdraw its representation at will. By blocking political appointments of liberal party members, the armed forces were able to divert some 46 percent of the budget to their own coffers. They maintained the support of the nation by assuming responsibility for education and by launching a massive propaganda campaign to curry favor with the citizenry. The government eventually became a puppet of the military, since the latter often used the threat of force to advance its militaristic designs within the cabinet (Finer 1988: 132–4).

While blackmail and threats may be used by the military to achieve specific goals, in democratic nations (where coups are rare) the military often seeks to achieve "influence" within the government by other means. Richard Betts (1991: 5) identifies two forms of military influence in democratic societies – direct and indirect:

> Direct influence flows from formal and explicit recommendations, or control of operations. Indirect influence flows from ways in which soldiers may control the premises of civilian decision through monopoly of information or control of options.

For example, during World War II the US Joint Chiefs of Staff (Marshall, Arnold, King, and Leahy) assumed a preeminent role in directly influencing President Roosevelt. They were instrumental in coordinating, with a reciprocal British Allied Command, the strategic direction of the war. Whenever Roosevelt and Churchill met, they were in sync with the advice of their respective military commanders, and it was clear that the American–British military top brass was responsible for the ground strategy and operations in each theater of war, except the South Pacific.

After World War II, the Joint Chiefs of Staff structure was formalized, and the power of the chairman of the Joint Chiefs declined when compared to the Roosevelt years. During most administrations since President Truman, the State Department has taken over as the dominant foreign policy advisor to the president. While the Joint Chiefs of Staff and its chairman have important influence on the president regarding military matters, they are forced to navigate the bureaucratic waters of civilian politics. This shift in domestic policy since the Truman administration compels the military to use indirect forms of military influence.

One major example of indirect military influence is the control of information. The military's information and intelligence system is often superior to civilian systems. Since the primary vehicle for information access is through this infrastructure, the military could have a significant impact on political decision-making, especially in wartime. For example, during the Vietnam War "the military intelligence and reporting systems had a greater impact on Vietnam policy than did direct military advice" (Betts 1991: 5). Gabriel Kolko agreed: "By early 1964 the Army alone in Vietnam was producing fourteen hundred pounds of reports daily," and "the information available to key officials in Washington, for all its limits, was certainly accurate enough to allow them to base policy decision on facts." The reliance on intelligence was also the result of generals who, unlike in World War II, often stayed in South Vietnam for only a year and failed "to comprehend the war's subtle, complex nature" and were less attuned to the military structure, body counts, and critical on-the-ground logistical efforts. The steady supply of military intelligence provided the officers with the opportunity to indirectly shape the options and opinions of policy makers (Kolko 1985: 194–6).

Another example of indirect military influence is charismatic leadership. In Max Weber's tradition of charismatic authority, Betts argues that "a few people's action, advice, and influence are relatively unconstrained by the formal limits of their office's purview" (Betts 1991: 174). Articulate and likeable military leaders, by virtue of their personality and the respect they command in important political and social circles, are able to influence government and society outside the formally prescribed channels of influence. Betts suggests that only a few twentieth-century soldiers possessed this kind of charismatic influence, and one of them was Douglas MacArthur (ibid.: 5, 174, 175).

Among his troops, for example, MacArthur understood how his role as commander was also one of role model, and that his military style was just as influential as his official managerial roles:

> There was enough of the actor in Douglas MacArthur to tell him that the good commander needs to be not only an able manager but a figurehead to whom the troops can look up with interest and admiration. In this second role a shrewd leader often cultivates some eccentricities of behaviour and dress, and particularly of headdress. MacArthur made himself a quickly recognizable figure by removing the wire from his stiff-crowned cap and wearing the cap at an angle, and by carrying a riding crop and wearing a turtleneck sweater and muffler.
>
> (Long 1998: 22–3)

Congressional or parliamentary debates and lobbying over military funding and arms acquisitions are also legitimate forms of influence the army seeks for its interests, which may also involve charismatic influence. During his early appointment as chief of staff, MacArthur showed the exemplary qualities of persuasion in the Congress and among the US citizenry when convincing them that the army's post-World War I condition was dangerously weak and had to be strengthened:

> Among the tasks that faced the new Chief of Staff ... were to obtain enough money year by year to maintain at least an efficient nucleus army and continue the training of civilian reservists, to take steps towards the

reequipment of an army that had few weapons beyond those it had possessed in 1918, and in particular to plan for increased mechanization.
During MacArthur's five years in the appointment he used his considerable
powers of persuasion to the utmost to convince Congress and the people
that the army was being dangerously reduced.

(Long 1998: 39)

Within the framework of democratic political channels, conflict may indeed
occur between the military and other national interest and political groups but
still be considered indirectly influential. For example, in 2007, the surge effort in
Iraq drew sharp criticism and debate from political circles even as military top
brass requested more time and patience for the surge to be fully implemented:

Lt. Gen. Raymond T. Odierno, the No. 2 commander in Iraq, told Pentagon
reporters that while he was not asking to delay a mid-September assessment
of the new military strategy that Congress has required, it would take "at
least until November" to judge with confidence whether the strategy was
working.... But the appeals by the commanders ... in three videoconfer-
ences on Capitol Hill and at the Pentagon, were met by stern rebukes from
lawmakers of both parties.

(Shanker and Cloud 2007)

These policy disagreements are considered moderate in the sense that blackmail
or the threat of force by the military is not used. Accordingly, the presence of
tempered conflict between the military and other domestic groups is also linked
with democracy. One scholar suggests that "the existence of a moderate state of
conflict is in fact another way of defining legitimate democracy" (Lipset 1981:
71). Or according to another scholar, a "mature political culture" (Finer 1988:
78–9) is able to control military influence through political channels, and most
would argue this is not considered a form of domestic military intervention.

However, the late J. David Greenstone, argues that political disputes over
policy are different from social, political, and/or religious cleavages that cannot
be resolved through an agreed-upon political process (1984: 2–3). In less democratic nations experiencing such deep-rooted conflicts, divisions are often the
result of basic differences in social and political philosophy rather than debates
and quarrels over specific programs or policies. Greenstone also indicates that
these types of divisions between the electorate and the government can shake
the foundations of a nation. Chapter 5, for example, will discuss Pakistan's
failure to come to terms with the East Bengali community within the ranks of
its military and throughout the political process. This social and political cleav-
age indeed shook the core of the young Muslim state until the Bengali
community had no alternative but to establish the separate nation of
Bangladesh in 1971.

A pluralistic society, on the other hand, allows for conflict and can include
the military with its vested interests attempting to influence non-military groups

with their own particular interests. Contention among the players may occur, but the foundations of a pluralistic government and society are left in tact. Domestic military interventions, such as coups, do not occur, but concordance or agreement among the military, the political elites, and the citizenry becomes the cornerstone of moderate conflict strategies (e.g., healthy debate and negotiated political process).

For example, in Iraq the US military reflects an institution that lobbies its interest in government and engages in posturing and debate that can promote moderate conflict between the military and the political elites. Military lobbying involves the development of a public relations network, largely the result of its involvement in industrial interests related to arms development, procurement, and the budgets required for military growth and maintenance. The rivalries and tensions between Congress and the president have often made private discords public, leaving an impression of strong military influence in government. In reality, the US military is forced to become another interest group that enters the US political system, creates relationships with other interest groups and law-makers, and embraces the political and social fabric of US society. The debate over the effectiveness of body armor used by US soldiers in Iraq is an example of the army defending its procurement interests in Congress:

> The service's top soldier equipment buyer, Brig. Gen. Mark Brown, said he plans to meet with lawmakers and staff this week after NBC News broadcast an investigative report Sunday claiming Dragon Skin – which uses a series of interlocking ceramic disks to stop armor-piercing bullets – outperformed armor currently issued by the Army. "Since the report, we have gotten a flurry of interest" from Capitol Hill, Brown said at a May 21 Pentagon briefing. "We're planning on going over to the Hill … for discussions with key members." … Army officials are fighting back with an aggressive campaign to undercut NBC's claims, which based much of its report on ballistic tests the network conducted in Germany and on the claims of Dragon Skin manufacturer Pinnacle Armor.
>
> (Lowe 2007: 1)

While many nations exhibit a paradigm similar to that of the United States, other nations see their military frequently crossing the line and threatening the process of legitimate influence in government. This latter scenario looms over many nations in which blackmail, intimidation, and coup are civil and military realities. Where the military has the power and the opportunity to aggressively assert itself, it often does. Understanding the unique conditions under which a military will intervene in domestic politics is one major goal of civil–military relations. As it currently stands, the civil–military relations worldview is a projection of two institutional realms, "the civil" and "the military," which often vie with each other for power and domination. Before looking at alternatives to this dualistic model and other factors that may be of consequence, it is important to know the origins and underpinnings of civil–military relations as it exists today.

The origins of civil–military relations

The separation and competition between civil and military spheres gained theoretical importance during the development of the Western European army in the eighteenth and nineteenth centuries. While Carl von Clausewitz is often considered the father of modern military strategy, the Prussian strategist has also been considered the writer who set the theoretical tenor for civil–military relations in the twentieth century. Clausewitz's depiction of the non-military "cabinet" as the policy making body for war and peace predates the post-World War II literature on civil–military relations. Clausewitz focuses on the importance of "civil" government and "civilian" values which are meant to check and control the military and warlike actions (Finer 1988: 128–30).

From Clausewitz's point of view, "war is a mere continuation of diplomacy by other means" (Clausewitz 1950: 16). This famous quote seems to exhibit highly militaristic overtones. Yet it is possible to extrapolate a basic theory of civil–military relations that considers civilian policy makers as the initial formulators of war. This perspective asserts a distinction between military and civil realms that is adopted by later civil–military theorists.

Clausewitz considers the "art of war" a battlefield performance or the execution of highly trained maneuvers. The "other means" mentioned in his famous quotation above alludes to a political body – "the cabinet" – that is distinct from a military body. In other words, war is determined by a political and not a military organ. In fact, he regards the planning and execution of a military enterprise by a purely military judgment as "irrational," and the decision to go to war should always be made by a political cabinet. Although the specific makeup of Clausewitz's "cabinet" is ambiguous with regard to military and non-military representation, it is clear that he makes a fundamental distinction between a civilian body that makes war policy and a military body that executes that policy. In sum, the art of war (based on force) is subordinate to political policy making that guides the decision to go to war (Clausewitz 1950: 117; Finer 1988: 128–30).

Clausewitz's framework sets the conceptual stage for the twentieth century phenomenon called "militarism." The *Oxford English Dictionary* (1971) defines militarism as the "spirit and tendencies of the professional soldier; the prevalence of a military sentiment and ideals among people; and the tendency to regard military efficiency as the paramount interest of the state." Similarly, noted scholar Alfred Vagts refers to militarism as the style of the military, the ideas and spirit that dominate the way the military perceives itself, and how the military influences the rest of society. A country embracing militarism "often places heavy burdens on its people for military purposes," to the point of wasting "the nation's best man power in unproductive army service." Militarism is contrasted to the "military way," which focuses on "the specific objectives of power" and bears a "scientific character" that is limited to winning wars. The military way focuses on military strategy and battlefield performance; it is the art of war preparation and execution. By contrast, militarism is an extreme example of military values dominating an entire society including its civilians (Vagts 1959: 13–15).

The values and spirit of militarism generally exist during peacetime. Military parades, marches, and other forms of propaganda demonstrate the nation's military buildup and extreme national patriotism. During wartime militarism often focuses on military leaders who pursue war for sheer glory and national reputation. Consequently, these military leaders and their nations have been described as militaristic.

Two modern examples of militarism are Germany and Japan during World War II. In the immediate post-World War II period, the Allies (especially the United States) attempted to demilitarize these countries with vast programs meant to both punish and educate these ill-spirited nations (Berghahn 1982: 50). Despite all the formal means of demilitarization, there still remained an underlying suspicion about spirits and sentiments that could not be attributed to the elusive state but only to the people who were citizens of that state. Such suspicions led many to believe that in every German there existed a Nazi, and that with the appropriate means, they had the capacity to recreate the militarism of the Nazi period. The Japanese also became targets of the public's view of militarism, especially after the attack on Pearl Harbor. The special internment camps set up during World War II demonstrated American distrust of the Japanese people even if they were US citizens.

We see this theme of labeling others as militarists recur in the debate on the emergence of the military–industrial complex (MIC). The MIC is said to exist in most developed and developing nations possessing the bureaucratic and technological expertise enabling them to participate in the arms trade. While the United States was extirpating Nazi militarism, it was also involved in a worldwide effort to export arms, military training, and troops to various parts of the world. Paradoxically, most Western nations do not call this militarism since Western democracies traditionally are not considered to be militaristic. As a clear victor of the war, it did not consider such activity to be militaristic because it had already defined militarism in terms of what it saw in Germany and Japan. Marxist scholars, however, viewed these international transactions as a new form of militarism with the distinctive characteristic of military imperialism – a major consequence of capitalism (Madgoff 1970: 337–42; Berghahn 1982: 85; Luxemburg 2003: 262).

The topic of militarism, much like the topic of civil–military relations, is shaped by those creating the concepts and exporting their implementation abroad. Militarism is found in Nazi Germany and World War II Japan because they were the Allied enemy. Militarism is generally not assigned to those nations who participate in the MIC because the MIC helped the Allies win World War II, it defeated militarism, and it made the world safe again. In sum, nations with historically threatening relationships with Western nations have been framed as militaristic, while those not posing a threat (but exhibiting similar domestic characteristics) have been framed in the more tolerable terms of civil–military relations.

Nations framed in terms of civil–military relationships (good or bad) are those that have been encouraged by Western nations to separate civil and military spheres. Civil–military relations standards are defined and implemented by those policy makers who provide a hegemonic determination of what the suitable civil–military relationship should be according to Western and US standards. In the cases of Japan and Germany, thwarting cross-national invasions across several continents justified labeling those nations militaristic. The case of civil–military relations, where the impact on foreign policy is significant but not as internationally compelling as World War II, allows for a more culturally and institutionally sensitive characterization of the relationship between military and society in distinctive nations.

The issue of continental invasions or high external threats becomes prevalent in the militarism literature, and is also at the heart of Harold Lasswell's garrison state hypothesis. Lasswell predicts that nations under high external threat conditions would develop into garrison states, where elite specialists in violence would assume control. These specialists are political elites who utilize science and technology to create coercive regimes. The elites are not necessarily military men but those who utilize the military for domestic coercive purposes, as well as external military adventures. In a typical Lasswellian society there is always an atmosphere of suspicion as the scope of military preparations call for the "surveillance of the entire community" (Lasswell 1954: 368; see also Lasswell 1962: 62–3).

Lasswell's main examples of the garrison state are the modern totalitarian states and especially Nazi Germany. In Germany, there was a close relationship between the civilian and military bureaucracies involved in research, development, distribution, and military armament production. All citizens were subjected to a disciplined and repressive lifestyle that conformed to the intentions of the Nazi elite. In addition, Adolf Hitler indoctrinated his civilians with militaristic values while maintaining domestic obedience as he sought to expand Germany's borders (Lasswell 1962: 54).

Although Lasswell uses the Third Reich as his prime candidate for a garrison state, he is also concerned about the possibility of a garrison state in democratic nations. Naturally, the internally repressive force would not resemble a police state such as the Nazi SS. Lasswell's concern, however, is heightened by new factors in the environment of democratic systems such as the growth of technology and capitalism. He is not terribly clear on the type of democratic garrison state he foresaw. His statement on this matter remains ambiguous: "the garrison state is not by nature non-democratic. This is left to empirical inquiry" (Lasswell 1962: 54). Despite his concern that garrison states could emerge in democracies, he did not articulate much beyond vague references concerning capital accumulation and resource basins.

Lasswell's essay regarding threats to privacy in democratic states focuses on the infringement by elite government organizations on the public in the form of "secret surveillance, such as phone taps, buggings and scrutiny of civil servants." Thus, even democracies, according to Lasswell, "can exhibit totalitarian features that emanate from elite government officials" (Lasswell 1952: 125, 136).

The use of Nazi Germany as the prototypical garrison state, as well as Lasswell's ambiguity concerning its democratic counterpart, makes it difficult to apply Lasswell's theory to nations lacking harshly repressive domestic regimes. Moreover, Lasswell does not consider the possibility of a garrison state that is unique to democratic nations – an altered form that may not involve political elites using highly repressive means of domestic coercion. For democracies, government and military elites may have difficulty managing specific economic pressures that result from issues such as high defense expenditures. Such pressures may manifest in national problems that are indicative of democratic or non-militaristic states in economic and/or political crisis.

During the 1980s, for example, scholars such as Paul Kennedy focused on the United States' economic weaknesses, the result of huge defense spending. The pressures born from military grand strategy were more complex than political–military elites in totalitarian states who harshly invaded the privacy of citizens. The United States' agricultural crisis, its lower share of global manufacturing, and its international debtor status were a few examples of critical domestic problems resulting from high defense expenditures. Though these did not result from dictatorial repression, US citizens still felt the backlash from military affairs in other aspects of their civilian lives.

In more recent years, however, scholars have been blunt about utilizing the term militarism to describe the United States. For example, Andrew Bacevich's *The New American Militarism* claims that US citizens have "fallen prey to militarism" by fostering a "romanticized view of soldiers" and "nostalgia for military ideals." Bacevich also mentions soldiers becoming more professional and separate as an institution after the Vietnam War. Turning the separation argument on its head, Bacevich argues that somehow the military's evolution after the Vietnam War places "war in a separate domain ... of military officers." While Bacevich agrees that US soldiers are "not warmongers," somehow they have "made militarism possible" (2005: 2–6).

In the context of criticizing US foreign policy on Iraq, Bacevich takes the concept of militarism outside the realm of totalitarian states. He does so without the intellectual rigor of placing "American militarism" in an appropriate theoretical and empirical framework that focuses on twentieth-century militaristic totalitarian states. In the end, we are left not with a description of a truly repressive American militaristic nation, but a discourse in civil–military relations which calls for a return to the American citizen soldier. Bacevich invites the military elite to participate with "the Left in rejuvenating higher education on matters related to national defense" (Bacevich 2005: 34–5).

With regard to the debate on militarism in a truly militaristic society, intellectual criticism and discourse on the military in higher education would simply be stamped out. Thus, Bacevich's eloquent discussion of the relationship between the officer corps, political elites, and the citizenry is well in line with the framework of achieving concordance in a civil–military relations context. It is not however, an accurate conceptualization of "militarism" within the fuller discourse of the prevailing literature (Bacevich 2005: 2, 33–4, 223–4).

The literature on the developing world, much like the literature on the military–industrial complex, does not readily attribute the word militarism to developing nations. The term civil–military relations is preferred. One reason is that policy makers were interested in affecting US policy toward Latin America, the Middle East, Asia, and other regions in a way that would see the military as a positive and developmental force in these countries. Moreover, these nations do not pose a military threat to Western nations as did Germany, Japan, and Russia. It therefore appears more constructive to label the relationship between military and society "civil–military relations" instead of "militarism."

Political development scholars, such as Lucian Pye, initially argued that the military could "play a crucial role in shaping attitudes toward modernity in other spheres of society" (Pye 1968: 69). They tried to disprove the assumption that the military was always an enemy of democratic forms of government. He argues, for example, that despite their authoritarian tendencies, armies in developing nations are often the most modern institutions in these countries and with proper support from Western nations they could help modernize and develop the Third World (Pye 1968: 69).

Other scholars such as Morris Janowitz agree that armies do possess certain "technocratic" features for social mobilization and development. Nevertheless, Janowitz and others warn that one cannot overlook the more traditional forms of authority that these militaries often possess. Janowitz did not deny that the military has the capacity to play a major role in the advancement of nation building; but he was more skeptical about the armies as agents of positive political and social development (Pauker 1959; Janowitz 1964). Nevertheless, Janowitz's social and cultural perspective on the military provides us with an alternative lens by which to focus on military studies. Janowitz and other scholars who value the study of both institutions and culture enable us to look beyond the traditional militarism literature and the civil–military relations dichotomy to embrace the multidimensional qualities of the role and function of the armed forces around the world.

3   Concordance theory

More nations today are engaged in the process of realigning and reorganizing their militaries than at any point since World War II. As a result, civil–military relations has reemerged as a vital topic of study for students of international relations, comparative politics, and military sociology. And now, more and more citizens around the world who previously cared very little about armies and militias are confronted with these issues in the daily news. We are compelled to understand how other nations organize (or, in some cases, do not organize) their armed forces.

One major conclusion of current civil–military relations theory is that the military should be physically and ideologically separated from political institutions. This approach calls for distinct civilian and military institutions like those found in the United States and other Western countries. It also prescribes such a separation as the best deterrent to domestic military intervention for Western and non-Western nations and the implementation of this separation into policy. In this chapter, concordance theory is presented as an alternative to the oft-adopted separation model.

Concordance theory argues that three partners – the military, the political elites, and the citizenry – should aim for a cooperative relationship that *might* involve separations *but does not require it*. Concordance theory sees a high level of integration between the military and other parts of society as one of several types of civil–military relationships. Because all such relationships reflect specific institutional and cultural conditions shared by the three partners, no single type is seen as necessarily leading to domestic military intervention. In essence, civil and military institutions need not be separate (like the US model) to prevent domestic military intervention.

Concordance does not preclude the separation of civilian institutions and the military. And, under certain cultural conditions, civilian institutions or the very idea of "civil" by Western standards may be inappropriate. Therefore, the specific type of civil–military relationship adopted is less important than the ability of the three partners involved to agree on four indicators:

- social composition of the officer corps
- political decision-making process

- recruitment method
- military style.

By the standards of concordance theory, it is not the separation of institutions which makes domestic military intervention less likely. Rather, it is the ability of the partners to agree on the indicators mentioned above, regardless of whether the "civil" and the "military" are separate or not.

Concordance theory achieves two goals. First, it explains the institutional and cultural conditions that affect relations among the military, the political elites, and society. For example, Chapter 5 describes the institutional partnership that takes place in India between the Congress Party, the three-tiered institutional defense committee, and the Indian armed forces. It also describes how the Indian caste system and British-influenced martial tradition underscored vital cultural relationships that encouraged broader post-independence recruitment patterns among mixed-caste units.

Second, it predicts that if the three partners agree on the four indicators, domestic military intervention is less likely to occur. For example, the case studies in this book on India, Israel, and post-revolutionary United States reflect successful partnerships between the three partners; the case studies on Argentina and Pakistan depict cases of discordance.

Concordance theory also resolves two problems found in the current theory of separation. First, the prevailing theory is derived largely from the experience of the United States. It assumes that to prevent domestic military intervention, the post-World War II US or Western-styled institutional separation should be applied to all nations. This book argues that the US case is grounded in a particular historical and cultural experience and may not be applicable to other nations. Concordance theory considers the unique historical conditions and cultural experiences of nations and the various other possibilities for civil–military relations, which may be different from the US and Western examples. Moreover, concordance theory shows that developing countries need not adopt the traditional Western model of civil–military relations in order to achieve greater political maturity. There exists a model of political partnership that includes agreement over the role of the armed forces and it can take on several forms (e.g., Israel, India, and the post-revolutionary United States). For example, India's successful civil–military relationship is contrasted to the Pakistani case where "discordance" led to domestic military interventions, civil war, and the eventual partition of Pakistan.

Second, the prevailing theory argues for the separation of civil and military institutions. Institutional analysis is the theory's centerpiece. Yet this method of analysis fails to take into account the cultural and historical conditions that may encourage or discourage civil–military separation. We see this deficit emerge, for example, in the post-revolutionary US example – a stark contrast to the post-World War II United States from which separation theory is derived.

Concordance moves beyond institutional analysis by addressing issues relevant to a nation's culture. Ethnic orientations and issues of multicultural diversity are often causes of domestic unrest throughout the world, most significantly in South Asia, Latin America, Africa, and the Middle East. Concordance theory operationalizes the specific institutional and cultural indicators mentioned above and explains the empirical conditions under which the military, the government, and the society may agree on separate, integrated, or other forms of civil–military relations in order to prevent domestic military intervention.

Challenging current theory

The more recent alternatives to Samuel Huntington's separation theory, as well as responses to concordance theory, look strikingly like the old separation theory. For example, agency theory argues that "civil–military relations is a game of strategic interaction." From rational choice modeling, agency theory notes "the 'players' are civilian leaders and military agents" (Feaver 2003: 58). "Each makes 'moves' on its own preferences for outcomes and its expectations of how the other side is likely to act ... the civilians cannot be sure that the military will do what they want; the military agents cannot be sure that the civilians will not catch and punish them [the military] if they misbehave" (ibid.: 10). The author admits that agency theory is "Huntingtonian in orientation" and it "preserves the civilian–military distinction – the *sine qua non of all civil–military theory*" [my emphasis added], and "it preserves the military subordination conception essential to democratic theory" (ibid.: 12). Finally, agency theory is applied to a single case study: post-World War II United States. The author admits that research may find that "agency theory only works in the US case" (ibid.: 10).

In addition to its limited application to case studies, rational choice models are very risky approaches to use in military studies largely because militaries affect the lives of real people, not abstract or modeled individuals. Donald Green and Ian Shapiro agree with the "reality" limitation on applying rational choice models to politics:

> We do not dispute that theoretical models of immense and increasing sophistication have been produced by practitioners of rational choice theory, but in our view the case has yet to be made that these models have advanced our understanding of how politics works in the real world.
>
> (Green and Shapiro 1994: 2)

With respect to military studies and policy making, rational choice modeling can have harrowing consequences. Lyndon B. Johnson and Robert McNamara found that out during Operation Rolling Thunder when Thomas Schelling's rational choice modeling approach was used to justify bombing escalation in North Vietnam. Army generals with real military experience, such as the army vice chief of staff, did not agree that escalated bombing would produce positive results, as McNamara notes in his autobiography (1995: 175). But civilian rational choice theory, completely divorced from the realities of war, won out in the end. Ultimately, the escalation did not modify the behavior or bargaining position of the North Vietnamese as the rational choice argument had predicted. It resulted in over 50,000 dead US soldiers and over 1.5 million casualties on both sides of the conflict (Kaplan 2005; Lebow 2006).

Discussion of how civilian and military roles play out on a day-to-day level (what agency theory is trying to show) should not be framed by abstract formulas or equations, especially in the US case. As discussed in Chapter 1, the vast majority of Americans are respectful and supportive of their military as an institution but are usually unaware of the realities of military life and government policy in military affairs. The late sociologist Charles Moskos called this "patriotism lite": "Oh it's good that somebody's fighting and dying for us so I don't have to do it myself. Those who are not serving are not willing to do any sacrifice, don't really pay much attention to those who are dying" (Moskos 2007).

The average US citizen and scholar should learn more about the day-to-day bargaining between military officers and political elites. But they do not need abstract models based on macroeconomic theory to gain insight into the partnering and lobbying efforts that take place in Washington. What is needed is concrete information and empirical expertise that allow citizens and policy makers to make sound and informed judgments on the conflicts in Iraq, Afghanistan, and other regions. Americans can and should respect the fundamental distinction between civilian and military realms in the United States; and they should partner with the political elites and the military on determining how distinct and separate those US-defined boundaries need to be. They should not, however, assume that those boundaries are necessarily applicable to other nations around the world. Rational modeling techniques – similar to the previously mentioned example regarding bombing escalation in Vietnam – irresponsibly take us further away from the realities of possible partnership among militaries, political elites, and citizens within their indigenous societies and cultures.

Another civil–military scholar claims to have an alternative to separation theory. But the title of his book is *Civilian Control of the Military*. He states that "the strength of civilian control of the military in most militaries is shaped fundamentally by structural factors, especially threats, which affect individual leaders, the military organization, the state, and society" (Desch 1999: 11). Again, this is simply a restatement of the separation theory favoring an institutional conceptualization of civilian and military relations. The author claims to focus on society and individuals, treating them as "intervening variables." The unfortunate part of that conceptualization is that society and individuals need to be studied as people in the context of their political and social environment rather than be characterized as "intervening variables" (ibid.: 13–17). This, coupled with an emphasis on the civilian control of the military, makes for another version of separation theory.

Douglas L. Bland also attempts to reconcile the civil–military relations dichotomy with a "unified theory" that is conditioned by regime theory or the "principles, norms, rules and decision making procedures around which actor expectations converge." He claims that the civil–military relationship is "maintained through the sharing of responsibility for control between civilian leaders and military officers" (Bland 1999: 9, 21). Bland rightly understands that most of the current theory is "too bound by the culture and national politics of their proponents" (ibid.: 8). He admits, however, that his unity theory "like most others, simplifies civil–military relations by describing a relationship between 'civilians' and 'the military'" (ibid.: 21). Through his use of regimes, Bland is noble in his attempt to offer an alternative perspective on domestic relationships, such as rivalries within the armed forces. Unlike the rational choice modelers, Bland understands why culture matters; but ultimately he affirms the old separation argument for distinct civil and military institutions.

One real problem here is that nobody wants to challenge Samuel Huntington's separation theory. A powerful and predictive theory of civil–military relations can make a definitive statement about the military's likelihood for domestic military intervention and provide meaningful institutional and cultural explanations. While current civil–military relations scholars desire alternative theories for their field, they hesitate to stray too far from Huntington's conceptualization. It's as if some unspoken boundary exists that cannot or will not be crossed in language and approach.

Over 50 years have passed since Huntington first conceived his theory; and still scholars are hesitant to appear too critical of the prevailing literature and discipline. No matter how inappropriate the separation model may be for specific nations, scholars often rationalize why Huntington's outdated model can still somehow fit. I firmly believe, as a trained political scientist, that adopting innovative language and culturally relevant approaches to explain the role of the armed forces in diverse and unique nations should also be welcomed by this field – a field that should comprise not only political scientists, but sociologists, anthropologists, peace builders, and policy makers, to name just a few.

Clearly current nation-building efforts in Iraq again point to the need for cultural and institutional sensitivity. Even the US military is actively recruiting anthropologists and sociologists to better understand its efforts in Iraq and to better advise the fledgling Iraqi military. Scholars' unwavering allegiance to Huntington and his followers points to good foot soldiering but also affirms a lack of innovative evolution in an intellectual and policy-making field that is all too relevant in the lives of real people and nations.

The perestroika debate mentioned in Chapter 1 also complicates current theoretical approaches. The trend in political science is toward rational choice models in an effort to move the field in the direction of more quantitative analysis. Unfortunately, as argued previously, these approaches are often out of touch with the realities of day-to-day politics. Rational choice has its place in economics, mathematics, and certain subfields of political science. But civil–military relations, which already superimposes an ethnocentric dichotomy on the rest of the world, does not need to become loftier. It needs to become more ethnographic. It needs to borrow from literature focusing on institutions *and* culture. It needs to consult scholars who conduct fieldwork and mingle with "the Other" or find the sources which take "the Other" and real people into account.

By contrast, concordance theory (as the US, Indian, Pakistani, Argentine, and Israeli cases will illustrate) demonstrates that division of the civil and military is indeed *not* the sine qua non of all civil–military relations theory. Concordance theory preserves the civil–military separation if that distinction is historically and culturally relevant to a particular country. If it is not relevant, as will be depicted in the post-revolutionary US and Israeli case studies, concordance theory can still explain why domestic military intervention does or does not occur in a nation (Anderson 1998; Schiff 1992, 1995, 1998).

Critiques of concordance theory

Before launching into the specifics of concordance theory, the partners, and the four indicators, it is worthwhile mentioning some criticism of the theory. As discussed in Chapter 1, when concordance theory was first published in 1995, Professor Richard S. Wells wrote a commentary to my piece published in *Armed Forces and Society* entitled: "Civil–military relations reconsidered: a theory of concordance" (Schiff 1995). The first comment dealt with the characterization of the United States with separate civil–military boundaries – the institutional separation argument:

> Schiff's characterization of "current civil–military relations theory" as emphasizing physical and ideological separation, and being dependent upon the American example, is in error to the extent that the American case no longer manifests the kind or degree of separation that she presumes.
>
> (Wells 1996: 269–70)

My response was and remains the following:

> Wells claims that the US case no longer manifests the degree of separation presumed by my article. To respond, the fact that US military and civilian institutions have shown degrees of intermingling over the years only points to the weakness of the current theory. The empirical situation in most countries, including America, changes; yet the longstanding theory of separate civil–military institutions has remained the same.
>
> (Schiff 1996: 278)

The point here is that case studies change constantly but the separation theory or "objective civilian control" remains inappropriately the same. Huntington affirms: "The essence of objective control is the recognition of autonomous military professionalism ... the objective definition of civilian control furnishes a single concrete standard of civilian control which is politically neutral and which all social groups can recognize" (Huntington 1957: 83–4).

I argue that there is no "single concrete standard of civilian control" nor should there be; nor is it always politically neutral; and social groups across the spectrum of ethnic and religious lines, for example, may recognize and relate to the military in vastly different ways. For example, the Buddhist monk community in Burma/Myanmar reflects a religious group completely at odds with the armed forces. Even the concept of professionalism can be different depending on national culture. In Israel, for example, it will be shown that the non-prim and sloppy-looking ZAHAL infantry uniform is, in appearance, opposite from Morris Janowitz's depiction of the professional American soldier; yet the ZAHAL uniform style is most appropriate to Israeli culture. A theory that is meant to explain the evolution of the military's role in changing societies is less useful when it relies on a single standard of analysis.

Another argument Professor Wells makes is that concordance is reminiscent of Huntington's conception of fusion:

> What Schiff calls concordance theory "highlights dialogue, accommodation, and shared values or objectives among the military, the political elites, and society." ... Just how this formulation differs from Huntington's concept of fusion is difficult to say. On the surface it doesn't.
>
> (Wells 1996: 271)

My counter to Wells remains the same – concordance does not assume or prescribe definitive types or forms of boundaries that characterize the role of a nation's military:

> I also challenge Wells's contention that concordance theory is similar to the concept of "fusion." Concordance theory does not advocate the blending or fusion of boundaries, nor does it advocate the separation of civil and military institutions. Rather, as stated in the previous article: Cooperation and agreement on four specific indicators may result in a range of civil–military patterns, including separation, the removal of civil–military boundaries, and other variations.
>
> (Schiff 1996: 278–9)

This latter point is important to the underlying cultural method of concordance theory. In the United States alone there have been historical periods when the blending of civil and military institutions and culture has been effective and appropriate. For example, in this book I focus on the post-revolutionary period when Washington and Hamilton aspired to create a separate and professional military, but the citizenry and many political elites preferred and defended the less formal citizens' militia. During World War II, US society had no choice but to join the war effort. Women and men, civilian and soldier, all merged to create an effective warfront against Nazi Germany and Japan. Superimposing separation theory on these two US case studies would be just as inappropriate as current US policy makers superimposing it on foreign countries. Theoretically, separation theory cannot explain these two critical US cases because the civil and military boundaries were not separate; yet the political elites, the military, and the citizenry were in partnership over the role of the military and the overlapping boundaries during these critical periods of United States history. This book will apply concordance theory to one of those US case studies (post-revolutionary United States); the theory will also be applied to nations that do not have overlapping civil and military boundaries.

Another comment posed by Professor Wells, and later by my colleague Ron Krebs, relates to the predictive and applied value of concordance theory. Wells states:

> To question the matter another way, if agreement of three partners on four indicators is an index of intervention, is agreement a condition of a subsequent state of intervention or nonintervention, or is intervention the condition of agreement? It would seem that the theory would have certain problems of application. How is one to distinguish between the absence of intervention and the presence of agreement? The argument seems to presume that agreement/concordance is somehow unrelated to forms of coercion/persuasion.
>
> (Wells 1996: 272)

Again, my response points to the need for cultural understanding of nations in order to determine positive agreement or concordance among the three partners versus hostile domestic intervention:

> With regard to concordance versus intervention, concordance theory does not presume that militaries are innately hostile and coercive institutions. Here again, concordance departs from a long-standing tradition in the field of civil–military relations. The field itself was largely developed as a result of many worldwide occurrences of domestic military intervention, including areas such as Latin America, Africa, South Asia, and the Middle East.... Nevertheless, smaller developing nations such as Israel and India contradicted the assumption that militaries were innately coercive.... A combination of archival research and cultural understanding is practically the only way to comprehend that the overwhelming influence of the Israeli military is, for the most part, not considered to be a negative form of domestic military intervention. In fact, with some exceptions, there is long-standing agreement among the political elites, the military, and the society over the role of the military in that country.
>
> While India is far more receptive to the current separation theory, the significant decline of civilian institutions in that nation should point to some form of domestic military intervention. Its neighbor, Pakistan, has in fact met this fate many times when its civilian institutions could no longer effectively influence the military and society. Separation theory alone, however, does not provide an adequate explanation for the professional Indian military. Again, India elicits the need for a theoretical framework that includes the unique British and Indian influences affecting the role of the armed forces in this society. The four concordance indicators offer a

more comprehensive prediction and explanation than the old theory for the role of the Indian military in partnership with the civilian elites and society at large. Therefore, presupposing that militaries are coercive or noncoercive institutions is not useful. Providing a framework that enables the scholar to conduct responsible research, both institutionally and culturally, is far more beneficial to the study of particular national contexts.

(Schiff 1996: 281)

This response also points to the usefulness of the three partners and the four indicators that are central to concordance theory. Below I will discuss how the role of the military should be looked at through the lens of the entire nation (political elites, military, citizenry) rather than dichotomously and institution-ally; the latter approach neglects the role of a nation's population which often serves in the military and should be part of the process which defines its national purpose.

I also focus on the four indicators which, with the exception of military style, have been identified by leading scholars of civil–military relations as key determinants of military function and role in most societies: social composition of the officer corps; political decision-making process; and recruitment method. The officer corps, for example, generally exists in some indigenous form within all militaries; yet the officer corps in specific nations may not be characterized by what are considered Western attributes. Determining agreement on the social composition of the officer corps is critical to concordance. It is often the case that if the officer corps is widely representative of a society, then concordance is more likely to be achieved. Broad representation, however, is not a requisite, since it is conceivable that the political elites, the military, and the citizenry could agree on a less broadly represented officer corps. The same may be true of the political decision-making process and conscription method indicators as will be discussed in more detail.

The structure and form of these four indicators, which are found in all mili-taries, are different depending upon the particular political structure and culture of each nation. This again points to the suitability of cultural interpretation in addition to the more conventional scientific methods that rely on measuring the success of institutions and political governance. As discussed in Chapter 1, this book employs a deductive causal methodology and considers the importance of cultural context. These indigenous contexts must be explored to understand the role of the armed forces in society. Prominent civil–military relations scholars such as Claude Welch understand how cultural analysis complements the more traditional forms of political science data collection:

I do not claim that only insiders of a particular culture can fully explain its inner workings; nonetheless, dialogue between academics and practitioners of different regional and academic backgrounds is essential. Indigenous scholars enjoy types of access to information and attitudes about interac-tions between armed forces and their societies by having been born within these cultures ... they can and should shape the research agenda and data collection more actively than in the recent past. Further, their officer colleagues could say and write much more, from their inside perspective, about modalities of transition.

(Welch 1992: 337–8)

This integrative approach to political science allows the concordance indicators to manifest and be described on their own terms with respect to each case study. Rather than superimposing Western institutional separations determining agreement or disagreement on the political decision-making process or military recruitment method suggests a richer understanding of the role of the armed forces in a particular society. Therefore, the indicators themselves may exist in all nations, but their composition and relationship to military, the civilian elites, and the citizenry will necessarily be distinctive in each nation.

An important comment and criticism I expect international relations scholars to raise is the issue of external threat conditions. As mentioned before, the realist school of thought views nations as unitary actors that exist in an anarchic international environment. A nation's strength is determined not by domestic factors such as civil–military relations but by the overall concentration of power and its balance of power vis-à-vis other states. In Chapter 1 I addressed why realism and the unitary actor model serve to reinforce the culturally deaf and theoretically dichotomous approaches to civil–military relations. Realism, by refusing to deal with unique domestic issues, only further precludes the importance of cultural analysis. However, Harold Lasswell (1954) argued that high external threat conditions would result in militarism and domestic military intervention. If this is the case, then why isn't external threat an explicit variable of concordance theory?

External threat conditions are important when considering almost any aspect of a nation's political system. Israel is certainly an example of a nation whose entire socio-political dynamic is largely the result of high external threats. The State of Israel emerged after World War II and the Holocaust, and the Israeli citizen's army was developed in response to the Arab–Israeli conflict. High external threat, however, did not give rise to Lasswellian militarism in Israel and did not promote domestic military intervention. While threat conditions were critical to the role of the Israeli military, it is concordance rather than threat that explains the lack of domestic military intervention in that nation. Israel, like all nations, had to achieve concordance under any condition of threat in order to prevent domestic intervention.

Concordance in nations with high external threat (e.g., Israel) may look different than concordance in nations under low or medium threat (e.g., Canada, India). Nevertheless, it is concordance between the military, the political leadership, and the citizens that hinders domestic military intervention. In other words, particular threat conditions should be considered in a discussion of any military organization. Each nation must be studied on its own merit to determine the success of concordance among the four indicators. It is concordance, however, and not particular threat conditions, that prevents domestic military intervention.

High external threat conditions also point to the importance of military strategy, which is often conditioned by both foreign and domestic pressures. Military strategy was alluded to in Chapter 2 when Alfred Vagts described the "military way." What Vagts was referring to was the art of war preparation and execution; this is military strategy. The logistical, technological, and operational concerns of warfare are essential aspects of the military way and traditional strategic studies.

Military strategy gains relevance in countries where external threat is high and domestic military intervention may seem inevitable. It will therefore be alluded to in the discussion of three of the four concordance indicators: social composition of the officer corps, conscription method, and political decision-making process. Although the officer corps indicator deals with social composition, a major function of many high-ranking officers is to develop and coordinate particular military strategies for a nation's grand military strategy. The conscription method of a particular nation is often conditioned by strategic plans and scenarios adopted by the military. Finally, the political decision-making process is frequently concerned with agreement or opposition to the strategic plans and operations of the military high command. Thus, all three indicators in some way point to the importance of military strategy.

One additional criticism and comment of concordance theory, offered by my colleague Douglas Bland (2001: 1), questions the limitations of predicting *coup d'état*:

> Extant theories and studies in America and elsewhere concentrate on solving or preventing the *coup d'état*, something that is a dangerous but, arguably, an occasional problem of civil–military relations in most states. "No coup? No problem, and so no further discussion is required." [Andrew J. Bacevich, "Tradition Abandoned: America's Military in a New Era," *National Interest* 48 (Summer 1997): 17]. The limitation in this approach is not that theories concentrate on the problem of military interventions in politics, but that they tend to overlook the other, perhaps more common, civil–military problems facing societies and their armed forces.

My primary response is that coup or the possibility of coup and other coercive forms of domestic military intervention, as discussed in Chapter 2, are not that rare. There are at least a dozen countries that are ruled by leaders who came to power via coup or are still influenced by previous military dictatorships. Many of these countries are located in critical regions such as South Asia, Africa, Southeast Asia, and Latin America where issues of oil, terrorism, water, and infectious diseases are prominent. The Western world is also confronted with serious policy making scenarios in Iraq and Afghanistan where newly created regimes are determining the role of their armed forces.

Nevertheless, concordance theory is limited by its causal objective, which is to predict the prevention or occurrence of domestic military intervention. Concordance theory does not pretend to be something it is not; nor is the theory meant to analyze all facets and problems facing the field of civil–military relations. But concordance theory is not a "mirage" either (E.A. Cohen 2002: 204). Concordance does successfully predict the likelihood of domestic military intervention.

Concordance theory

The current civil–military relations theory emphasizes the separation between civil and military institutions and the authority of the civil sphere over the military to prevent domestic military intervention. By contrast, the theory of concordance highlights dialogue, accommodation, and shared values or objectives among the military, the political elites, and society. Concordance theory accomplishes two goals. First, it explains which institutional and cultural conditions – separation, integration, or another alternative – prevent or promote domestic military intervention. Second, it predicts that when agreement on four specific indicators prevails among the three partners, domestic intervention is less likely to occur. In some nations, like Israel, agreement may include the blurring of civilian and military boundaries. In other nations, like post-World War II United States, the boundaries may be more distinct. Regardless of how permeable the boundaries may be, the central argument is that if the military, the political elites, and the citizenry achieve concordance on the four indicators, then domestic intervention is less probable.

Concordance theory explains the specific conditions determining the military's role in the domestic sphere (i.e., the government and society). Concordance does not require a particular form of government, set of institutions, or decision-making process. But it usually takes place in the context of active agreement, whether established by legislation, decree, or constitution. It is also based on long standing historical and cultural values.

In contrast to the prevailing theory that emphasizes the separation of civil and military institutions, concordance encourages cooperation and involvement among the military, political institutions, and society at large. In other words, concordance does not assume that separate civil and military spheres are required to prevent domestic military intervention. Rather, intervention may be avoided if the military cooperates with the political elites and the citizenry, regardless of its separate or integrated status. Cooperation and agreement on the four specific indicators may result in a range of civil–military patterns, including separation, the removal of civil–military boundaries, and other variations.

The military, the political leadership, and the citizenry

Concordance theory views the military, the political leadership, and the citizenry as partners and predicts that when they agree about the role of the armed forces domestic military intervention is less likely to occur in a particular state. The first partner, the military, can be defined quite simply. It encompasses the armed forces and the personnel who represent the military. The officers and the enlisted personnel are usually those most dedicated to the armed forces. In some nations, other security services may also comprise the armed forces. Generally, the military is the institution publicly recognized by society and the political elites as the institution that defends a nation's borders.

The second partner, the political leadership, can best be defined in terms of function. The exact nature of governmental institutions and the methods of their selection are less important when determining concordance. What is more relevant is identifying the elites who represent the government and have direct influence over the composition and support of the armed forces. Thus, cabinets, presidents, prime ministers, party leaders, parliaments, and monarchs are all possible forms of governmental elites.

The third partner, the citizenry, is by corollary even more heterogeneous than the political leadership. Usually it is comprised of individuals who are members of unions or associations, urban workers and entrepreneurs, rural farm workers, those who may have the right to vote, or other groups that may be disenfranchised. It is also best defined by function. How do the citizens interact with the military? Is there agreement among the citizens themselves over the role of the military in society?

The current civil–military relations literature, which focuses on the institutional civilian and military separation, does not consider the citizenry but relies instead on political institutions as the main "civil" component of analysis. Although the relationship of civil institutions to the military is indeed important, it only partially reflects the story of civil–military relations. By contrast, concordance theory does not lump political and civil institutions together. It considers the citizenry an important partner distinct from the military and the political elites. After all, it is the citizens who cooperate with and legitimize the power of the other two partners. Thus, concordance is not restricted to an institutional analysis but incorporates additional elements of society that affect the role and function of the armed forces.

On what levels can the government and the citizenry affect the military's role in a nation? It is argued here that there are four indicators of concordance: (1) the social composition of the officer corps; (2) the political decision-making process; (3) the military recruitment method; and (4) the military style. In the past, the first three have been discussed in the context of theories emphasizing political and military separation. Concordance borrows important concepts of civil–military relations from the current literature but places them in a wider historical and cultural context that allows richer theoretical conclusions and enables better evaluation of empirical case studies. The four indicators are important elements of concordance because they reflect specific conditions that influence agreement or disagreement among the three partners. Thus, depending on particular cultural and historical conditions, the indicators will determine whether relations among the military, the government, and the society take the form of separation, integration, or some other alternative. The crucial point, therefore, is the cultural and historical context that shapes the relationship among partners and the indicators.

The social composition of the officer corps

Composition of the officer corps is a primary indicator of concordance. Most militaries have an officer corps that is in charge of the broad institutional and day-to-day functioning of the armed forces. These are the career soldiers who dedicate their lives to soldiering and to the development of the military and who help to define the relationship of the military to the rest of society. The officer is distinguished from the rank-and-file soldier; and, as leaders of the armed forces, the officer corps provides not only critical links between the citizenry and the military but also between the military and the government.

A particular composition of the officer corps exists in all modern militaries. In democratic societies, the officer corps usually represents the various constituencies of the nation (e.g., middle class, Brahmin, Muslim, African American). Broad representation or democracies, however, are not requisite conditions for concordance, since it is conceivable that the society and the military could agree on a less broadly representative corps. In Israel, for example, ultra-orthodox Jews are exempt from military service yet concordance prevails (not without some tension around this issue) because this is a mutually agreed arrangement among the political elites, the military, the non-religious citizenry, and the ultra-orthodox constituency. In India, while the military is broadly represented, the militarily skilled Sikh community, which comprises only 2.5 percent of India's population, has at least a 10 percent representation in the Indian officer corps. Again, tension has prevailed around the leveraging of Sikh martial qualities with high officer representation; but, for the most part there is agreement on this military and cultural arrangement.

By contrast, the Pakistani alienation of the Bengali community because of their supposed absence of martial qualities created deep discordance among the citizens, the military, and the political elites. These examples affirm that particular historical and cultural traditions prevail, and that those traditions can affect agreement or disagreement over the composition of the officer corps.

The political decision-making process

The political decision-making process involves the institutional organs of society that determine important factors for the military such as budget, materiel, military size, and structure. This process *does not* imply a particular form of government – democratic, authoritarian, or any other. Rather, it refers to the specific channels that determine the needs and allocations of the military. For example, budgets, materiel, size, and structure are issues decided by open parliaments, closed cabinets, special committees, and political elites that may or may not involve the participation of military officers. Often, the military makes its needs known through a governmental channel or agency which takes into consideration both military and societal resources and requirements. In many countries there is a close partnership and in some instances a collusion between the military and industry, a military–industrial complex. Such a partnership may have the support of the citizenry who may be persuaded that external threat conditions warrant a close relationship between the military and industry. Also, the domestic economy may play a role, as both the business sector and citizens stand to gain from the creation of new industry and employment. The critical issue is that agreement occurs among the political elites, the military, and the citizenry over the political process that best meets the need and requirements of the armed forces.

Much discussion has evolved around democratization of developing nations. Americans and Western Europeans certainly favor democratization and in many instances have fought long and hard to establish democratic governments and institutions. The post-revolutionary United States (discussed in Chapter 4) is a case in point. Nations, however, evolve differently and often encompass and incorporate values that may challenge modern Western democratization. Concordance among the military, political elites, and citizenry is more likely to result in a type of government based on widespread agreement, quite possibly a modern-day democracy.

The theme of this book, however, is domestic military intervention not democratization. Here we are examining the conditions that are likely to result in military overthrow or forms of domestic military intervention. Therefore, the type of government that keeps the military in check or creates a partnership with it may be democratic, or authoritarian, or fall somewhere in between on a continuum of political development and societal concordance.

Recruitment method

The third indicator of concordance is recruitment method – the system for enlistment of citizens into the armed forces – which may be coercive or persuasive, a distinction borrowed from Samuel Finer's "extraction–coercion–persuasion cycle" (1975: 95–6). Coercive recruitment refers to the forcible conscription or extraction of people and supplies for military purposes. Demands are made upon the citizenry, through conscription and taxation, to supply the needs and obligations of the military. Such demands are often harsh because citizens are forced to cooperate against their will. Consequently, this form of recruitment usually does not allow concordance between the military and the citizenry.

Persuasive recruitment can take the form of voluntary or involuntary enlistment and is based on beliefs. The population may believe the sacrifice of military service is worthwhile for the sake of security, patriotism, or any other national cause. The government is not forced to coerce its people into military service when they "willingly offer themselves" by volunteering or accepting the need for enlistment (Finer 1975: 95–6). Persuasive recruitment implies an agreement among the political leadership, the military, and the citizenry over the requirements and composition of the armed forces.

Military style

The final indicator of concordance is military style. This refers to the external manifestations and inner mental constructions associated with the military: what it looks like, what ethos drives it, and what people think about it. Why is style so important? Style is about the drawing of social boundaries or their elimination. It is the mode by which members of particular elites relate to each other as peers and differentiate themselves from members of other elites and the members of non-elite groups. Style is important because it reflects how something appears, and appearance stands as a symbol that conveys and connotes a type of power or authority.

The late sociologist Charles Moskos (as cited by Williams 2007) stated: "A uniformed service – including police officers – is a way for both members and outsiders to define who is serving their country and community ... It highlights the sacrifices that are expected of uniformed personnel." Military style deals directly with the human and cultural elements of the armed forces – how the military looks, the overt and subtle signals it conveys, the ritual it displays – which are all part of a deep and nuanced relationship among soldiers, citizens, and the polity.

Military style is not separate from the other indicators of concordance. On the contrary, it manifests itself within, among, and throughout the substance of the other variables. It is usually part of the historical development associated with military traditions and symbols. The uniform, for example, has always been one important symbol of respectability, professionalism, separateness, or cohesiveness depending upon the character of the nation and its armed forces. Other military symbols and rituals include military parades and marches, military music, social traditions, and ceremonies that capture the sense of belonging to the armed forces. Symbols and rituals may be found in the officer corps and in the methods used to induct soldiers. More importantly, it informs core civilian values including the institutional processes that determine the needs and requirements of the military.

Summary

Both the current theory of civil–military separation and the theory of concordance are descriptive as well as prescriptive. Separation theory describes the United States and other Western nations. It prescribes separation as the best deterrent to domestic military intervention for nations throughout the world. By contrast, concordance theory describes a concordance or agreement among the military, the political elites, and the citizenry, found in a wide range of cultures (including the United States) where there has long been substantial agreement among all sectors of society about the role of the armed forces. It prescribes this theory as a deterrent to domestic military intervention that flexibly applies to cultures different from each other and from the United States.

The separation theorists and policy makers believed they could export US theory and practice to developing nations, thinking all "they" had to do was become more like "us." The developing world suffered from coups and domestic military intervention because their civil and military institutions were disoriented, without the advantage of modern US civil–military separation and the US soldier. The problem is that civil–military relations scholars never really bothered to go beyond foreign institutions and into the "Other" culture – a culture perhaps more complex than that of the United States – with strategies other than the familiar civil–military dichotomy.

These scholars should have heeded Ruth Benedict's advice about understanding foreign cultures: "The cases of cultural disorientation may be less than it appears at the present time. There is always the possibility that the description of the culture is disoriented rather than the culture itself" (1934: 228). To assume that "civil" as it appears in post-World War II United States should apply to all nations, even non-Western ones that may possess no real history of the civil or a variant society, is to offer imported assumptions about the indigenous and historical character of a nation. In the following chapters, this and other issues are addressed through concordance theory within the context of five case studies: post-revolutionary United States, India, Pakistan, Argentina, and Israel.

4 Post-revolutionary United States (1790–1800)

A nation as it exists today differs vastly from its initial form. Cultures evolve, institutions mature, and decision-making strategies change. Citizens of Western nations often forget that nation building is a long, complicated, and arduous process that requires attention to indigenous institutions and culture. For those living in the United States, the century-long nation-building process in all of its grueling glory is now buried under centuries of history. It seems appropriate, therefore, to bring forth in memory the post-revolutionary United States – a case which looks quite different than the present-day United States.

Drawing from the resource development profession and fundraising terminology, nation building is the difference between an annual gift and an institutional infrastructure that spends years cultivating endowed million-dollar contributions. At Harvard University, for example, one principal gift could take anywhere from five to ten years to cultivate, solicit, and close – and that does not include the post-gift stewardship process. In addition, a university of that caliber would already have a well-developed infrastructure, an endowment the size of the GNP of several small nations, and probably the best fundraising army in the world.

In the context of nation building, Westerners might expect the process in Iraq or other regions to be quick, like an annual gift. In reality, the process more closely resembles soliciting a principal gift. The creation or remaking of an entire nation that relies on significant capital to build its military and socio–political infrastructure is likely to be an extended period of development and evolution, not an overnight task. The US post-revolutionary case reminds us of this. Despite initial success, nation building is not without conflict, setbacks, and even subsequent military action, as exemplified by the American Civil War. In other words, building a nation is a prolonged activity that almost certainly involves domestic civil–military encounters with diverse cultures and institutions – a notion separation theorists would oppose or regard as being not very orderly.

For too long scholars have applied the modern US model deliberately to developing nations around the world. Nations in Latin America, Asia, Africa, and the Middle East were presumed to separate their civilian and military institutions accordingly. That is as tall of an order for developing nations today as it was for the United States during its first 25 years of independence. From a similar standpoint, President Washington wanted for his young nation a more professional and British-inspired military – a military style appropriate for British cultural space. But the British model was not adopted, and the founders opted for a militia-style, dual-army system that was more in-line with the US culture of the revolutionary era.

The early US case study turns separation theory on its head. The nation rejected President Washington's separate and professional military configuration, maintaining permeable military, civilian, and political institutional boundaries. Furthermore, it was a young nation under very high external and internal threat conditions that managed to escape domestic military intervention (or praetorian government). In other words, separate military and civilian institutions did not predict non-intervention. And having collaborative institutions, like the early United States, did not necessarily mean the military would intervene in civilian life.

Separation theory cannot explain the success of the post-revolutionary US case. It focuses on separate civil–military spheres and predicts domestic military intervention, or praetorian government, to form the new American nation – a situation that did not occur in the early United States. Separation theory also cloaks the United States' evolution from a nation of permeable civilian and military boundaries to one of separate military and civilian institutions by not mentioning the early American period but relying on the post-World War II scenario. More important, both culturally and institutionally developing nations today (despite advances in technology) significantly resemble the early United States in their army formation and their struggle for military, political, and citizen cooperation.

This chapter explores the deficit of separation theory as it applies to post-revolutionary United States (1790–1800). As an alterative, concordance theory is applied to shed light on a situation where the militia army provided an effective blurring of civilian and military boundaries under high external threat conditions. In the early United States, almost no domestic military intervention occurred despite its presence in everyday life. US political elites, military, and society experienced agreement regarding the four concordance indicators. Concordance was achieved, and domestic military intervention was averted.

Brief mention should be made regarding the history of the US militia and the sensitivities that existed surrounding a standing army just prior to the nineteenth century. The early American colonists utilized the militia to fend off Native American attacks. Most male colonists participated in the militia system, although certain exceptions were allowed: the Quaker community for example did not participate for pacifist reasons, and wealthy citizens could pay others to take their place for militia duties. Prior to the Revolutionary War, General Washington was deeply concerned about the militia's ability to truly defend colonial territory in time of war. Indeed, it was the ill-disciplined militia, fraught with lack of regular troops, poor military skills, and insufficient guns, that Washington inherited to fight the British from 1775 to 1783. Eventually the minutemen militia was developed into a standing Continental Army, while the regular militia protected the homestead against Native American attacks and slave rebellions, both instigated by the British. The Continental Army was composed of about 100 battalions (11,000 troops) and was really a mega-militia to which each state, in proportion to their population, contributed men. The difference between the Continental Army and the militia was time commitment and military discipline: soldiers in the former had to commit for three years of service and were taught basic military skills by officers who had been trained in the European tradition; soldiers in the latter militia served sporadically and frequently showed up in ragtag farm clothing and often without a weapon.

By contrast, the British army in its regal redcoat style was far more experienced than the American colonial militia. By 1760 Britain was an empire that extended throughout America, Africa, and Asia. Its army and navy were the best-trained force in the world – well-disciplined, well-armed, and battle-tested throughout the globe. Moreover, by 1707 the United Kingdom included the Scottish military and was centrally controlled from London. It did not hesitate to ship thousands of troops across 3,000 miles of water to fight the colonists. From the start, it appeared that the American militia would be no match for the Royal Navy and infantry. What the British did not anticipate was the resilience and determination of the American colonists, in addition to Washington's adoption of British and Prussian military tactics throughout the War of Independence.

After the war, the Continental Army was abolished and American debates began over the future of the militia versus a standing army. Although a small standing constabulary force was immediately established in 1784, it was relegated to the Appalachian Northwest region, and the average term of service was one year. In 1786, "Congress tripled the authorized strength of the army, ostensibly to prevent Indian War in the Northwest but actually to crush the uprising of debtor farmers in western Massachusetts led by Daniel Shays" (Skelton 1992: 4). Due to insufficient funding and recruitment of the expanded standing army, it was the Massachusetts militia that ended up quelling the rebellion and not the newly authorized armed force.

A similar incident occurred in 1791 during the Whiskey Rebellion (described later in this chapter) when federal troops were raised to put down the rebellion; but local militiamen and political leaders, many of whom had fought with the rebels during the Revolutionary War, ended up quelling that uprising. By 1800, the standing army and its War Department bureaucracy showed moderate growth, but despite Federalist preference for a full-fledged professional army, the militia army remained influential and was greatly supported throughout the Jeffersonian period.

Post-revolutionary United States: high external and internal threat conditions

The US post-revolutionary period faced so many external and internal threats that Harold Lasswell would have readily predicted a garrison state disaster for the young republic. The key external threats included military hostility from

Britain, France, and the Barbary States and economic threats resulting from trade embargoes and US ship assaults, while internal threats came from Native Americans and citizen uprisings, most notably the Whiskey Rebellion. The Federalists recognized these severe domestic and foreign threats on the American continent, noting "the territories of Britain, Spain and of the Indian nations in our neighborhood do not border on particular States, but encircle the Union from Maine to Georgia" (Madison *et al.* 1961: 163).

External hostility from France and Britain had an acute presence during the United States' early years. Britain had military posts on US soil in the Northwest and would not consider removing them until two years after signing the controversial Jay Treaty – the 1794 agreement that thwarted another war between Britain and the United States. Despite the treaty, tensions with Britain still existed. The Jay Treaty also created problems with France who interpreted the treaty as benefiting Britain during an era of continuous hostilities between the two countries. The treaty also became a source of friction between France and the United States in 1797, although the United States had tried to remain neutral during this period (Millet and Maslowski 1984: 96).

While external threats involving alliances and sovereignty persisted, threats to the United States' maritime trade and related economic factors were also encountered. Both Britain and France controlled major US waterways during the 1790s. In addition, the United States could not fully protect its citizens while navigating the Mississippi River through Spanish-occupied New Orleans (Weigley 1973: 41). In addition, France used its warships to aggressively capture US merchantmen at sea (Beach 1986: 36). The Barbary States of Algiers, Tunisia, and Morocco also proved relentless in capturing US ships and merchantmen in the Mediterranean Sea. As a result, the Barbary States established a formidable white slave trade based on captured merchantmen, including Americans (Hitchens 2004: 56): "No longer shielded by the British navy and with no navy of its own, the United States had to pay tribute" to prevent further capture of its citizens (Beach 1986: 26). Britain, France, and the Barbary States enriched themselves at the expense of the American nation, while the young country struggled to protect its borders and maritime activity.

Related to US trade route troubles were economic threats imposed by Britain and France in the form of trade restrictions. Prior to the American Revolution, the North American colonies had a type of "most favored colonies" status. In 1768, annual exports to Britain averaged £1,752,142. After the Revolution, however, exports fell to £749,395 and rose only slightly to £1,191,071 in 1790. After 1793, "France increased its depredations against US shipping" (Millet and Maslowski 1984: 96). All major US staple exports, including tobacco, rice, and wheat, "dropped alarmingly" in the post-revolutionary period (Musselman 1980: 15–16). Britain even excluded US shippers from the profitable West Indies trade as well as trade with Canada. In all, the dangers of maritime trade and the strict trade restrictions induced crippling economic conditions for the young republic.

In addition to national defense and economic instabilities, internal conflicts also placed the emerging nation in jeopardy, namely "a ring of hostile Indian tribes from the Saint Laurence River to the Gulf of Mexico" (Faber and Faber 1989: 127). The hostility was largely the result of divided allegiance among the Native Americans during the Revolutionary War. Many tribes had supported the British to prevent further expansion into Native American territory. During the war, Native American villages were often attacked by the American army and sacked for food supplies. After the war, US territorial expansion frequently resulted in massacres, such as the 1779 Sullivan Expedition in upstate New York when over 40 Iroquois villages were destroyed.

With hostilities between the United States and Native Americans elevated, attempts at peace agreements began to emerge. The United States attempted a series of treaties among several tribes in 1784–6. Such policies included land payments, trade regulations, and boundary determinations. But Native Americans in the wilderness west of the Mississippi River often rejected US sovereignty and peace attempts. Additionally, Britain and Spain supported native revolts with money and arms and "[the British] were doing their best to stir discontent at every opportunity" (Slaughter 1986: 171). Moreover, as John Jay pointed out, Native American hostilities were frequently provoked by the "improper conduct of individual states" (Faber and Faber 1989: 12). In other words, member states would not support national policies regarding peace efforts with Native Americans. For example, Americans searching for land would often incite the Native Americans rather than respect the fragile treaties that attempted to reconcile land rights with early American territorial expansion. Also, unreliable state policies caused uncertainty over proclamations of state versus national rights in states such as Georgia and New York. These internal conditions consistently undermined government attempts at peace with Native American tribes.

But internal conflict was not limited to US–Native American hostilities. Resistance from its own citizens over government policies also weakened US sovereignty. This was perhaps best exemplified during the Whiskey Rebellion – an event that led Britain to believe Western Pennsylvania might be "ripe for British plucking" (Slaughter 1986: 171).

The Whiskey Rebellion

The Whiskey Rebellion of 1794 was a clear example of internal insecurity and regional conflict. It became President Washington's foremost civil–military relations problem. A new federal excise tax was placed on whiskey, causing Pennsylvania farmers to revolt against the supervisor for collections. In Eastern Pennsylvania, the excise tax seemed reasonable because it was simply a tax on distilled spirits. In the West, however, whiskey was used as currency to purchase items that could not be grown or produced in the rural areas. As a result, settlers from the West marched to Pittsburgh with the intention of overthrowing the local government. The rebellion reflected regional insecurity and President

Washington's primary civil–military relations dilemma (Slaughter 1986: 116–18, 158).

When farmers confronted General John Neville (the supervisor for collections) at his home in Bower Hill, shots were fired and several protesters were wounded. The following day protesters were joined by the local militia that had coincidentally been summoned by President Washington to fight the Native Americans. The militia sympathized with the protesters and began to take control of the situation. When militia commander James McFarlane heard that Neville had fled, McFarlane demanded the militia soldiers leave. They did not, more shots were heard, and the Neville house was set on fire. Two or three people were killed and several were wounded at Bower Hill (Faber and Faber 1989: 155–6).

President Washington was very concerned about the incident at Bower Hill. He "worried about anarchy if rebels were permitted to continue trampling on the law without being punished" (Faber and Faber 1989: 163). In response, he assembled an army of 13,000 men – militias from Maryland, New Jersey, and Pennsylvania. Two months after the rebellion began, President Washington and Alexander Hamilton sent the troops to Pittsburgh to assess the situation. Alongside a federal judge, a marshal, and an attorney, an official inquiry ensued. Only 18 minor figures in the rebellion were arrested, and all were either acquitted or pardoned. The incident proved, however, that "the federal government would use the army, if [it] needed to enforce the law" (ibid.: 163).

The Whiskey Rebellion was less of a threat to the government than President Washington feared. In the end, "the moderate elements were able to restrain the mob" (Faber and Faber 1989: 158). Many local government officials and many of the business elites believed that the farmers had a moral right to protest the excise tax but did not have the legal right to incite a riot and cause physical damage. It was the protesters' use of the militia that caused President Washington to assemble additional militia troops with allegiance to the federal government. At first it appeared that the people's army was turning on the government. In reality moderation prevailed, and the larger military force called in to quell the incident proved unnecessary.

Indeed, the young American nation was beset by significant threats. Britain, France, the Barbary pirates, and Native Americans all posed high external and internal threats. President Washington experienced what he considered a significant civil–military conflict in the Whiskey Rebellion. Any one of these threats should have been enough to undermine the tenuous political and economic condition of the new nation. All of them combined should have resulted in an oligarchical praetorian government at best, with the end result being complete anarchy by the citizens at large. Concordance, however, was achieved throughout the Federal period (1790–1800).

The success of this case is the result of the development of political and military institutions and their compatibility with the US culture of the time – most notably the citizens' militia army and citizen–soldier mentality. Had a standing army been created or had the militia been completely federalized as Washington,

Hamilton, and Knox preferred, anarchy by the citizenry would have likely been the outcome. However, the nation's founders chose to create military institutions and a political decision-making process in concordance with the military recruitment and the predominant culture. As a result, concordance was reached between the three partners – the military, the political elites, and the citizenry – regarding the four concordance indicators.

Concordance in post-revolutionary United States

The social composition of the officer corps

To understand the composition of the officer corps, we must first understand the militia system organization – the localized bodies from which the officer corps was comprised. In 1776, the British arrived in New York with a superior navy and 31,625 soldiers of all ranks and military skill. General Washington could only collect 19,000 men – half of whom lacked military skill and discipline – to defend his budding nation. There were never enough officers and rank-and-file soldiers during the American Revolution to tactically meet British military proficiency. Washington tried in vain to model his Continental Army as closely on the British military as possible. But there always remained a deficit of soldiers due to the militia system and the engrained militia mentality.

The Continental Army's composition was indeed "continental" in flavor. It was comprised of militias from every North American colony, with the troops and formations remaining loyal to their colonial affiliation first and foremost. Often, citizen soldiers from all regions of the colonies were called to reinforce the tiny Continental Army in important battles, including New York and Boston (Wright 1983: 43, 44).

The army officer corps members, like the rank-and-file members, also had a history that was steeped in the militia system and indeed reflected the prevailing "opposition to the notion of a standing army" (Wright 1983: 43, 44). As a result, these officers and their troops remained in the service of their colonial governments while serving only temporarily in the centralized Continental Army. Though no research has comprehensively studied the Continental Army's officer corps composition, the majority is thought to have been wealthy community elites. In other words, citizen constituencies coming from farming or artisan backgrounds had little representation in the officer corps.

Because both citizen soldiers and the elites of the officer corps had loyalties to the militia system and resisted the British-styled standing army, the US Constitution institutionalized "the dual-army tradition." This tradition placed the federal government in authority over both a standing army and the militia. Although the president, as commander in chief, would call the army, navy, and militia into service, the states still had significant authority over their respective militias including the appointment of officers and their training. The states, however, were not allowed to maintain warships or non-militia soldiers (Millet and Maslowski 1984: 89, 95, 96).

A federal infantry company in 1792 was highly organized and efficient in both training and makeup: "the make-up was one captain, one lieutenant, one ensign, six sergeants, six corporals, two musicians, and eighty-one privates" (Urwin 2000: 33). By contrast, the militia members were called up two or three times a year for rather sporadic and ineffective military review and training. Despite the less efficient militia army, allowing the states to appoint militia officers and train the militia troops was considered far less threatening to the local citizens than federal oversight of the military (Larkin 1989: 274; Urwin 2000: 33).

In 1796, the political differences within the officer corps began to emerge with Washington's authorization of more than 3000 regular troops. The armed force was a "constabulary" army – established largely to guard northern US borders against Native American incursions and internal revolts such as the Whiskey Rebellion. President Washington sent the force to the frontier – far removed from the main centers of cities and towns. Despite the army's remote location, senior military officers assisted the secretary of war, the secretary of navy, and the president with the day-to-day operations of the military. These senior officers – believed to be the political elites of the time – influenced military decisions and thus made President Washington's army the focus of controversy.

In the political debate over military structure, the Federalists wanted a large force and the Republicans opposed a significant standing army. During Adams' presidency in 1798, an additional 12,000 men were included in the Federalist-inspired constabulary army. President Adams reluctantly accepted the larger army on the political urging of Hamilton and Washington, perhaps due to conflict and possible war with France. This military supplement was filled mainly with Federalist and Southern officers. The Southern officers in particular, "with their stress upon the ethic of honor, often aspired to the titles of general and colonel" (Chambers 1999: 599). Despite a move toward a larger, centralized army, Adams understood the citizens' preference for the militia system with its close cultural connection to the average post-revolutionary civilian.

Nevertheless, Secretary of War Henry Knox (with Hamilton's support) encouraged Congress to completely nationalize the militia in an effort to strengthen the standing army and its officer corps. Members of Congress, in-line with President Adams' intuition, declined full military federalization. Many had fought in the Revolution and understood the social and political significance of the militia and its connection to the states. Consequently, Congress approved a provisional force – an army to be raised only during wartime. Also, under the maritime plans of Secretary of the Navy Benjamin Stoddert, Congress had approved additional navy frigates and a million dollars to build them. However, peace with Algiers and France and President Jefferson's later preference to create a small gunboat fleet would stall the building of a serious navy. Despite the examples of France and Great Britain with their well-disciplined infantries and magnificent navy fleets, US congressional representatives demurred from a nationalized military in favor of provisional forces (Weigley 1973: 45; Millet and Maslowski 1984: 89, 95, 96).

By the late 1790s the army officer corps was composed of Federalists and many Southerners, and commanded by Washington and Hamilton. The geographical composition of the officer corps, however, was relatively well balanced among northern and southern states:

> Although New England was somewhat underrepresented in the officer corps as a whole, Yankees predominated in the upper ranks, claiming nine of the twenty officers at or above the rank of major. At the unit level, geographical concentrations are more evident ... 48 percent of the officers of the Second Infantry whose origins are known came from New England, 52 percent of those of the Third Infantry from the South, and 50 percent from the fourth infantry from the Middle Atlantic States.
>
> (Skelton 1992: 19–20)

In the end, while there was fair geographical balance among the corps, the political composition of the officer corps was considered to be largely Federalist.

According to military historian William B. Skelton, by 1803 "Federalists outnumbered Republicans in the army by a majority of 140 to 38" (1992: 73). The officers strove to have a more disciplined and British-styled military but were often unequipped and socially disparaged by non-officers and the population at large. There was far too much social debate over the role of the preferred citizens military and the new constabulary force for the latter to become fully institutionalized and professionalized along British lines. Moreover, there was tremendous overlap between the military and political arenas with respect to the officer corps. "Even though the Articles of War prohibited regulars from speaking disrespectfully of high federal and state officials, many officers used their political contacts to pursue their own interests both inside and outside the army" (Skelton 1992: 73). The counterbalance to the officer corps was always the militia, which prevented the establishment of a large standing army and encouraged a unique albeit tense partnership between Congress, the president, and the citizenry.

The political decision-making process

The political decision-making process was stimulated by a constant Federalist versus Republican debate on the nature of the military and foreign policy. In the background was the citizen–soldier mentality and culture that Republicans fully embraced and the Federalists yielded to largely because the citizens distrusted a standing army. In contrast, Federalists were concerned about the constant threats to the nation from the French, British, Barbary pirates, and Native Americans. In light of these persistent threats, President Washington (on Hamilton's advice) created the constabulary force. President Adams was less inclined to yield to Hamilton but in the end agreed to bolster the army and navy as Congress saw fit. It was Hamilton who greatly influenced President Washington to intervene with an overabundance of militia troops during the Whiskey Rebellion. And it was

Hamilton's desire to form a large force and a federalized militia with the Federalists at the helm of military and political power.

Had Hamilton gotten his way, a large standing army would have been created – a type of oligarchical praetorianism where the monopoly of power was in the hands of a few elite groups in collusion with military officers overseeing the federalized force. The result likely would have been social and political revolt and anarchy by the citizenry, many of whom were militiamen during the American Revolution. They favored a citizens' army that could not be manipulated and abused by the government. Many of those citizens were now members of Congress who could officially place a check on grand military designs. Consequently, even Hamilton's final proposal for an elite reserve was neither a regular army nor a militia, but something in between – the constabulary force. Hamilton knew the citizen culture too well, having also fought in the Revolution. He tried to enhance Federalist political power by compromising with the political elites and the citizenry who were concerned with national security but were just as worried about Federalist political abuses through a standing army. In the end, Congress and the citizens kept Hamilton and the Federalists at bay in concordance with the nation's values and political culture.

As an alternative to Hamilton's oligarchical praetorianism, President Washington devised an executive establishment and decision-making process that had not been delineated or even mentioned in the US Constitution. The departments of Treasury, State, and War were created, and holdovers from the Continental Congress were in most instances reappointed: John Jay to secretary of foreign affairs, Henry Knox to secretary of war, and Alexander Hamilton (eventually) to secretary of treasury.

President Washington's executive style was highly personal. He was fully aware of the citizenry's "fears of executive power, and especially the corruptions of the British patronage system" (McDonald 1974: 39–40). After Congress approved his appointments, these appointees and cabinet heads were directly responsible to President Washington, and he expected departmental subordinates to be responsible to their superiors as the superiors were to the president. There were few codes or procedures (except for Hamilton's Treasury Department), and President Washington closely managed his appointees and their daily activity.

An additional 350 posts, including the judiciary, were assigned by President Washington. His standard for appointments was based on merit and public service record. President Washington was concerned with political loyalty, but he was also conscious of local community relationships and the acceptance of his appointments within those communities. This process of appointing skilled officials acceptable to the distinctive localities or quasi-autonomous republics was President Washington's strategy for achieving legitimacy of the federal government. He masterfully created a "web of loyalty" based on talent, merit, and community confidence that went a long way in unifying the nation and legitimatizing the political decision-making process (Elkins and McKitrick 1995: 55).

President Washington's sensitivity to local communities made the establishment of a standing army impossible. He had always wanted to professionalize the military along British lines. But the militia army mentality was too deeply embedded inside the psyche of the average American. While courting the local leadership, he also listened to Hamilton's Federalist ambition to create a strong and British-styled military. In the end, President Washington created a small and rather ineffective constabulary force of 3,000 men dispersed along the frontier – far enough away from the communities of militiamen who despised the idea of a standing army. As president, Washington skillfully bent the culture and aspirations of those whose "web of loyalty" he had so carefully cultivated in the establishment and implementation of the new United States government.

Recruitment method

Military recruitment during the post-revolutionary period was grounded in the concept of a "militia organization and distrust of centralized standing peacetime forces" (Chambers 1999: 594–5). As a result, Congress and military elites depended on regional militias for centralized army recruits. Regional militia officials enlisted and mobilized local men when necessary to provide troops for the colonies and later for the nation. Even during the Revolutionary War, Congress allowed enlistment to be left to the states' discretion.

Coercion as a recruitment strategy for the American Revolution's Continental Army – the centralized army of the time – was out of the question "because of its potential to create desertion or even a riot" (Chambers 1999: 594–5). Additionally, the militiamen were not accustomed to the type of military rituals and rules we often associate with a professional military, such as a lifestyle based on hierarchy and discipline. As a result, a persuasive though highly ineffective recruitment system ensued. For example, the Continental Congress resorted to bounties and finally a draft to entice men to enlist in the centralized army for a period of at least three years. But citizens could pay a fine or hire substitutes to take their places. As a result of ineffective recruitment methods and a culture that feared centralized militaries, Congress declared that "standing armies in times of peace were inconsistent with the principle of republican government" (Raphael 2001: 94). Consequently, they disbanded virtually the entire Continental Army.

The day after the disbandment, however, Congress once again made an attempt to create a standing army. It ordered certain states to recruit 700 militiamen for a year of service on the frontier, later to be replaced by regular soldiers (Chambers 1999: 594–5; Raphael 2001: 94). Though Congress and President Washington successfully established this small constabulary army, still "a standing army did not fit naturally into the ideological landscape of the new republic" (Urwin 2000: 32). As a result, the army suffered from geographic isolation, being located in the new republic's hinterlands, and was not well kept nor well staffed. For example, recruits were usually found among the poor – those considered to be less successful in a young nation with burgeoning opportunities. Pay was low, earning a private $3 per month "with $1 deducted for medicine and clothing" (Urwin 2000: 32). Additionally, the constabulary force was largely devoted to defending the young nation against Native Americans and pirates – a task of low merit during this period. Finally, the constabulary force offered little benefit or assistance to state militias due to the army's small size and geographic separation (Urwin 2000: 123). Recruitment patterns in the newly nationalized army were therefore inconsistent and difficult to maintain.

Overall, military recruitment among the rank and file was persuasive and not coercive, but the citizenry had little respect for the small and separate constabulary force. This is a clear example in US civil–military relations and nation building where a separate and more regulated military was out of sync with the US culture of the time.

Militia recruitment, by contrast, was dependent upon individual state policy and mainly attracted men when regional threats were high. The militia was created during the colonial period to defend against Native Americans and powerful colonial competitors such as Spain, France, and Britain. The method of recruitment during the colonial and post-revolutionary period was created among local militia districts and was persuasive and not entirely effective. The wealthy could pay the state and others to opt out of military duty. Like the centralized Continental and constabulary armies, forcible coercion was out of the question since the political culture was largely anti-military. Men across the country resented recruitment and training "both for the time it took away from their work and the subordination to commanding officers it presupposed" (Larkin 1989: 247). Desertion was high among militiamen who often wanted to return home to harvest their crops and be with their families. The citizenry simply preferred to have the militia called up when absolutely necessary for national security; but, they were clearly opposed to a formal standing army that could have augmented the defense of US borders and its shipping trade.

The Federalist political elites, including Hamilton and President Washington, were forced to compromise with the citizenry, and the congressional political decision-making process sprung from the post-revolutionary culture. In the end, that culture persuaded the political leadership to allow individual states to determine the makeup and recruitment process for the republic's dual-army system.

Military style

The militia style during the Revolution permeated the post-revolutionary period with informal spirit, anti-hierarchical organization, and blurred civilian and military boundaries. The common militiaman, usually 16 years or older, often left his farm to serve the state if only for a short period of time. The officer corps during the Revolution, including George Washington, complained of the militia's "unbounded freedom" and lack of subordination. In 1775, he wrote "such a dirty, mercenary spirit pervades the whole, that I should not be at all surprised at any disaster that may happen" (Raphael 2001: 54). European-born Baron von Steuben "observed that in Europe an officer had only to say 'do this' and he doeth it. In America the officers had to say 'this is the reason why you ought to do that'" (Raphael 2001: 94). Since the militia in most cases elected their non-commissioned officers, the officers in turn compromised with the men who could vote them out of official duty. Overall, the federal and local political elites had no choice but to compromise with the citizen soldier whose informal agrarian style pervaded the culture of the time.

Even the most basic stylistic attributes such as uniform and hats were frequently discussed among officers and militia regulars – the latter of whom shunned the formal military style. Infantry officers in the 1794 constabulary force wore rather ornate uniforms for the times: "dark blue breeches and coat with red collar, cuffs, and lapels, lined with white; a black hat and boots. His buttons, belt plate and spurs are of white metal, as is his epaulette ... his sword has a brass hilt, and the scabbard is of black leather" (Copeland 1976: 6). By contrast, a militia rifleman might be found in a "black flat-brimmed hat with feathers ... a white hunting shirt, and brown overalls," looking more like a Davy Crockett figure than a professional soldier (Urwin 2000: 28). Often without an appropriate weapon, most militiamen wore their daily civilian clothing or some form of it to annual drills, thereby further blurring civilian and military boundaries. The military style of the militia soldier, in contrast to the constabulary soldier, exemplifies how concordance took place not through the separation of citizen and military but through their overlap; the ornate uniform was therefore out of context with militia society, and the constabulary force was clearly less preferred as the nation's military.

In order to conduct some form of fieldwork regarding the military uniform of this early US period, I traveled to Old Sturbridge Village in Western Massachusetts on August 8, 2004. There, a program called "From Redcoats to Rebels" featured a special reenactment of American military units from the 1600s to the Civil War. Old Sturbridge Village is known for its authentic cultural reenactment and display of a typical US village during the early 1800s. I asked several of the soldiers at this event about the militia units during the 1790s. They all agreed that most militia citizen soldiers, unlike the regular army, mainly wore their daily civilian clothes during military drills and practices.

In an odd but meaningful way, this overlap of civilian and military culture in society prevented civil–military disaster during the Whiskey Rebellion. President Washington was concerned about the rebels from Western Pennsylvania. But the Whiskey Rebellion was less of a threat to the government than President Washington had anticipated. In the end, the moderate local officials were able to bring the protesters under control. These officials and many business elites believed in the farmers' right to protest the excise tax but were not in favor of inciting violence against the government. The Pennsylvania citizens – many of whom had fought side by side with the protesters and the national government leaders during the American Revolution – were able to restrain the protesters from fomenting anarchy. The wealthier local leaders sympathized with the protesters "but not to the commission of violent acts. They understood the meaning of protest but sought to channel it through peaceful petitions ... representative assemblies, open meetings or political societies" (Slaughter 1986: 168). This unique social and political partnership among the citizens, soldiers, and political elites ultimately sustained an underlying respect for government law and order (Slaughter 1986: 168; Faber and Faber 1989: 158).

The foundation of this respect for governance was grounded in colonial constitutional history. The Constitution of 1787 was formally a new document. While there was no tradition of union or "united states," there did exist a constitutional tradition in the pre-revolutionary colonial ideology. Constitutional dialogue before and after the American Revolution may also help explain why moderates were able to quell protesters during the Whiskey Rebellion. The militia tradition in the United States was rooted in citizens fighting side by side against British abuses, yet respecting constitutional concepts and colonial implementation of law and order. Bernard Bailyn captured this sentiment in the *Ideological Origins of the American Revolution*: "the colonies demonstrated military effectiveness of militia armies whose members were themselves the beneficiaries of the Constitution and hence not likely to wish to destroy it" (Bailyn 1967: 84). Bailyn points out that even among the lower classes who emigrated to America, the attraction to a simpler life with "special freedom in their politics" was prevalent (ibid.). It was this respect for constitutional tradition that fostered the delicate balance between citizen in arms and rule of law.

Military style in the United States during the 1790s was grounded in a militia culture. Political elites such as President Washington and Hamilton strove to create a larger, more professional, and British-inspired military establishment. However, the citizens who comprised the militia and many congressional political representatives who had fought in the Revolution opposed a large standing army. It was not compatible with the military and societal culture of the time. The militia may not have been the most effective military for defending the nation; but the young republic and its people were protecting a culture inspired in a state constitutional heritage, an informal agrarian lifestyle, and the values of freedom and liberty – often opposing the hierarchical disciplined style of a Western and European standing army. In the end, the military, the political elites, and the citizenry learned to respect and work with the overlapping and the blurring of civilian and military boundaries. The three partners came into concordance over the military style which reflected the post-revolutionary culture of the time.

Summary

The current civil–military relations theory of the field is grounded in the separation of civil and military institutions. Separation theory is based on the post-World War II US experience and has been exported to nations around the world. The civil–military dichotomy indeed works in the present-day United States and many Western nations. It does not, however, apply to the US post-revolutionary case study (1790–1800) when citizen life, military decisions, and respect for the law were intricately intertwined. All three partners came to agreement over officer corps composition, political decision-making process, military recruitment method, and military style. Domestic military intervention by the constabulary army's officers or militia factions did not occur as a result of institutional and cultural concordance. Despite high external and internal threat conditions and lack of a separate and standing military, concordance prevailed in the young American republic where a dual-army tradition was established.

Why is this case study important? The US case study during two distinct historical periods provides important examples of both modern-day military expertise and the development of early political and military institutions. Certainly the institutions of the eighteenth and twentieth centuries were vastly different as were the military cultures of the time. While there are distinct differences in terms of culture, technology, and political formations, some nations today, such as post-Saddam Iraq and Afghanistan, are still in those critical nation-building stages, while others are near to or have achieved the final stages of nation building, such as Pakistan and Serbia. But regardless of the stage, military cultures and political institutions differ, making each nation-building experience unique. And domestic military intervention may be prevented but for completely different reasons. For the post-revolutionary United States, it was not the separation of civil and military realms that prevented military chaos in the young nation; rather, it was the incorporation of informal colonial values and priorities of the militiamen into military life that deterred domestic military intervention.

Separation theory cannot account for the success of both US case studies. Nor should it be applied to other countries that differ in culture and circumstance from that of the modern-day United States. An alternative explanation is needed, one which helps the observer of nations understand and determine the institutional and cultural contexts of both periods. Concordance theory offers that solution. It does not superimpose a predetermined and favored case study upon another nation. Rather, concordance explains why nations with indigenous political institutions and militaries suffer from or are able to prevent domestic military intervention.

5 Concordance in India and discordance in Pakistan

At first glance, India does not appear to be a case that challenges the theory of civil control (i.e., separate civil and military institutions). The Indian armed forces still exhibit the influence of the many decades of British rule. The legacy of British professionalism and the related subordination of the Indian armed forces to civil institutional control are often put forth as major reasons for the prevention of domestic military intervention in India and as examples that support separation theory. So why should we concern ourselves with concordance theory if civilian control provides an adequate explanation of civil–military relations in India?

Despite the traditional separation between civil and military institutions, the Indian political system throughout the 1980s and 1990s underwent significant changes. These changes greatly weakened the central government and subsequently the civilian authority over the military. Many of these changes were prompted by domestic social violence, as well as economic problems resulting from the post-Cold War environment. It is argued here that despite a weakened government, the military adapted to the political transformations and chose to remain loyal to its civilian authority.

One major reason for this adaptation was that India did not limit itself to politically controlled institutional relationships among the three partners. Since independence, the military as an institution, and in conjunction with civilian authorities, has groomed Indian soldiers to adapt to the changing and often conflict-ridden political and cultural landscape of Indian society. In other words, the military and civilian authorities have cooperated in situations that called for clear military leadership within the context of Indian political leadership. This process has nurtured agreement among the military, the political elites, and the citizenry about the role and function of the armed forces in India. It is this long-term concordance that has enabled the military to meet the challenges of critical stages in Indian state building without domestic military intervention.

Conditions in present-day India

Before embarking on India's civil–military relations story, deserving of mention is India's recent geopolitical "renaissance" – economically, militarily, and politically. India is the world's largest democracy and the world's youngest. Fifty percent of its population is under the age of 25 with 1.2 billion residents and an additional 20 million living outside of India. Economically, India has become an epicenter for outsourcing, development, and research among important multinational companies. Companies such as IBM, Intel, and Cisco Systems are investing billions of dollars into India. Co-sourcing and outsourcing to India-based firms are profitable in the information technology and pharmaceutical drug fields. India provides highly skilled, English-speaking, and inexpensive labor compared to the United States and Europe. Moreover, Indian corporations like Tata Group, Wipro Technologies, and Ranbaxy Laboratories Ltd are becoming multinational players. Not only do they compete with companies such as IBM and Pfizer, they often prove more nimble than these well-established rivals in areas of business strategy and growth (Kamdar 2007: 8, 11–13).

India's fast growing economy and relations with China, the United States, and Europe affect not only its economic growth but its military growth as well. For example, its trade relationship with China, a long distrusted one, "is growing more than 40 percent per year. ... China will unseat the United States as India's biggest single country trading partner" (Kamdar 2007: 7). China's relationship with Pakistan is less threatening now to India as India favors the benefits of a market economy and long-term trade agreements with its Chinese neighbor. Indian–US trade has also grown dramatically over the last decade – over 400 percent between 1990 and 2006. In 2007, bilateral trade between the two countries grew by 21 percent. As US companies in a variety of areas (from IBM to Wal-Mart) are poised to present opportunities to the Indian economy, direct investments will increase multilateral trade agreements and assist in growing the Indian economic trade infrastructure that will only bolster its economic and foreign policy relationships (Kamdar 2007: 38–9).

Militarily, India is the world's largest purchaser of weaponry. "India's $5.4 billion dwarfed the $3.4 billion number two buyer Saudi Arabia spent and the mere $2.8 billion spent by China" (Kamdar 2007: 262; see also SIPRI 2006: 477–80). India partners extensively with the United States in dual-use technologies such as nuclear, nano-, and bio-technologies. For example, in 2005 Prime Minister Manmohan Singh and US President Bush signed "Next Steps in the Strategic Partnership" (NSSP). The highlight of this deal would end a "US moratorium on nuclear trade with India, provide US assistance to India's civilian nuclear energy program, and expand US–Indian cooperation in energy and satellite technology" (Pan 2006). Countering concern over the onset of regional nuclear proliferation, the US administration argued that India served as a counterbalance to China's nuclear arsenal, and NSSP was critical to India's domestic energy requirements. In 2007, the deal was sealed and a joint United States–India statement announced it would create "enhanced energy security, a more environmentally friendly energy source, greater economic opportunities, and more robust non-proliferation efforts" (Labott 2007: 1). US Republicans and Democrats also agreed that the deal would be a "bonanza for American business" interests in the region. Conversely, India would continue to become a dominant military and economic power in the world (Kamdar 2007: 269–71).

This economic growth and partnering is partly the result of India's initial historical grappling with the development of its armed forces and eventual understanding of its external military threat condition. The leadership and philosophies of Mahatma Gandhi and Jawaharlal Nehru in the 1940s created an early disdain for all things military in favor of non-violence and diplomacy. Nehru, in particular, observed the Pakistani domestic military interventions and wanted to avoid a similar situation in India. He therefore tried to minimize the military's role in foreign and domestic policy. This was not always easy especially in the early stages of independence, when nationalists such as Subhas Chandra Bose challenged both Nehru and Gandhi by advocating violent resistance against the British Raj. Bose developed the Indian National Army (INA) from Indian expatriates in Southeast Asia. The army, along with Gandhi's non-violence strategy, helped to inspire the Indian independence movement.

Nehru's strategy to underplay the role of military strategy did not last long as external conditions required military involvement. In the early 1950s, India was forced to formalize British-initiated treaties with countries such as Nepal and Bhutan. Later, Pakistan's alliance with the United States became a regional threat to India. Additionally, India's invasion of Goa – which allowed India to absorb this former Portuguese–Indian colony into the subcontinent – angered the United States. To the north, India's relationship with China appeared calm until conflict arose between the two and India's military was unexpectedly defeated in 1962. Additionally its performance against Pakistan in 1965 led India's political leadership to reassess its external threat condition and foreign military alliances.

India's current technological revolution is partially the result of former Prime Minister Indira Gandhi's military buildup against Pakistan and its Cold War alliance with the Soviet Union. In exchange for weaponry, India "became a supplier of many light industrial products and a wide variety of consumer goods to the Soviet Union" (S.P. Cohen 2002: 143). India also began to develop its own secret weapons and detonated a nuclear device in 1974. Overall, India's external military threat condition could be characterized as medium to high depending on the current state of affairs in Kashmir and with China. While India would never become a major arms exporter, India's early military alliances with Britain, the United States, and later the Soviet Union encouraged the political leadership to partner domestically with its military while boosting its industrial, manufacturing, and research sectors to new heights.

As we see in the case of India, economy and military growth were inextricably linked, and a philosophy of non-violence soon gave way to a more practical understanding of politics in a volatile region. India's leadership realized that to avoid suffering the domestic fate of Pakistan it would have to resolve political and military exigencies by partnering with the military and the citizenry. Concordance was achieved throughout India's recent history because the political and military leadership safeguarded the continuity of Indian history, a blend of modern and traditional elements. The leadership also realized that close military and economic alliances with foreign partners such as Britain and the Soviet Union would also enhance its domestic relationships, since the nation as a whole and specific multiethnic groups would benefit from a stronger economy and entrance into India's military and political institutions. Concordance was really the result of Indian leadership insisting on preserving its historical and cultural roots while embracing their global realities in the twentieth century.

Technology, history, and the modernity of tradition

The current twenty-first-century technological revolution has also enhanced India's modern and traditional political system. India is historically hierarchical – a democracy rooted in a caste system that is hundreds of years old and has often prevented mass social mobility for as long. While India is regarded as a secular state, the caste system is identified with Hinduism dating back to the fourteenth century BCE. The caste system provided India with a structure for an orderly society, a division of labor, and the integration of foreigners into Indian society.

Throughout India's history Muslims and Christians have also observed the caste structure and its focus on socioeconomic status. The caste categories influenced all aspects of society including employment, marriage, and daily social interaction. For example, when the young Mahatma Gandhi pursued his legal studies in Britain it was required that he ask for permission from his subcaste before leaving India. The British codified the caste system, while more recent Indian governments have created affirmative action programs for lower castes. Regardless of the Indian government's formal attempt to level the playing field socially and economically, Indians know the difference, for example, between Brahmins (the highest caste level historically identifying with Hindu priests and scholars) and Shudras (the caste that historically consisted of farmers and artisans); although South Asian scholar Anit Mukherjee notes that in some regions one subcaste could dominate while its correlating subcaste could be suppressed in another region (telephone interview, October 2, 2007).

Early Indian state building is an amalgam of twentieth-century liberalism, modernity, and centuries of "the traditional obligation of the ruler to recognize and uphold the jurisdiction of prior social groups" (Rudolph and Rudolph 1987: 68). The new technological world – within the context of an evolving parliamentary democracy and the government's move to diversify the military ranks – has led to a far less rigid view of caste and social hierarchy. As Mira Kamdar clarifies, "a young person's prospects were largely determined by his family's status, connections, and wealth. India's information technology companies have changed this" (2007: 43). A merit-based employment system allows the world's youngest democracy to grow its socioeconomic pool of labor, while increasing its GDP from 5.6 percent in 2001 to about 8 percent by 2008 (Asian Development Bank 2001, 2007).

In addition to the recent technology revolution, there are also several fortuitous and historical conditions that shaped India's evolving democracy: India's partition from Muslim Pakistan encouraged a secular parliamentary structure; Gandhi, Nehru, and Patel provided a solid and effective founding leadership; the incorporation of the princely states into multinational entities thwarted attempts to create a monarchy; and decades of parliamentary practice under British rule strengthened democratic institutions (Rudolph and Rudolph 1987: 64).

Grounded within these fortuitous events is a complex amalgam of traditional and modern conditions that overlap, contradict, and often complement the evolution of India's democracy. "Modernity of tradition" is a contextual interpretation that refuses to relegate "tradition" into a "historical trash heap" (Rudolph and Rudolph 1972: 3). It is a meaningful diagnosis of why India has thrived as a democracy and has maintained an extraordinary relationship between the government, the citizenry, and the armed forces. Moreover, it influences several case studies in this book, including Pakistan, Israel, and Argentina. When scholars and policy makers begin to think more hermeneutically and less dichotomously about nations and their culture, we will be in a better position to interpret and influence nations on their own indigenous terms.

The "modernity of tradition" – like the "civilianization of the military" in post-revolutionary United States and the Israeli case to be discussed – challenges the dichotomies that fit the comfort level of scholars and interpreters of nations. This concept suggests that modern and traditional aspects are not mutually exclusive. In other words, modern and traditional characteristics can exist concurrently and even jointly influence political, military, and civilian institutional practices.

The phrase "modernity of tradition" was first coined in 1964. Yet today, we are not much further along than the dichotomous approaches of the previous century. Current foreign policy exigencies in the Middle East and elsewhere are demanding a more rigorous and sensitive approach to cultural interpretation, yet scholars still cling to the Western-bound political science interpretations. Certainly in the field of civil–military relations (still called "civil" and "military" relations, thereby implying a bifurcated relationship) we are entrenched in highly inflexible theoretical frameworks of how the military should interact with the political elites and the citizenry. The modernity of tradition implies a "misdiagnosis" of modern society and its efforts to dichotomize.

Many theories and interpretations of the modern world operate on a continuum "where traditional features have either disappeared from view or are pictured as residual categories" (Rudolph and Rudolph 1972: 4). The modernity of tradition allows for a "range of sentiments, psychological predispositions, norms, and structures" that helps describe nations' institutional conditions in terms of the traditional and modern at the same time (ibid.: 5).

As revealed in Chapter 4 on concordance theory in the United States, a complex struggle between the modern and traditional took place following the American Revolution. President Washington, on the one hand, was tired of commanding a ragtag militia army that was often ineffective and looked unprofessional. He believed the modernized British military to be the ideal because it commanded respect in appearance and aptitude. The citizens' militia army, on the other hand, prevailed because US citizens in the eighteenth century trusted and valued their colonial tradition. They had won their independence with the slapdash and often makeshift militia and had developed deep and long-lasting relationships and sentiments among fellow revolutionary citizens: "a web of shared habits, loyalties and memories nurtured in the camps of the Continental Army – in effect, a common socialization into military life" (Skelton 1992: 14). These deep societal and historical bonds among local elites and common citizens would assist in brokering peace with local insurgencies as in the Pennsylvania Whiskey Rebellion. The traditional social norms and structures of colonial America would influence the military's evolution into the "modern" version existing in the United States today.

With respect to India, the modernity of tradition has informed the relaxation of caste tradition and the evolving democratic political institutions, along with the more recent technology revolution. For example, the concurrent existence of the caste system and democratic institutions has foundations in both the traditional and the modern. Sacred fifteenth- and sixteenth-century Brahminic texts revealed "considerable social mobility and change ... [by] castes to establish themselves within the traditional system" (Rudolph 1972: 5). In fact early political caste mobilization is characterized vertically, horizontally, and differentially.

In each of these interpretations there is a dynamic "marshalling of support" by political notables, local elites, and community leaders, and the direct or indirect involvement of political parties and community associations. The result is the infusion of modern democratic systems of participation into a centuries-old caste tradition:

> leadership in the caste association is no longer in the hands of those qualified by heredity ... the availability of association leaders is conditioned by their ability to articulate and represent the purposes of the caste association, and for this purpose they must be literate in the ways of modern administration and new democratic politics.
>
> (Rudolph and Rudolph 1972: 34)

In a true dichotomous fashion, British ethnographers portrayed the caste culture as part of "traditional and timeless India ... [the British] took for granted the reinforcement and preservation of tradition and hierarchy" (Cannadine 2002: 42–3). In other words, they shunted the dynamic evolution of the caste system aside. Nevertheless, the British Raj (or the period of British rule over India) fostered India's political transformation – one that bridged traditional norms and values with modern social advancement.

This example of caste system evolution within the context of Indian democracy reinforces the inappropriateness of the usage of dichotomous interpretations. India is a thriving democracy that is neither modern nor traditional: it is both. While modern political and social institutions exist, they continue to be influenced by traditional structures, norms, religions, and cultures.

I recently spoke with the scholars who coined the term "modernity of tradi-tion." They had just returned from a conference in India related to the impact of technology on India's educational system. After visiting one of the largest soft-ware companies in Bangalore, they depicted the initial blend of modern and traditional elements in ethnographic detail:

> There was an initial outpouring of men from corporate headquarters dressed in suit and tie with white shirts, while the women were mainly dressed in traditional Indian garments, all on their way to the brand new fitness center on the corporate grounds.
>
> (Rudolph and Rudolph 2007)

In addition to capturing the stylistic overlap of modern and traditional dress and routine, they voiced concern for the Indian educational system and the impact the technological revolution would play on the established curriculum.

India has solid civil institutions, inherited from the British Raj, both separ-ate from and in control of the military. Similar to India's caste system, however, Indian civil–military relations is in fact a partnership among the political elites, the military, and the citizenry that incorporates a wide array of institutional and cultural influences keeping a large, battlefield-ready and cul-turally diversified military at bay:

> The raw material of the army, the *jawan*, or ordinary soldier, is still drawn from the villages of India. Here he is inculcated with traditional notions of obedience, but he remains tied to the village authority structure ... Thus today's armed forces, especially the army ... represent the melding of ancient practices, recently invented "traditions," and modern professional norms.
>
> (Cohen 2001: 21–2)

Domestic military intervention in India is avoided not because of civil–military separation but as a result of a complex partnership that respects and integrates the modern and traditional structures, values, and rituals of Indian society. To demon-strate the agreement that has been achieved among the military, the political elites, and the citizenry of India on the question of the military's role, it is necessary to examine the four indicators of concordance as they apply to India. These reveal a substantial evolution since independence from Britain, and they are sharply con-trasted with the Pakistani case study discussed later in this chapter.

Concordance in India

The social composition of the officer corps

For many years after independence, the Indian officer corps was considered the "last outpost of the British Raj" (Cohen 2002: 182), since the corps preserved the style and selective recruitment of the British. The British sepoy armies (armies comprised of Indian soldiers but under the control of the British) were divided into regiments covering three provincial regions: Bengal, Madras, and Bombay. All had contained a mixture of religious (Hindu and Muslim) and caste groups (from the high Brahmin to the lower caste groups of Kshatriya and Shudra). Hindu Brahmins nevertheless predominated. The Bengali regiment was drawn mostly from a narrower population than the other two. After the Mutiny of 1857–8, the British retained this selective recruitment policy but especially favored individuals from the Punjabi Sikh and Hindu Brahmin communities.

In the wake of independence, this profile of the officer corps initially did not change much. The recruits to the officer corps remained largely Hindu Brahmins and Punjabi Sikhs. The latter constituted about a third of the cadets. Aside from the high proportion of the recruits from Punjab, another 15 percent came from Delhi. Officers from other regions, such as Madhya Pradesh and Kerala, composed less than 5 percent of the officer corps (Cohen 1971: 183).

Unlike Pakistan, as will be shown, there was no effort by the post-independence Indian political establishment or the military to aggressively alienate its minority citizen populations. Yet, similar to Pakistan, early officer corps recruitment was influenced by the British-inspired "martial races." The theory of martial races, as it applies to both Indian and Pakistani military history, evolved in the late nineteenth and early twentieth centuries. It was coined by British commander Lord Roberts of Kandahar who was interested in building up the Indian military to meet the Russian external threat. This theory argued that "some Indian peoples were warlike by tradition and others were not" (Omissi 1991: 7). In other words, some "races" of people were more physically inclined and predisposed for military service. For example, the Punjabi Muslims and Sikhs became part of an established warrior class, and that status gave these select groups social and political privileges that were initially denied to other groups.

As the martial race tradition became more culturally entrenched in British India, it affected the recruitment of officers and the rank and file. Consequently, those who were considered part of the privileged elite (or martial races) were more actively recruited in the prestigious British-Indian military. The wealthier classes selected by the British included groups such as the "Punjabis, Muslims, Sikhs, Dogras, Jats, and Rajputs" (S.P. Cohen 2002: 62). Indian families were most concerned about the placement of their sons in the military and professional mobility therein. The British, in turn, were careful to prevent tensions among the recruited castes.

Prior to the establishment of the British system, "Indian noblemen were allowed to raise and lead their own men in battle" (S.P. Cohen 2002: 62). Under early British rule, Indians could become the "viceroy's commissioned officers, but they could never be promoted to senior appointments (all held by the British KCOs [King's Commissioned Officers])," nor could they raise their own troops (ibid.: 62). By the 1920s, the British relaxed their commissioned officer requirements as Indians now constituted 25 percent of the king's officers. Indian officers were also allowed to enter the Royal Military Academy Sandhurst, the elite officer training establishment in Britain.

Since the 1980s, the Indian military no longer privileges certain classes based on supposed warlike tendencies. Now the officer corps draws more from the middle class and reflects a greater diversity of regions. This change has revealed both conscious recruitment practices and socioeconomic factors. For example, many wealthier Indian families have declined to send their sons to cadet school, and the military pay scale (lagging behind inflationary trends) has persuaded many potential officers to seek more lucrative jobs. Nonetheless, it is unquestionable that the officer corps has now become significantly more representative of Indian society than it was during its early years of statehood. The British historical legacy, Indian socioeconomic and cultural reality, and evolving recruitment patterns have become the cornerstone of the ethnic and social composition of the officer corps (Barua 1992: 131–2):

> The transformation in the social base of the officer corps … accelerated after 1970. The young officers now entering the Indian military – the generals of 2030 – are very much like their predecessors. The officer corps has become even more middle class in composition.
>
> (S.P. Cohen 2002: 215)

Similar to the caste system in India, the officer corps has a combination of modern and traditional elements. The post-independence military represents "the melding of ancient practices, recently invented 'traditions,' and modern professional norms" (Cohen 2001: 22). Officer corps training includes Western-influenced logistics, tactics, and weapons training. In addition, "individuals in the officer corps whose childhood and upbringing did not include a strong traditional component are rare" (ibid.: 183). The Indian officers have "honeycomb personalities" as they "must shift rapidly" and often "from a purely technical encounter to a traditional home or personal life" (ibid.: 183). Officers have a highly structured military life in the British cantonment system, but often experience a life outside the military context that embraces indigenous Indian values and customs.

I recently spoke with a self-declared former Indian "military brat" whose father had been a colonel in the Indian army. Her father was recruited into the military after Indian independence and partition from Pakistan. She acknowledged the structured cantonment system that was separate from the traditional Indian civil servant lifestyle. The cantonments had special amenities such as large homes, telephones (rarely found in Indian homes during the 1950s), and good schools (mainly missionary-led schools where English was spoken). The officers and their families also moved frequently according to assignment. The moves, according to this woman who is now a physician and distinguished university professor, exposed her to a diversity of cultures and language dialects throughout India.

She confirmed that while the cantonment existence was separate from mainstream Indian culture, there remained a fluidity between Western British and

Indian customs in her upbringing. For example, when her father was sent to a military post in the hinterlands, the family was sent to her grandmother's house. Unlike the cantonment, only Punjabi was spoken and strictly vegetarian Indian meals were served. In the cantonments, by contrast, English was the common language with some mixture of Hindi. Breakfast usually consisted of soft-boiled eggs served in English egg-cups, and there was always some form of meat available. When her father came to her grandmother's house, he arrived in a British-styled military uniform. Yet he would also settle into her home by changing into traditional Indian garments for leisure and rest, and speak to his mother in Punjabi only.

Indeed, this was a "honeycombed" existence for the army brat and her family where modern and traditional worlds collided and nourished each other. Her British-trained father was never far from his indigenous language and customs, and their lives consistently shifted from a Western lifestyle on the military cantonment to a traditional Indian experience at home.

The Indian officer corps is a unique combination of structure and style embedded in centuries of multicultural influences. Post-independence India has carefully blended the culture of caste, Western impression and authority, and linguistic and socioeconomic diversity with the exigencies of Indian national defense and domestic politics. The officer reflects the continuous intermingling of modern and traditional elements that foster military professionalism suited to the demands of Indian military requirements and social contexts. Sociologically, the dichotomous lens of Indian civil–military relations, or separation theory, simply does not capture the profound intermingling of officer corps development, Western influences, and recruitment patterns within the mosaic of Indian society.

The political decision-making process

With respect to the political decision-making process, the Congress Party and a respected military tradition emerged during the early development of the Indian state. The Congress Party, India's dominant political party, was founded in 1885 and gradually became a far-reaching organization that embraced a comprehensive range of ethnic, religious, and social groups. An organized hierarchical structure was established during pre-independence, and with millions of active participants, the Congress Party became an agent and symbol of political emancipation.

After independence, with respect to the political establishment and the military, India established a three-tiered committee system that remains in place today. It consists of the Defence Committee of the Cabinet (DCC), the Defence Minister's Committee, and the Chief of Staff Committee (CSC). In matters of security, the prime minister's council delegates its authority to the DCC and what is now called the Political Affairs Committee (PAC). The result is that the civilian component of the three-tiered system has been the major partner in military affairs, and the armed forces have responded professionally. Thus, the army has maintained the British-inspired three-tiered system and has conformed to the prevailing political system and ideology implemented and formed by civilian elites. Consequently, the Indian military is regarded as a "professional corps" by Western standards.

To some scholars, the officer corps may be considered *too* professional especially in strategic military planning. The military has been inculcated with the attitude that "it is wrong for the army to try to make policy; their business is to be concerned with military tactics" (S.P. Cohen 2002: 175). This may appear to be an idealized professional military separate from civilian elites and institutions; but with respect to important issues such as nuclear procurement, the civilian ministries are often in need of integrative strategic planning that includes a military perspective. Opting for über-professionalism and complete disassociation of the military in policy making may not be appropriate in all contexts.

During the early post-independence years, which resulted in conflicts with Pakistan and China, the Indian military realized that "political understanding" was just as important as military professionalism (S.P. Cohen 2002: 177). While political elites became suspicious of officers in uniform, an enlarged joint chiefs system would encourage a more coordinated relationship that enhanced a strategic partnership with the political elite. Indeed, the Indian political decision-making process moved toward a "system of planning and inter-service coordination" (ibid.: 220, 170), a system that encouraged more cooperative strategic planning among civilians and officers.

Despite military efforts at political neutrality and strategic integration, the Indian political center relative to the armed forces weakened significantly during the 1980s and the 1990s. This weakening of civilian institutions resulted from: (1) the political center's failures to control Hindu–Muslim violence; (2) the challenge of preserving the secular state; (3) India's post-Cold War economic conditions; and (4) increased government scandal and corruption as well as a power shift toward regional parties and bosses. The central government confronted heightened religious and ethnic turmoil in the 1990s. In an effort to quell this domestic violence and terrorism, the military was called on to aid civilian authorities. During that time, one Indian scholar summarized the situation as the "disintegration of India's dominant political institutions" (Kohli 1990: 306; see also Ganguly 1991: 22).

The military's aid to the civil institutions has both positive and negative consequences for Indian politics and the armed forces. On the positive side, the military frequently assists in providing important infrastructure and crowd support: "road repair, flood control, disaster relief, or distribution of food and medicine in times of famine or epidemic ... the military is [also] used to help patrol *melas* (religious fairs or gatherings)" (Cohen 1971: 127). These kinds of interactions with the citizenry promote the military's image as a nation builder and protector. It also provides soldiers with a break from routine military duties.

On the negative side, aid to the civil also means quelling riots and uprisings. Between 1951 and 1970, the military "was called in to suppress domestic violence on approximately 476 occasions" (Cohen 1971: 202). The creation of specialized police and paramilitary forces had lessened the military's domestic presence but heightened tensions in Kashmir. Additionally, the Punjab – a resentful Sikh population especially during the 1980s and 1990s – created dangerous scenarios for the Indian military. One culmination was the occupation of the Golden Temple at Amritsar in the mid-1980s and subsequent assassination of Indira Gandhi by Sikh extremists (ibid.: 202).

It is also important to note that the Indian paramilitary force at 1.3 million personnel is now larger than the Indian army. The paramilitary force is the world's second largest next to China's paramilitary which stands at about 1.5 million personnel. The Rashtriya Rifles, in particular, was created by the Indian army in 1990 as a counterinsurgency force for special missions in Kashmir. This special force both bolsters the local security establishment and assists the army in securing and defending the borders against Pakistani guerrilla forces.

Why has the Indian military and paramilitary forces only assisted with civilian issues and not intervened in the dominant political structures (via coup for example)? Civilian control over the military cannot be the sole explanation, for the theory of civil control looks only at institutional mechanisms shaping the relationship between the civilian government and the armed forces. The concordance surrounding the role and function of the armed forces that arose among the military, the political elites, and the citizenry during tremendous political and social changes since independence must be taken into account as well.

Despite civilian institutional weakness, the military remains adaptive to the current decision-making process that often utilizes the military for civilian purposes. A diverse officer corps and a broad rank-and-file recruitment policy undergird this political situation. Military cultural diversity, in conjunction with a well-organized military that partners with political elites, creates a "coup-proof" Indian scenario. In other words, the role and function of the armed forces in partnership with the political establishment and the citizenry, as well as long-standing agreement over officer corps composition and political decision making, contribute to a distinctive institutional and cultural concordance in India (S.P. Cohen 2002: 222–3).

Recruitment method

Within the military's rank and file, recruitment is both voluntary and persuasive. As in other democratic nations, many of India's less wealthy citizens are motivated by patriotism, loyalty, monetary remuneration, and quality living conditions. Furthermore, the Indian military is an internationally respected institution that has performed well during wartime. Past successes have given the armed forces prestige and a meaningful role and function in Indian society. Thus, recruits are often persuaded to join the military for both nationalistic and personal reasons.

The post-independence Indian army has pure and mixed battalions. A pure battalion does not mean a single caste unit but could by tradition be recruited primarily from a particular region or from a long tradition of military families.

The Gurkhas from Nepal are an example of a pure unit. The Madras regiment, on the other hand, is mixed – it recruits all eligible southern Indians from varying religious backgrounds including Muslim, Christian, and Hindu.

A turning point in military recruitment occurred under the British after the Mutiny of 1857 when Indian soldiers rebelled over various economic and judicial grievances. One critical reason Hindu and Muslim sepoys revolted was to protest the use of greased rifle cartridges that were considered religiously offensive. In the aftermath of the Mutiny, the Peel Commission took a more comprehensive look at recruitment and diversification based on region and caste:

> After the Mutiny most Indian regiments were reorganized into mixed battalions where one company might be made up of Sikhs, another of Punjabi Muslims, a third of Dogras and a fourth of Rajputs. Only a few "loyal" regiments – Sikhs, Gurkhas, Marathas – were allowed to continue intact ... Recruits were drawn not only from particular races, but very often from the same clans and villages, with sons following fathers and nephews following uncles, so that over the years, a strong tradition of kinship developed within each regiment.
>
> (Allen 1977: 105)

An important recruitment ramification of the Mutiny was that the proportion of Indian soldiers to British soldiers would decrease significantly (nine to one versus three to one). To prevent future rebellion, homogenous regiments were limited in favor of "class companies" where, for example, Muslim Punjabis would fight alongside Pathans and Rajputs. Nevertheless, homogenous Sikh and Gurkha regiments remained in order to preserve elements of the martial class tradition (Farwell 1991: 50–1).

Unlike the British recruitment process, post-independence India dissolved single-caste units and diluted the British-inspired martial tradition in an effort to broaden recruitment. It also increased the army's size and effectiveness. Even before independence, when the British utilized Indian troops during World War II, "the ratio of British to India officers changed from 10.11:1 to 4.1:1, and more than 8000 Indians were serving in almost every fighting unit" (S.P. Cohen 2002: 144). Sikhs, who were considered to have great martial qualities, have always had a high percentage of army representation (8 percent at independence and 10–13 percent in the 1980s) relative to their demographic status (about 2.5 percent; Khalidi 2001: 1).

Although in the past Hindus and Sikhs provided a disproportionate number of recruits, since independence the ranks continued to be diversified by caste and region. For example, in a Mahar or Dogra regiment one can find recruits from geographical areas as diverse as Punjab and Uttar Pradesh and from different caste backgrounds. While there remain specific regiments reserved for specific classes, the newer mixed-caste units "have developed their own martial myths," and many officers view these units with pride as they truly "symbolize the Indian nation" (S.P. Cohen 2002: 188–9).

As recruitment continues to broaden the societal base of the corps and ranks, the likelihood of ethnic or religious cliques diminishes. One exception, as mentioned above, was in the 1980s when the government announced plans to broaden military recruitment patterns. This decision, along with other significant grievances, led to a Sikh uprising and the assassination of Indira Gandhi. Complaints from Sikh officers and soldiers were generally "couched not in ethno-religious terms but on grounds of combat efficiency." With 20 percent of the officer corps made up of Sikhs, for generations, this group was regarded as superior warriors; they wanted combat effectiveness preserved (Khalidi 2001: 1).

During Indira Gandhi's leadership and after, military recruitment patterns continued to diversify taking into consideration the proportion of the states' populations vis-à-vis the national population. While specific data on the ethnic and religious composition of the military remains inaccessible, it is estimated that the army's composition is about 70 percent mixed. It is relatively open to all classes of society and has remained an attractive career path through the 1990s:

> India's three services (army, air force and navy) have always been long-service, all-volunteer forces, and general conscription has never proved necessary. The normal securities of regular service life in contrast to the low average per capita income of most civilians have helped make military career attractive for both the jawans and the officers, at least until the economic liberalization of the early 1990s.
>
> (Khalidi 2001: 1)

India's persuasive military recruitment method has embraced the regional national diversity and has provided an important professional and social outlet for Indian citizens. The recent growth of technology opportunities and progressive weakening of caste has made the recruitment of the upper and middle classes challenging, as these groups often prefer more lucrative occupations. Nevertheless, the abundance of Indian human resources and wide socioeconomic differences (about 40 million people live in urban slums; and 27.5 percent of the overall population lives in poverty) still make the military an attractive employment outlet and occupation for many Indians. Despite India's demographic and governmental challenges, especially during the 1980s, the Indian government and military have been sensitive to and successful in establishing concordance with respect to the military recruitment method.

Military style

Recruitment of the rank and file is intertwined with military style in significant ways because post-independence recruitment incorporates a revised view of the martial tradition. It is a "secular" interpretation that "permits the continuance of strong martial traditions within a broad egalitarian framework" (S.P. Cohen 2002: 191). In other words, there is still an effort to embrace a martial tradition, but it is done within a framework of a voluntary recruitment method that allows virtually all Indians to participate in the military including women (although women's roles are non-combative).

The public face of the military is reflected in rituals such as military award ceremonies. The military and the government take great care to include a wide range of caste, religious, and ethnic communities in the military award receptions and distinctive cross-cultural events and festivals:

> The ability to develop an army culture through common celebration of religious and cultural festivals, and respect for diverse beliefs certainly serves as ethnic cross-pressure, preventing stereotyping and prejudice among the troops. This necessarily implies recruitment of all ethnic and religious groups in India, as absence of particular groups from its rank and file may lead to biases based merely on ignorance.
>
> (Khalidi 2001: 1)

Despite more egalitarian trends in recruitment, the Indian martial tradition is still heavily influenced by British military history. Indian military style often exhibits the British "brusqueness" and swagger-stick manner; and of course English is the language used within the officer corps. Soldiers live and train in secluded British-inspired cantonments. Under the Raj and during the early years of independence, the cantonments were separate from the rest of Indian society and created almost a super-caste above the established caste system – distinct, regimented, and militarily ceremonial.

The British Raj was indeed fixated on military protocol and symbolism. Throughout India, British ceremony was so extensive and ornate that by the early twentieth century the empire's extravagance reached an "elaborative zenith." It was commonly suggested that "the British Raj depended less on justice and good administration than on precedence, honors, and minute distinctions of dress" (Cannadine 2002: 51). With respect to the military, among the princely states for example, "they were carefully ranked and ordered, they were obsessed with protocol and the number of guns they received in salute, and they delighted in 'flamboyant assertions of ritual sovereignty and extravagant contests for symbolic precedence'" (ibid.: 45). The British focus on status, rank, and hierarchy shaped the style of the military uniform and the interaction among officer and soldier. It was an extravagant display of ornate social hierarchy and deference that would inspire current trends in post-Raj military style.

Yet despite this British influence, the Indian army is a true example of the integration between Britain and native India. The most evident illustration of this integration is the military uniform. Since the 1800s Indian uniforms have been characterized by "native costume and European fashion" (Knotel *et al.* 1980: 276–7). One such uniform is the infantry's prim and well-kept British khaki, highlighted by a native Sikh turban. The uniform and general style of the officer corps and rank and file symbolize a successful bridge between colonial presence and Indian independence.

Summary

The post-independence Indian case demonstrates how the theory of separation of civil–military relations is inadequate when explaining a particular example of relationships between the military, the political elites, and the society. The composition of the officer corps, military recruitment method, and military style, in conjunction with the political decision-making process, are essential to an understanding of Indian civil–military relations. They draw attention to the importance of specific cultural and institutional contexts – such as religion, caste, language, and domestic conflicts – not to mention the integration of a British legacy into these indigenous societies. In addition, military training has provided officers and the rank and file with British-inspired technical skills while still embracing native Indian culture and diversity.

The historical and cultural conditions found in India are distinctive and bear significantly on the way in which the military views its role in that nation. India integrates British colonial history into its rich native culture. Strong civil institutions are important political constructions, but they alone do not explain the complexity of Indian civil–military relations. In India, particularly during the 1980s and 1990s, those institutions were weakened yet the military refrained from the interventionist fate of Pakistan. Thinking about Indian civil–military relations in terms of concordance, with respect to the role and function of the armed forces among the military, the political elites, and the citizenry, captures a more accurate depiction of the true civil–military condition in India today.

Pakistan

Pakistan's current international dilemmas mirror their early civil–military conflicts: deep ethnic divisions among diverse minorities and the government's inability to integrate these populations into a peaceful political process. Both institutionally and culturally, Pakistan is sharply contrasted to Indian in terms of civil–military relations. In both case studies, however, concordance theory, rather than separation theory, provides a more adequate explanation for why one country has not experienced domestic military intervention, and why the other has had a history riddled with military governments.

Pakistan has had four episodes of military rule and several failed coup attempts since its founding. During the early 1950s there were high hopes that Ayub Khan's implementation of "basic democracies" would yield a successful domestic political relationship and a secure foreign policy. This chapter highlights many aspects of Ayub's regime (1958–69), because this early condition of discordance and domestic military intervention has continued throughout much of Pakistan's history.

As we will see in this section, Pakistan should not have experienced early domestic military interventions and widespread coup activity. It initially embraced the British–Indian decision-making process and the tradition of parliamentary government, both of which lead to concordance in its neighboring country of India. Further, a large proportion of the Pakistani officer corps had been trained at Britain's Royal Military Academy Sandhurst or the Indian Military Academy. Clearly, Pakistan initially welcomed a British model to its civil–military relationship and civilian control of the military.

Fragile political leadership and a weak political decision-making process ultimately offset the established infrastructure and military professionalism. These early political problems resulted from the fact that "[no] real leader emerged who had the prestige, power, or determination to forge unity among power contenders" (Feit 1973: 64). By contrast to the profound and enduring Indian founders, Mahatma Gandhi and Jawaharlal Nehru, Pakistan suffered leadership setbacks with the untimely deaths of Ali Jinnah and his successor Liaquat Ali Khan. Despite Pakistan's inheritance of civil parliamentary institutions, subsequent unstable governments provided no effective mechanism for political stabilization, viable constitution making, direction for the armed forces, nor peaceful decision making regarding critical issues such as national elections; domestic unrest prevailed and military intervention followed.

Religious and cultural conflicts

Weak civilian leadership and institutions, however, were not the sole explanation for Pakistani domestic military intervention. Also contributing to Pakistani political instability were the religious and cultural difficulties faced while establishing a new Islamic state. In the nineteenth century about a quarter of India's population was Muslim. Not until 1930 did the idea of a separate Muslim state emerge – a state that would be carved from several British Indian provinces.

Pakistan's founder Mohammed Ali Jinnah became president of the Muslim League in 1916. Later when called back to reorganize the party in 1934 he sought to promote the establishment of a separate Muslim state. Jinnah tried to utilize Islam as a tool for nation building by including Muslim legal codes from the *Sharia* while integrating the civil service and political infrastructure inherited from the British. However, his philosophy was intended to be moderate, inclusive of all minorities, and more prone to a secular perspective. While he envisioned the new country as a haven for Muslims, Jinnah also preferred to keep religion out of the day-to-day governance of the nation (Haqqani 2005: 12).

The integrative difficulty for Pakistan was balancing the exigencies of the new state (subdivision of provinces, creation of political and economic infrastructure, and migration of millions of refugees to and from Pakistan and India) with the concept of a Muslim nation. The Muslim League won 75 percent of the Muslim vote in the 1945–6 elections. Pan-Arab movements, such as the Arab Muslim Brotherhood, supported Pakistan. Its leaders, like the former grand mufti of Palestine Mohammad Amin al-Husayni, were often visitors to Pakistan.

Following partition, independence, and universal franchise, the Muslim League could not retain a majority because there were varied and conflicting interpretations about the nature and character of the new Islamic state. After his premature death, Jinnah left his successors "divided, or confused, about whether to take their cue from his Independence Eve call to keep religion out of politics or to build on the religious sentiment generated during the political bargaining for Pakistan" (Haqqani 2005: 10–13). The intense competition with India also encouraged Pakistani political leaders to define "Muslim Pakistan" in stark contrast with "Hindu India" (ibid.: 19).

The resulting balance of power was maintained by creating a nexus among religious leaders, "the country's military establishment, civilian bureaucracy, and intelligence apparatus, which saw itself as a guardian of a new state" (Haqqani 2005: 15). Pakistan's political and religious complexity would not be resolved. As a result, the entrance of a dominant military was an attempt to integrate key elements of Pakistani statehood into a political decision-making process that would jump-start the new nation into a meaningful and effective Muslim nation.

Discordance in Pakistan

The social composition of the officer corps

In the aftermath of Pakistan's independence, founder Muhammad Ali Jinnah made it clear to the officer corps that it was the civilians who "make national policy" while the armed forces remain the "servants of the people" (Cohen 1984: 117). In fact, by the end of British rule, the military appeared to be fiscally and administratively separated from and controlled by the civilian political elites. The professional Pakistani military had intended to follow the tradition of civilian law and order as well as professional military insularity.

Ayub Khan (1958–69), for example, was schooled at Sandhurst in Great Britain and understood the Western officer's respect for civilian authority. What followed was a military regime under Ayub that promised "basic democracy" and transition to civilian rule. In fact, Ayub established military rule with very limited forms of democracy that never became fully entrenched in Pakistani political life. Ayub's leadership reflected the officer corps' "organizational ethos of hierarchy, order, and discipline" but, unlike India, the corps itself did not represent a full cross-section of Pakistan (Cohen 2004: 124).

The lack of diverse representation and the alienation of the Bengali population was the major downfall of Pakistan's inherited tradition of military professionalism. In newly created Pakistan, Punjabi Muslims constituted about 60 percent of the sepoys and officers. The rest of the corps was divided among members from the North-West Frontier Province, Sindh, Baluchistan, and Azad Kashmir. Bengalis were conspicuously absent in the configuration of the Pakistani officer corps. During World War II, no regular Bengali Muslim army units were formed. In contrast to the Punjabi Muslims, who were considered a "martial" class, Bengali officers had developed a reputation quite antithetical to the martial spirit by the 1850s (Jacob 1857: 106; Cohen 1971: 34; Moran and Goodlander 2007: 42, 52).

The Bengali non-martial reputation would stick to the eastern Bengali population during the creation of the Pakistani nation, its military, and its officer corps. From the start, the eastern wing of Pakistan would consistently receive far less attention in budget allocations, political representation, and social status. For example, between 1950 and 1969 Pakistani defense expenditures were approximately 56 percent of the federal budget. "Significant is the fact that out of the total defense expenditure, barely 10 percent was used in East Pakistan, where large revenue collections were made through taxes" (Kodikara 1993: 127). With respect to officer recruitment, by 1967 only 5 percent of the army officers came from East Pakistan. In the navy and air force the total numbers hovered around 10 percent. Although recruitment of the Bengali officers gradually increased, there existed a "considerable distaste for the quality of Bengali officers and other ranks" (Cohen 1984: 43). Officer corps discrimination against Bengalis pointed to discordance between the military and a large sector of the Pakistani society.

Despite the fact that the establishment of Bangladesh in 1971 sealed the fate for an oppressed and now ceded minority, the Pakistani leadership did little to subsequently open up the social composition of the officer corps. Unlike India, which tried to remodel the British martial traditions to accommodate wide social diversity, Pakistan remained wedded to reinforcing the martial Punjabi traditions hailed by the British under the Raj. By 1979 the Pakistani Military Academy was composed of 70 percent Punjabi Muslims and the poorer provinces such as Baluchistan remained underrepresented at 1–9 percent.

Within the Pakistani officer corps, the element of continuity so often valued by professional militaries is often misplaced. For example, Ayub Khan created a narrow promotion system whereby senior officers promoted younger officers who came from similar socioeconomic backgrounds. While generational continuity is preserved, so is lack of diversity among the officer corps. Moreover, the notion of the army as a conduit to military power and politics has stuck since Ayub's days and has severely diminished respect for the officer corps among the citizens. While Ayub's regime was regarded as an initial protector of military and national interests, that view would severely diminish with Pakistan's military defeat by India in 1965, the loss of East Pakistan, and subsequent military coups.

Other examples of misplaced continuity are in the Muslim nation concept and martial tradition, both of which focus on India as enemy number one, rather than on the ways in which the religious and cultural uniqueness and diversity of Pakistan can contribute to the diversification and effectiveness of the officer corps. The British under the Raj used the martial myths to limit recruitment of specific Indian classes and castes into the officer corps. Pakistan adopted the martial tradition "as a way of demonstrating to foreign supporters and to the Pakistanis themselves that a small amount of assistance to Pakistan could offset the Indian behemoth" (Cohen 2004: 103). Pakistan, since Ayub's regime, has been fixated on India and on achieving military superiority over the Hindu nation. Ayub was certain that India wanted to "browbeat Pakistan into subservience" and was determined to utilize Muslim concepts and martial myths to overpower India's military (ibid.: 62). Again, Pakistan's defeat by India in 1965 and the loss of East Pakistan in 1971 emphasized the officer corps' often misplaced notion of continuous traditions. These traditions, while grounded in important religious and historical origins, were often misused and detracted from the real need to diversify the officer social recruitment process for broader and more effective representation and military effectiveness.

The political decision-making process

Focusing on the political decision-making process rather than simply "civil institutions" as a concordance indicator gains relevance with the case of Pakistan. Pakistan has a long history of British influenced civil institutions, yet neglected both the institutional and cultural dimensions that resulted in political instability. The Pakistani armed forces initially did not want to challenge the legality and form of the British inspired parliamentary institutions. The unfortunate saga of the early Pakistani story was that there was plenty of political talent – individuals who had acquired parliamentary experience under the British Raj. The Bengali community, for example, had the most experience with democracy, but even they were not successful at creating that important shift toward constitutional government. Concordance theory is not dependent upon nor does it advocate the development of democracy or constitution; rather it identifies the condition of agreement among the political elites, the military, and the citizenry over the role and function of the military *regardless of a nation's political system of government*. However, in the case of Pakistan, there was hope among the citizenry and the initial founders that a constitutional democracy, not a foreign concept to most Pakistanis, would be the preferred political decision-making process that would keep the military professional and abiding by civilian authority. Ultimately, Pakistan's discordance, and successive military coups, resulted from the government's and the military's inability to create the institutional stability and the cultural/ethnic integration needed to fuse agreement over the role of the armed forces.

Nevertheless, even after seizing power from civilian authorities in 1958, General Ayub Khan was "concerned about the legality of [his] initial action and the subsequent acts that [he] and [his] subordinates committed under the rubric of martial law" (Cohen 1984: 120). This was not a situation of rogue officers who were determined to seize power because of their disagreement with the concept of civil institutional control. Rather, this was a situation where ten years of political interlude forced professional and Western-trained generals to enter politics. As a result of their exposure to the concept and reality of civilian control in British India, they remained concerned about the institutional viability of the state.

Ayub's "Basic Democracies" was established to create a more effective political decision-making process and to enable the military to have a more secure role and mission. While Ayub opposed an elaborate parliamentary democracy,

his new system, which resulted in a 1962 constitution, created an indirect electoral system whereby local governments and union councils would impose taxes
and initiate rural development such as education and sanitation programs. The
urban centers had a similar structure whereby municipal laws were established
to fulfill economic reform and to connect with the unions and national governmental representatives. Eventually an electoral college was formed to elect the
president, assemblies, and councils. Ayub's Basic Democracies ultimately did
not become entrenched long enough to make a real difference in the nation's
political stability, decision-making process, and important areas of infrastructure
such as land distribution and agricultural production.

One key weakness was the lack of true rural political mobilization, as Ayub's
focus was on economic and military development and not political participation.
Unlike Argentina's Juan Perón, Ayub was less interested in reaching out to the
masses for political support and mobilization. Although Perón, like Ayub, would
ultimately reign personally over the nation, in the early years Perón managed to
create a condition of concordance between the political elite, military, and
unions and *descamisados* (shirtless ones). By contrast, as with the social composition and recruitment of the Pakistani officer corps, Ayub's Basic Democracies
failed to truly integrate wide sectors of the population.

Although the Basic Democracies did not achieve concordance among the
political/military elite and the citizenry, this was not a situation where civilian
institutions per se were the point of contention; rather, it was the civilians' and
the military's inability, in the earliest years of Ayub's rule and before, to con-
struct an effective decision-making process that would protect the military's
long-held professional ethic and create true political partnership with the citizenry. This condition of discordance resulted in subsequent domestic military
interventions.

In each of the four Pakistani coups, the general in charge tried to "straighten
out" Pakistan by "introducing major constitutional changes" or by "allowing
civilians back into office" (Cohen 2004: 124–5). In many instances, the army
tried to fill the political vacuum by instilling the army's hierarchical and disciplined ethos into the political process. In most instances, however, Pakistan was
ruled by martial law.

Ayub Khan, Yahya Khan, and Zia-ul-Haq assumed that the military's "professional competence" – a tradition acquired from its British and Indian roots –
could help manage and evolve Pakistan's political decision-making process.
Yahya Khan and Zia-ul-Haq were more adamant about the military's role in
defining the political regime. There was less of an attempt to create a partnership
between the military and the political system and more of a "patron–client relationship." Ayub Khan and more recently General Pervez Musharraf tried to use
the military as a role model to bolster weak political institutions. Musharraf
attempted to follow Ayub's endeavor to make "social and political changes" that
would prevent future military interventions (Cohen 2004: 125). The tragic
events in 2007, however, show the failure to create needed institutional and
social partnerships. The assassination of Benazir Bhutto threw the country into a

new round of domestic volatility. The pattern of discordance among military/political elites, the military organization, and the citizenry continues Pakistan's history of political strife without effective leadership. Moreover, a 2007 poll by a Washington-based nonprofit organization "showed that Osama bin Laden was more popular in Pakistan than Musharraf, polling 46 percent support against 38 percent for the president" (Gall 2007: 2).

Militant Islamic terrorist threats along the Afghan border, the 2007 standoff between Islamic militants and Pakistani troops at Islamabad's Red Mosque, and the recent removal of Supreme Court justices only further weaken the possibility of achieving concordance between the political elites, the military, and the citizenry. Pakistan's generals – from Ayub Khan to Musharraf – have tried to realign the nation's political decision-making process, but a history of domestic political disaffection and regional strife compels the generals to administer military rule of law over a gradual partnering with political groups and the citizenry.

Recruitment method

Lack of cooperation and disagreement among the military, political leadership, and the citizenry is continuously evident in the area of military recruitment. The Pakistani military is organized along British lines and is composed of an army, air force, and navy. As one of the most "central institutions" in Pakistan, citizenship is largely determined by participation in the military (an important cultural reality we also see in the chapter on Israel). Soldiers volunteer for seven years and may enroll for a maximum of 18 years of service. Similar to the British-inspired Indian military, the Pakistani ranks live in military cantonments that provide well-furnished facilities for military training and extracurricular activities such as sports and education (Cohen 1984: 66).

The upper ranks of the Pakistani military are discouraged from mingling with the lower ranks, and the army has acquired preeminence over the navy and air force. For example, the Pakistani counterpart to the chairman of the Joint Chiefs is recruited solely from the army at the expense of the other services (Siddiqa 2007: 61).

Historically, recruitment among the rank and file also reflected a disproportionately small number of Bengali soldiers. The recruitment method appeared both voluntary and persuasive, which according to concordance theory should have encouraged partnership among the political elites, military, and society at large. Whereas many from West Pakistan were encouraged to join the ranks, significant discrimination occurred with respect to East Pakistan. This fact was instrumental in the events that led to domestic strife, the imposition of martial law in East Pakistan, and ultimately to civil war.

In the early years, the British-influenced cantonment system "enhanced the esprit de corps of the army" and ensured that ready supplies of recruits "always therefore exceeded demand" (Feit 1973: 66–7). The ready recruitment supply, however, was mainly from West Pakistan and most predominantly drawn from the Punjab region. The eastern Bengali sector, although comprising 60 percent of Pakistan's population, provided only three battalions (3,000 men) in an army of 300,000. Furthermore, the Bengalis constituted the only single-class units in the Pakistani army, whereas the West Pakistani Muslims were combined in different units. As a result of this overt discrimination and political disparities directed against the East Pakistanis, the Bengalis, during these early years, felt threatened by their lack of representation in one of Pakistan's most vital institutions (Cohen 1984: 40–1, 43).

Today, recruitment is still quite homogenous with about 75 percent of a 650,000-strong army drawn from the Punjab districts. Another 20 percent comes from the North-West Frontier Province (NWFP), while Sindh and Baluchistan combined contribute only 5 percent of the personnel. While the recruitment of the lower middle class results in broader economic recruitment patterns, the social component of military recruitment remains much the same with the obvious elimination of Bengali recruits. There are only about 200 ethnic Baluch and even fewer ethnic Sindhis in the military (Siddiqa 2007: 59, 60). As Ayesha Siddiqa notes (ibid.: 60):

> The myth of Punjabis and Pathans from the NWFP as the "martial races" was propagated even after the county's independence in 1947, and served the purpose of retaining the ethnic composition and inherently elitist fabric of the armed forces. Moreover, the British bias against recruitment of Bengalis, Sindhis and Baluch was maintained. The continuation of the recruitment pattern also fed into the tension between the centre and the smaller provinces, particularly Baluchistan.

Unlike India, which has carefully broadened the military ranks at all levels, social and demographic discrimination prevails in Pakistan. Moreover, the military often looks down on civilians as incompetent and untrustworthy. The military, however, takes care of its military retirees via an elaborate military welfare system. This system ensures a recruit's livelihood throughout his lifetime with employment opportunities, pensions, housing, and other perks. This system, however, accentuates the military's homogenous recruitment patterns since approximately 72 percent of the welfare budget is located in the Punjab versus 2.64 percent in Sindh. Inequality in wealth distribution only encourages resentment among the ranks and in the minority provinces (Siddiqa 2007: 2, 16).

Military style

A disproportionate officer corps composition and discriminatory recruitment of the rank and file are also relevant to the final indicator of concordance: military style. This concordance indicator directly expresses the human and cultural elements involved in the armed forces. It is often part of the historical evolution associated with military tradition and symbols.

One important military tradition of the British-Indian and Pakistani militaries is the theory of "martial races." As described previously, the theory of martial races argues that certain groups of people were more fit for military service: Punjabi Muslims and Sikhs are well known examples. As the martial races tradition became more culturally entrenched in British India, it affected the recruitment of soldiers, because those who were considered part of the privileged elite were more actively recruited in the prestigious British-Indian military.

During its post-independence period, the Indian Army (in contrast to the Pakistani military) tried to demythologize the concept of martial races developed under British rule. One way this was accomplished was by gradually recruiting officers and soldiers from wide sectors of the Indian population thereby preventing the alienation or domination of any one group. This broad recruitment process helped India avoid domestic military intervention. In Pakistan, however, the mythology of the martial races remains embedded in the armed forces, thereby fostering discrimination against the so-called "nonmartial" groups, such as the Bengalis (Cohen 1984: 43; Barua 1992: 131–2).

The concept of the martial races in Pakistan was thoroughly embraced in the 1950s by "the American Generation" of officer corps. These officers were trained by Americans and received knowledge in US problem-solving, military structure, and American-made army equipment. Unfortunately, US military training coupled with the ideology of the martial races resulted in strategies such as the use of guerrilla warfare and special forces to fight Pakistan's own population in East Bengal (Cohen 2004: 103–4). The martial races idea, along with US military influence and over-exaggeration of Pakistani military tactics, served to embolden the Pakistani army at home. Rather than address Bengali grievances, Ayub Khan and his successors utilized Pakistan's US-imported military tactics not for building democratic institutions with a stronger military but to treat "the Bengal movement as a counterinsurgency exercise, not a political puzzle to be painstakingly and patiently resolved" (ibid.: 74–5).

Where British India used martial races as a tactic for military recruitment and perhaps caste-based discrimination, it never manifested in post-British India to a full-fledged tradition, ideology, or mythology within the military. India allowed various military traditions and mythologies to evolve naturally among a diverse rank and file. Concordance was thus maintained.

In Pakistan, by contrast, this military martial races mythology was not only used in military recruitment but also as justification to turn on one of its nonmartial race populations which happened to be the largest sub-population in Pakistan. Part of the problem was that Pakistan was consistently being compared to and compared itself to India. Pakistan wanted to show the world that it could gain military superiority over India with a small amount of foreign support and domestic adherence to military mythology. Thus, Ayub Khan "elevated the martial races theory to the level of absolute truth" (Cohen 2004: 103–4). As a result, Pakistan saw military style, embedded within a martial race mythology, used against it own people.

In the end, stable political institutions were sacrificed for domestic military conflict that alienated the Bengali population, fomented civil war, and ultimately resulted in discordance. The culture of military traditions, inherited from British colonial rule, continued in Pakistan. This was reflected in the recruitment of the officers and rank-and-file soldiers. In the case of the East Bengalis, this overt form of discrimination, coupled with additional political and social grievances, led to civil war, the downfall of Ayub Khan, and the eventual creation of Bangladesh in 1971.

Pakistan also failed to reconcile the state's Islamic identity with its political and military infrastructure. There was a constant tension between "adapting to a British-dominated environment, while simultaneously supporting and exploiting traditional allegiances and structures" (Cohen 2004: 167). The problem that continues to haunt Pakistan is the state utilizing "religion and religious groups for political purpose" and the military stepping in to "deal with the symptoms of the chaos generated by religious–political agitation, without any effort to deal with its causes" (Haqqani 2005: 21). Early US support for Pakistan fostered economic growth and additional foreign alliances with the Soviet Union and China. Pakistan's aspiration, however, in becoming a "haven for Indian Muslims" and a "stable and prosperous Islamic state" would be short-lived (Cohen 2004: 3). While India succeeded in modifying the martial races theory through broad military recruitment in its officer corps and rank and file, Pakistan used religion and martial class mythology to restrict military participation and diminish a successful partnership between the military, the political elites, and Pakistani citizens.

Summary

This section has focused on Pakistan's early yet significant state of discordance that led to a history of domestic military interventions. Separation theory posits a dichotomous power relationship between civil and military spheres; it also suggests that military intervention in domestic politics is prevented if civilian institutions are in control and maintain a check over a professional military. Conversely, it holds that military intervention in internal politics is more likely to take place if civilian institutions do not exist or are greatly weakened. As we have seen this was not the case for Pakistan. For Pakistan, separation theory could not be the sole explanation for the military's interaction and intervention within the civilian realm. Separate military and civilian institutions existed yet military intervention still occurred. The military historically maintained a certain respect for and support of civilian rule over the armed forces, even to the point of questioning military rule from a legal and constitutional standpoint.

Concordance theory, however, presents a more viable picture for the civil–military relationship that exists in Pakistan today. It was cultural and institutional discordance that resulted in domestic military intervention, civil war, and the country's eventual partition. Pakistan never recovered from this early inability to organize inherited British-Indian political institutions vis-à-vis the military. Civil institutions were not absent in Pakistan. Domestic military interventions occurred and a state of discordance continues to exist because Pakistan lacks political stability and a partnership with the citizens at large.

Pakistan's continuous domestic discordance has resulted not only in domestic conflict but international difficulties with the United States, India, and Afghanistan. The current international dilemmas faced by Pakistan mirror their early civil–military conflicts, stemming from deep ethnic divisions among diverse minorities. Pakistan's military government faces tribal conflicts along the Afghan border that are fostering terrorism and jihad in Kashmir, Afghanistan, and Pakistan. This is the result of years of sectarian conflict between Shiites and Sunnis. As a consequence of these ideological clashes, militants are intimidating Pakistan's local border communities and encouraging Taliban networks. The local schools in the poorer rural provinces have become recruiting grounds for pro-Taliban militants. The Pakistan government is once again uncertain about how to cope with tribes and sectarian hostility. It is also under increasing pressure from the United States to reign in the tribal regions and to prevent the further spread of Taliban attacks in Afghanistan.

Pakistan's inability to quell al-Qaeda extremism has contributed to a lack of domestic confidence in General Musharraf's political agenda. While Musharraf had initial support from the military and the citizenry, he continued the discordant political and social relationship (begun by his predecessor Ayub Khan) with the imposition of martial law. Largely as a result of Khan's initial and dramatic alienation of the East Bengali community, Pakistan has continued to fail during many subsequent historical periods in partnering with diverse domestic political groups and the citizenry and in gaining credibility – a credibility vital to domestic concordance and international foreign policy. Instead, partnerships often remain severed despite an early history of separate military and civilian institutions, which has lead to unrest in present-day Pakistan.

This current situation in Pakistan also illustrates the close connection between international relations and civil–military relations. Pakistan's failure to contain tribal conflict and Taliban activity ultimately poses a threat to countries outside its borders – the United States, neighboring regions, and other countries worldwide, all of whom see Taliban activity as a major threat to their own national security. Most obviously, these conflicts create political, economic, and societal tension within Pakistan itself that foster a context for discordance rather than concordance.

This chapter has focused on the development of concordance with respect to India's civil–military relations and Pakistan's early yet significant state of discordance, which led to subsequent domestic military interventions. On a regional level, discordance is far more prevalent, and India operates in a South Asian environment where domestic military interventions are not uncommon – Pakistan and Bangladesh being clear examples. Moreover, the influence of China in the region cannot be overlooked, since India's defense policy is often a reaction to the role of China and the presence of conventional and nuclear forces.

The proliferation of nuclear weapons, and who will control them, threatens a delicate balance in a highly volatile region where China exerts enormous influence on neighboring states including Pakistan. An argument could be made that

India's domestic concordance between the military, the political elites, and the citizenry contributes to the preservation of regional stability because India has chosen both to maintain its regional strength vis-à-vis China and Pakistan, and to continue to search for a peaceful solution to the nuclear issue with allies such as the United States. India's most recent and ongoing nuclear deal with the United States, originally struck in 2005, is an example of the delicate synergies taking place to offset potential threats from China, Pakistan, and Iran, while maintaining domestic military and technological muscle (S.P. Cohen 2002: 164–5; BBC 2007). In other words, the domestic partnering among military officers, political elites, and society at large is extended to regional partnering among India's allies and adversaries. We can at least begin to surmise that successful domestic concordance may contribute to foreign policies that can affect regional stabilization. In Chapter 8, it will be shown that India's booming technological revolution, within a stable domestic civil–military relationship, also contributes to higher levels of social responsibility in the area of multinational partnering and corporate philanthropy.

While India's successful domestic course encourages partnerships among international political and corporate allies, Pakistan's continuous domestic discordance has resulted in recent difficult relations with the United States, India, and Afghanistan. Pakistan's inability to quell al-Qaeda extremism contributes to a lack of domestic confidence in General Musharraf's political agenda. Needless to say, Pakistan's history of discordance may also affect the delicate South Asian nuclear balance should al-Qaeda gain control of these destructive weapons. The domestic political regime remains volatile as military and civilian institutions and leaders grapple for power and support from the citizenry. Musharraf's legacy remains a question mark at best in the history of Pakistani generals who have ruled the nation at the expense of institutional agreement and cultural partnership.

Acknowledgment

Portions of this section were adapted from the following book chapter originally published by Westview Press: Schiff, R.L. (1998) "Concordance theory: the cases of India and Pakistan," in D. Mares (ed.) *Civil–Military Relations*, Boulder, CO: Westview Press.

6 Argentina's Perón period (1946–55)

For too long the US post-World War II case has been studied and applied deliberately to developing nations around the world. Nations in Latin American, Asia, Africa, and the Middle East were supposed to model their militaries after the US military and their separate civilian institutions accordingly. That is a tall order for newly developing nations with distinctive cultures. Argentina also has a distinctive military and political culture. During the first Perón presidency (1946–55), Argentina had a well-established military subordinate to a political authority, at least in the early years. It was a military supportive of Perón's early social programs, but whose officer corps receded in importance vis-à-vis the president and his wife Eva Perón. In the end, the military toppled Perón because his economic programs did not succeed and he lost the support of the unions. The concordance theory of civil–military relations is applied here to the Perón period in Argentina.

Scholars persist in superimposing the Western separation model on Argentina, as we find in John M. Anderson's naval post-graduate work – a thesis insisting that a culturally limited theory be applied to a nation with a distinct historical and cultural mosaic (Anderson 1998). Anderson begins his critique of concordance theory as it applies to Argentina by marrying the field of civil–military relations with studies of democracy: "I argue that each nation must find its own way to democratic forms. Once memories of old patterns of authoritarianism have been supplanted by more democratic experiences, then concordance will have the opportunity to take hold" (ibid.: xi).

Concordance theory, however, is not about trying to create a more democratic government, nor is it a consequence of democratic government. It is independent of democratic ideology and organization, though a democratic nation (like an authoritarian nation) may experience concordance. As stated at the beginning of this book, concordance theory explains conditions for domestic military intervention or non-intervention in a particular nation *and nothing more*. Concordance explains both institutionally and culturally why some nations fall prey to domestic military intervention and others do not. Domestic military intervention may include forcible actions such as *coups d'état*, palace revolts, or other forms of takeover by a nation's military.

Concordance is not meant to measure levels of democracy, authoritarianism, or any other form of government. A central premise of concordance theory is to avoid superimposing a particular type of government or culture upon a nation. Hence, more concordance does not necessarily result from more democracy; and more democracy does not necessarily result from greater concordance. Rather, domestic military intervention may be averted if there is agreement among the military, the political elites, and the citizenry over the four indicators highlighted throughout this book, regardless of a nation's form of government.

One final comment on Anderson's work and critique of concordance theory. Anderson examines Argentina from 1930 to the early 1990s then qualifies his examination; specifically, he argues that separation theory may not apply from about 1930 to 1983, but it may have relevance from 1983 onward (Anderson 1998: 43, 74).

Concordance theory does not pretend to be all things to all historical periods. If a theory can be applied rigorously to select case studies, its strength is enhanced and its applicability is sufficiently demonstrated. This chapter on Argentina identifies a short but critical time frame in Argentine history (1946–55) and applies concordance to that time period alone. Moreover, it is argued that in the early Perón years concordance was achieved, if only briefly, and the chapter reflects the evolution from agreement among the three partners to eventual discordance and the fate of domestic military intervention.

Conditions in Perón-era Argentina

Argentina has a distinctive military and political culture. As in India, the military was influenced by the British but developed its own style of officer corps, recruitment, and relationship with the political elites and the citizenry. For example, from 1930 to 1945 the military governed Argentina either under the guise of democracy or often through direct military control. During the first Perón presidency (1946–55), Argentina had a well-established military which remained subordinate to Perón's authority at least in the early years. There was initial concordance among the officer corps, the citizenry, and Perón over the creation of Peronist economic and foreign policies that initially brought Perón to power. It was Perón's connection to the unions and the underprivileged *"descamisados"* (shirtless ones), which earned him sweeping political recognition in a country that was largely divided by class and income and was fraught with domestic military interventions. The citizenry benefited from Perón's efforts as secretary of labor to achieve more equitable work conditions. The officer corps – a victim of misdirection and international criticism by US Ambassador to Argentina Spruille Braden – embraced Perón's leadership, uniting both as victims of Braden's accusations of fascism. The Braden–Perón controversy galvanized labor and the military in support of Perón. Both the working class and the military would be integrated into Perón's vision for Argentina's future:

> Perón and his supporters expanded the political, economic, and social policies that first appeared in 1944. He shifted the focus from the reactionary

and secretive concerns of the military officers toward a new era of state-directed reform and development. He moved groups that were once ignored or repressed to the center of a movement he defined as revolutionary.

(Lewis 2003: 99)

The officer corps and Perón achieved initial agreement on the projects of industrialization through military support and promoting Argentina internationally – a reaction to vocal US diplomatic interventions and Perón's political outreach efforts to the officer corps and working class. A fair election and wide social support for Perón created the hope that the "New Argentina" would usher in participatory politics and agreement on the role of the armed forces. For the first few years of his presidency, the army was in agreement with Perón's efforts to rebuild the economy and the military. Discordance with the military by 1949 and Perón's eventual overthrow was the result of Perón's effort to centralize power into one party, his Peronist party, and his unfulfilled domestic economic promises. Had the economy flourished and had all segments that supported Perón's initial rise to power remained collaborative partners, Perón's political and social concordance likely would have remained more constant, and overthrow may have been averted.

Internal and external threat conditions

The pre-Perón period faced significant internal and external threats, and Argentina suffered a number of domestic military interventions during the early 1930s. The most prevalent were internal and external economic threats. The socioeconomic landscape in Argentina had changed drastically from 1920 to 1936. The Great Depression in particular created an economic crisis in the rural sectors, which lacked the capital and machinery to keep up with the competition of imported goods. While rural producers struggled to adapt to the industrial landscape, opportunities in the countryside receded as factory growth and manufacturing increased in the cities – "As new factories opened, they attracted laborers who settled in the country's expanding urban and suburban centers ... the expansion of domestic industry increased the number and weight of the industrial workforce" (Lewis 2003: 88).

From an external standpoint, the Argentine economy was initially successful until World War II when Nazi war efforts curtailed European trade with Argentina. For example, Argentine exports to Britain were drastically reduced. US foreign policy decisions regarding Europe also alienated the Argentine economy and resulted in economic crisis. The Marshall Plan allowed European nations to buy US and Canadian products in an effort to rebuild the war-torn continent. Much of Perón's political base included ranchers, grain producers, and public servants who were detrimentally affected by the new European situation. "Wheat production dropped so low that the government had to import grain for the first time since 1898" (Lewis 2003: 105–7). Argentina's mother industries continued to be negatively affected when export prices dramatically increased during the Korean War and when drought ravaged the Argentine farm-lands. These economic conditions were critical factors in Perón's loss of partner-ship and support among the citizens and the military.

The United States also provided economic and military aid to southern nations such as Brazil – a nation that supported US foreign policy and was mili-tarily feared by Argentina. While the United States saw Brazil's economy as compatible, Argentina's export economy of meat and grains was viewed as competition. Moreover, Argentina did not break with Nazi Germany until the last few months of World War II – a key factor in US–Argentine tensions. David Mares (1988: 466) writes:

> Argentina refused to accept diplomatic subordination to US definitions of defense requirements in 1940, and in 1942, joined temporarily by Chile, it did not break diplomatic relations with Nazi Germany … Chile succumbed to US pressure after one year. Argentina, however, held out completely until 1944, when it severed diplomatic relations with the Nazis but continued to be friendly toward them.

During this time, Argentina had built the most powerful military in South America, thereby increasing the rivalry with Brazil. The consequence for Argentina was internal economic difficulties and a perceived military threat from its southern neighbors (Lewis 2003: 88, 90). By the early 1940s the world condemned Argentina as fascist and continued to mount significant economic pressure. It was under these conditions that Perón rose to power.

Prior to the 1945 elections, Perón gained vast union support by promising to stimulate economic growth and redistribute national income. The business elite and property-owning oligarchy, many of whom supported the Nazi regime, would ultimately remain intact under Perón's rule. Yet during his rise Perón criticized their privileged position while embracing the unions and their "shirtless" workers (*descamisados*) who migrated to the cities from the countryside.

Additionally, Perón's officer standing assisted in gaining military support for his popular economic agenda that promised a better life for the military and citi-zenry. The military elite initially opposed Perón's rapid rise but realized during the regime prior to Perón that the military needed direction and popular citizen support to survive: "the military leaders had not faced the long-term question of what policies to follow once they were in power" (Francis 1977: 201). In 1943, the military attempted to remove Perón from the political scene, but this was fol-lowed by massive citizen demonstrations that frightened the military into rein-stating him. It was Perón who appeared to offer political direction through his five-year economic plan and his desire to elevate Argentine interests internation-ally with industrialization backed by military support.

In 1945 Perón and his wife Evita did not simply rely on the separation of the civil and military institutions but achieved concordance or partnership between the military, the citizenry, and the presidency. The Peróns came to power through support from the working classes, the military's protection of the general election, and their collaborative efforts to improve Argentina's military and foreign-policy standing internationally. Institutional boundaries could co-mingle due to Perón's dual status as president and former military officer. He utilized both positions to influence the military and the citizens and to persuade them to support his policies. By contrast, throughout his presidency and certainly by 1955, Perón had not fulfilled his promises to restore long-term economic prosperity and a successful international foreign policy. Failing economic programs, waning popular support, and eventual distrust among the military ranks resulted in the toppling of Perón. Below are the concordance indicators that reflect the early concordance and eventual discordance in Perón's Argentina.

Concordance and discordance in Perón's Argentina

The social composition of the officer corps

Prior to Perón's presidency, the officer corps was largely unorganized and split between the pro-Allies and pro-Axis wings of support for the war in Europe. Certain officer factions attempted to prevent Perón's rise, but those efforts did little to influence the military commanders whose support was critical for any organized defiance or serious coup effort. As Perón rose to power, he understood the importance of integrating military and industrial interests in an effort to create an international Argentine presence among the larger economic and political players. He was intent on expanding military armament development by cultivating close ties with the United States. The US–Argentina relationship, however, was not completely positive because of Argentina's partial support for Germany during World War II and Spruille Braden's interpretation and influence on the matter. The outcome of the Braden fiasco (discussed later in this chapter) brought the officer corps and Perón closer in focusing on greater defense spending and development and attempting to establish Argentina as a formidable international presence.

After World War II Argentina was in the unique position of having significant cash reserves. This resulted largely from the efforts of close Perón advisor and Central Bank President Miguel Miranda who initiated the Institute for the Promotion of Trade (IAPI). This agency controlled Argentine imports and exports including lucrative commodities such as meat and grains. By December 1946 anticipated profits reached 2 billion pesos. It was the IAPI surplus that would fund Perón's ambitious five-year plan. That surplus, however, would be dissipated quickly through corrupt mismanagement of funds, IAPI's pricing practices, drought, and fuel shortages. For example, by 1948, Argentine banks were over $200 million in debt, and gold reserves had dropped dramatically (Potash 1980: 53, 60, 63; Rock 1987: 295–9). Nevertheless, during the early years of Perón's regime, the initial financial surplus enabled Perón to invest in the senior officer corps and in military armaments:

Efforts to depoliticize the military included awarding the officer corps several pay increases, reportedly raising the salaries of some senior ranks above those of their counterparts in the United States … Meanwhile senior officers continued in high government posts and as managers of state firms in the energy and transportation sectors. Whenever he could overcome or ignore continuing American reluctance, Perón also provided the military with new weaponry; in 1947, for example, he made a large purchase of British jets.

(Rock 1987: 281)

Perón's early concordance with the officer corps was the result of his vision that the army, navy, and air force work cooperatively under a central authority. The military was pleased with Perón's presidency and programs of industrialization, modernization, and achieving international prominence. He had also connected with the people, including the *descamisados* who trusted Perón's partnership with the citizens and the military – a situation unique to Latin America where distrust was more frequent among these stakeholders.

In 1946 the military responded positively to Perón's relationship with the citizens by assuring a peaceful and honest election, a move that "won praise from all political sectors, the press and foreign observers" (Potash 1980: 44). Institutionally, Perón furthered his partnership with the military by creating the Defense Ministry that constituted an organizational link between the commanders in chief of each force and the president. Through Minister of War Sosa Molina, and improved professional and social benefits, Perón was able to keep the military professional and somewhat separate from politics (although key officers had ministerial positions). Perón was also deeply interested in improving the army's domestic and international reputation through the modernization of military facilities and weapons acquisition:

If War Minister Sosa Molina was able to preserve the Army's autonomy from unwanted civilian intrusions, he was also highly successful down to 1949 in keeping the Army from becoming involved in civilian politics. In part, this resulted from the sense of professional well-being that President Perón fostered through pay increases, improved housing, and other social benefits, and through the energetic support he gave to weapons acquisition and the construction of new military facilities.

(Potash 1980: 87)

Perón, however, did not simply rely on a separation between civilian and military institutions to determine the role of the armed forces; he also leaned heavily on creating an effective partnership with both the military and the nation's citizenry. In turn, the military subscribed to Perón's political outreach to the unions and the *descamisados*.

Perón paid special attention to the NCOs – "the *suboficiales* or noncommissioned officers" (Potash 1980: 117). Perón could identify with these officers from his early years in the military and therefore had "keen insight into their professional and personal concerns." As a second lieutenant, Perón had been popular with the soldiers and was assigned to the School for Noncommissioned Officers, which later earned him entrance to the Superior War School (Lewis 2006: 143). As president, Perón knew that "efforts to reduce distinctions between them [noncommissioned officers] and the commissioned ranks," without altering the basic hierarchy, would have a profound impact on the entire corps. Improvements in housing and social programs for the officers as well as changes in the military uniform "enabled senior NCOs to appear more like officers" (Potash 1980: 117).

Attention paid to the NCOs was part of his movement "directed to the social classes from which most enlisted men came" (Potash 1980: 117). For example, Perón supported a scholarship program that enabled sons of lower-class workers to enter *liceos militares* – secondary schools run by the army. While affecting the lives of the NCOs, Perón continued to embrace the working and labor classes who were the cornerstone of his economic and social policies (ibid.: 86).

The Defense Ministry included a national defense council, external security cabinet, and coordinated military staff. Initially, Perón had intended to overhaul the defense system and achieved early partnership in this regard with the commissioned officers. However, by 1949, economic conditions in Argentina suffered and Perón found himself in a discordant relationship with the military. Adding to the friction were verbal attacks on Perón's wife. As Evita gained her own political stature, the older officer corps members criticized her for becoming more involved in Perón's political decisions and for her possible intention to run for office. Perón, however, remained loyal to his wife and the officers backed down, but not without consequence. General Molina now had diminished authority over the troops as the Defense Ministry receded into the background.

Though initial concordance was achieved through initiatives such as NCO equality and the three-pronged Defense Ministry, discordance regarding the social officer corps composition prevailed. Contrary to his electoral promises, the military (along with the labor unions and *descamisados*) was less included in Perón's decision-making process than originally intended. Additionally, Perón proceeded to select officers who paid allegiance to him, Evita, and the Peronist political party (Fraser and Navarro 1980: 96; Pion–Berlin 1997: 156). Six out of 21 ministerial posts went to military officers who showed loyalty to Perón (Pion–Berlin 1997: 155–6).

Furthering the discordance was the prospect of Evita becoming Perón's vice-presidential running mate. In Argentina's male dominated culture, "this suggestion greatly disturbed the military … especially since, in the event of Perón's death Evita would become not only President but Chief Commander of the Armed Forces" (de Elia and Queiroz 1997: 140). In particular, the officers staffing military installations throughout the country and the military and naval colleges opposed Perón's reelection with his proposed elevation of Evita to the vice presidency. It also became clear that Perón's hold over the unions and the working classes was not completely solid, as widespread strikes occurred which required military mobilization to quell protests against the regime. Moreover, one officer decided to launch an ill-fated coup against Perón:

> General Benjamin Menendez, a retired cavalry officer, attempted an ill-planned coup, supported by only three tanks, a handful of junior officers, and two hundred men. Although the coup was immediately silenced by the government, Perón saw that the alliance he had proclaimed between the army and the people was beginning to crumble.
>
> (Rock 1987: 305)

Additional economic and political problems, including fuel shortages, US credit loan delinquency during the Korean War, and the shutdown of the Argentine newspaper *La Prensa*, diminished his support among key military officers. "Of its more than 400 officers, including course directors, professors, and officer–students, perhaps 80 percent were alienated from Perón in 1951." The military remained "a key foundation of the regime," but Perón's treatment of the older retiring officers, his policy of favoritism in promoting non-commissioned officers, as well as the diminishing national economic returns significantly affected his relationship with the officer corps (Lewis 2003: 108). This evolution sparked discordance with the officer corps and the eventual demise of Perón's regime.

The political decision-making process

Argentina's constitutional government, devised in 1853, was inspired by the US Constitution. The Argentine political system is based on a separation of power among the three branches of government: the president, the Congress, and the judiciary. The president is elected by an electoral college which in turn is elected by a bicameral legislature. Both the president and the Congress are elected for a fixed term. Unlike the US system, the Argentine Congress has historically augmented the executive powers:

> Argentine presidents did not need to seek legislative confirmation when appointing members of their cabinet or other executive offices; they had broad regulatory powers by means of decree; they combined the positions of head of state, the government, the public administration and the armed forces.
>
> (Llanos 2002: 19)

One particular power that has varied among Argentine presidents was the legislative veto. Historically, the veto would be used to object to congressional bills, which would then be sent back to Congress for reconsideration. Similar to the US system, two-thirds approval by both chambers of Congress could override the veto. Beginning with Perón in 1940s, the veto was used more often, and the judiciary provided an ambiguous definition of the veto power, which only added to its frequency of use and augmented executive authority. Perón would ultimately reform the entire constitution, including the veto privilege, to give presidents unprecedented and often autonomous authority, cementing his reign of power.

During Perón's rise to the presidency, he was less concerned about the Argentine congressional system but embraced those who would support his presidency: the labor party and the unions. Under the previous military government, Perón had requested a new appointment to Secretary of Labor and Social Welfare. Through this new position, Perón introduced labor laws that empowered the workers with decent wages and conditions and, in turn, gave Perón the support he needed to assume power:

> There would be an eight-hour day, clean and healthy factory conditions, accident and health insurance, annual paid vacations, and compulsory contributions by employers and workers to pension funds. Going further, he not only insisted on the workers' right to form unions but launched a drive to unionize all previously unorganized workers, even rural labor ... Clearly the Law of Professional Associations would give Perón the power to bring the entire labor movement under his control, giving him a mass base from which to pursue his obvious political ambitions.
>
> (Lewis 2006: 145, 146)

Indeed, when then President General Edelmiro Farrell and other conspiring generals arrested Perón in 1945, the unions and the workers mounted a mass rally to gain his release. Perón had won the support of the citizens who had once lived in destitution but now were given legal and economic opportunities to pursue their livelihood and hope for a more just and inclusive Argentina. The citizen support gathered during his tenure as secretary of labor and social welfare was key in Perón's upcoming campaign and eventual election to the presidency.

The 1946 presidential election was considered legal and fair. At this point Perón could have easily maintained concordance among the citizens, the military, and the political elites and "might easily have governed democratically" (Lewis 2006: 146). He had won the election by a wide margin and was a career officer who had achieved extensive support among the workers and unions in a political atmosphere receptive to participatory politics. His wife Evita was winning the hearts of the common citizen through her targeted speeches and national charity programs aimed at alleviating poverty. Moreover, Perón had won the election against the backdrop of the antagonizing US diplomatic efforts of Spruille Braden and the publication of the *Blue Book* – a documented study by the US government that was released in Argentina just prior to the 1946 election and cast Perón and his supporters in a negative light.

Braden's *Blue Book* attempted to accuse not only Perón but also a number of army corps officers as being Nazi sympathizers, angering the military. In addition, as US secretary of state for Latin American affairs, Braden had painted a picture of Argentina that was opposed by many US institutions, including the Pentagon and Corporate America (MacDonald 1990: 142). Though these accusations might have destroyed Perón's chances for citizen support Braden had in fact tipped the balance in favor of Perón among the citizens. Campaign signs popularizing Perón's position asked citizens to choose – "Braden or Perón?" Backed with pro-labor reforms and the popularity of himself and his wife, Perón's campaign gained acceleration rather than deterioration. Braden also brought the military and Perón closer than ever before as both were being labeled as Nazi sympathizers. The nationalist sentiment against Braden, and Perón's alliance with the military, would give Perón the goal of establishing a formidable Argentine presence worldwide, but it did not convince him to establish a true participatory decision-making process in government.

Differing from the then-established constitutional process, the early political decision-making process revolved around Perón, Evita, and Perón's party of union supporters and the *descamisados*. The unified party was soon changed to the Perónist party, "Partido Peronista," which during the interim congressional elections defeated the opposition and paved the way for constitutional reform. That reform centralized power in Perón's hands with a number of new changes:

> The most controversial provision was to permit an incumbent president to seek reelection to an unlimited number of six-year terms. Also the electoral college was abolished allowing the direct election of the president ... The Constitution of 1949 thus established election by plebiscite, eliminating the sectional and regional weightings that were legacies of nineteenth-century federalism. Furthermore, it widened presidential authority to intervene in the provinces and gave the president discretion to impose "a state of internal war" to protect against rebellion or insurrection.
>
> (Rock 1987: 288–9)

Perón created a type of "legal" coercive regime, where he held the power over the military and the citizenry to quell unwanted internal protest. Perón's regime abided by the "formal" constitutional structure of government yet essentially made the political parties, Congress, and provincial legislatures irrelevant. For example, "Perón exercised direct influence on the nomination of candidates, so that the party remained too weak to generate a middle level political elite by itself" (Llanos 2002: 25–6). By giving practically unlimited power to the president, Perón's reforms eventually rendered the other decision-making branches helpless.

He also ruled with a tremendous amount of charismatic authority that tempered the uglier repressive side of his rule. Perón and Evita were able to lavish the nation with persuasive oratory and exuded a love for each other that permeated the entire country. Everything was done in the name of democracy, inclusion, and hope for the "New Argentina," but anyone who crossed Perón's authority was either banned or jailed.

Once he achieved control and replaced the labor party with his own, Perón began to curb political activities and leadership initiatives that countered his authoritative rule. He also proceeded to censor the newspapers that criticized his authoritative form of participatory politics and even acquired a monopoly over the ink used to print the newspapers in order to control the printing presses.

Evita's role as first lady showed the same false front as her husband's "constitutionally sound" regime. Though a proponent of women's suffrage and founder of the Female Perónist Party, Evita's national charity abandoned the *descamisados* in favor of more profitable partnerships. Shortly after her ascent to power as first lady of Argentina, the popular base of the *descamisados* was run by political patronage similar to Perón's regime (Fraser and Navarro 1980: 103, 107):

> Her efforts were directly responsible for the enfranchisement of women in 1947 and for the creation of the women's branch (Rama Feminina) of the Peronist party of 1949 ... Having taken a leading part in the subjugation of the unions, Eva Perón afterward directed the creation of the lines of communication between the upper hierarchy and the base. Her charity was directed to the same goal. As she dispensed succor to scores of daily supplicants at her foundation, she revived on a grand scale activities of traditional political boss, exchanging favors and benefits for support and allegiance.
>
> (Rock 1987: 287)

The Peróns had won the support of the Argentine masses who longed for better economic and social conditions. They embraced Perón's military background and his apparent plans to uplift the lower classes through legal and constitutional means. Evita was his partner who exuded style, compassion, and hope in her foundation activities and first lady role. But the constitution's "emphasis on freedoms and rights of the individual was replaced by corporate rights emanating from the state" (Rock 1987: 289). A condition of concordance or partnership among the military and the citizenry was gradually replaced with centralized presidential authority; by 1949, the "Perónist Revolution evaporated" (Fraser and Navarro 1980: 103).

Perón's rise to power was won by a legitimate concordance between the presidency, the officer corps, and the citizenry. Initially, he had been inclusive enough to ensure that the role of the military was determined by congressional approval with support from the officer corps and labor. Through constitutional reform, however, Perón gradually sowed the seeds of alienation and centralized his power, His coercive regime would eventually alienate the officer corps (who ultimately only had superficial control over officer and rank-and-file recruitment) and the citizens (who did not benefit from economic reform).

Initially, Perón's strong union support discouraged worker strikes. Perón mobilized police and security forces to oppose political rivals and assist with the 1952 election. Evita died before the election and Perón suffered a huge personal and political blow. "Her supervision of the party's women's auxiliary organizations, her manipulation of union leaders and army officers, and her skill as a spokesperson for the government and the president had helped maintain Perón's control over the country" (Lewis 2003: 109). Perón won the election, but he was losing his grip on the country. His new five-year plan suffered setbacks because of continuing foreign export restrictions. Argentina still had difficulty increasing exportable products, and inflation continued to grow at significant levels. Perón, with union support, placed restrictions on his political opposition among workers. But the unions finally lost patience with Perón and began to strike in 1954.

The final blow came from the Catholic Church, which had seen Perón and Evita as competitors even after her death. The Eva Perón Foundation's charity competed with Church funding, and Perón's efforts to have Evita canonized did not gain Church support. Neither did Perón's proposed laws to legalize prostitution and divorce. Perón effectively alienated key political constituencies: the military officer corps, the unions, the Church, and the land-owning oligarchy. In addition, his regime was often at odds with the United States and her allies. Perón's regime was eventually toppled in September 1955 (Lewis 2003: 110–11).

The political decision-making process began with Perón's early connection with the unions during his time as secretary of labor and social welfare. It was then that he began to partner with the citizenry who elected him and allowed him to announce his five-year economic plan, rebuild domestic military strength, and improve Argentina's international standing. Perón's early presidency appeared participatory while working with Congress, the military, and the supportive labor constituency. After implementing constitutional reform, however, the concordant relationships shifted from one of partnership to more authoritarian control and political disaffection. The evolution from a labor-based party to Perón's own party, the abolition of regional elections and the electoral college, and the latitude of executive veto power enabled Perón to rule authoritatively often with the appearance of establishing democratic legislation, such as women's right to vote: "Yet Perón's repressive acts were performed simultaneously with the enactment of numerous and significant social reforms, some of which had the effect of making Argentine institutions more democratic" (Fraser and Navarro 1980: 105).

The constellation of economic and foreign policy obstacles, along with the military's disaffection regarding Eva Perón's political stature and Perón's eventual unwillingness to embrace participatory politics, led to a discordant political decision-making process. Coupled with the alienation of the officer corps and a flawed military recruitment method (discussed in the next section), Perón's Argentina reflects an evolution from a state of initial concordance to one of discord and military coup in 1955.

Recruitment method

The Argentine recruitment method during Perón's period was largely persuasive and compulsory. Commissioned and non-commissioned officers, reserve officers, and the rank and file were all petitioned for participation within the Argentine armed forces. In 1943, resulting from significant urban industrialization, a large percentage of Argentines were living in the cities. "Each year tens of thousands of men and women, and after 1943, over 100,000 annually, came to Buenos Aires looking for jobs and excitement" (Potash 1980: 2). The military "absorbed 6% of Argentina's gross national product." The army benefited the most from the defense budget, acquiring about 65 percent of the budget in 1945. The recruitment of generals was largely urban: "At least 50% of the generals on active duty in January 1946 were immigrants' sons," and the preponderance came from Buenos Aires (Potash 1980: 5). All generals and rank-and-file soldiers who were commissioned started as cadets in the Military Academy (*Colegio Militar*). The non-commissioned officers had a more diverse background – "some had only completed the sixth grade of elementary school; others had finished one or more years of secondary school" (Potash 1980: 6–7).

With Perón in power, the armed forces establishment decreased by about 5 percent each year. For example, in 1946 there were 87,273 conscripts among the enlisted personnel. By 1950, that number had dropped to 68,500. While the regular officer corps hovered between 4,700 and 5,700 officers, the reserve officers (similar to the conscripts) declined significantly (Potash 1980: 83–4):

> Contrary to some impressions, the Argentine Army declined in strength, dropping by some 14 percent between 1946 and 1949. This reduction was achieved primarily by cutting back sharply on the number of one-year conscripts while retaining the number of permanent enlisted men at about the same level ... By 1949, in contrast to three years before, the Army budget provided for more than 900 additional regular officers to command a force that was smaller than 17,000 men ... this trend toward a larger regular officer component in an overall smaller force was continuing.
>
> (Potash 1980: 83–4)

There was less reliance on reserve officers and more dependence on career officers in all areas of the armed forces. Some speculate that Perón saw an opportunity to allow the "sons of working-class families and other social sectors" (Potash 1980: 84) to become a significant part of the officer corps. This process of "social integration" was in line with Perón's populist strategy that integrated labor and the *descamisados* into his political agenda (Potash 1980: 83–4). As mentioned previously, the army in particular began "democratizing officer recruitment related to *liceos militares*" – boys coming from low-income families who received an education and were integrated into the military (ibid.: 86). Perón saw this as part of his effort to support the non-commissioned officers he related to early on in his military career:

> Indeed the cultivation of their support was a goal that he had been pursuing for some time. Having served at the Escuela de Suboficiales at earlier stages in his own career, Perón had a wide acquaintance among army sergeants and a keen insight into their professional and personal concerns. He was

aware that efforts to reduce distinctions between them and the commissioned ranks would have a profound impact, and he was prepared to make
changes in areas that did not affect basic hierarchical principles.

(Potash 1980: 117)

There is much debate, however, over the effectiveness of the *liceos militares*
recruitment process, and there is no firm documentation on how many soldiers
were recruited into the *liceos militares*. On paper and in his speeches Perón
spoke about the integration of all classes into the armed forces. In fact, the
Defense Ministry was far more hesitant to implement this social program, being
concerned about the quality and performance of the soldiers from less-educated
backgrounds. While Perón saw the military as an institution for social integration, the Defense Ministry from 1946–9 "made little effort to alter its system of
recruiting future officers" (Potash 1980: 85).

Perón was a master at publicly acknowledging the critical partners who gave
rise to his presidency, in particular the military and the citizenry. The military
and its recruitment method under Minister of War Molina was for the most part
kept professional, separate from politics, and publicly supportive of Perón's outreach to labor and the *descamisados*. The earliest days of Perón's presidency
were based on a concordance or support from the military, Congress, and the
average Argentine.

Problems began to occur, however, when Perón made his real political
agenda too overt and began to alienate the officers and rank and file who did not
benefit from the regime. As discussed previously with respect to the officer
corps, prior to 1949 Minister of War Molina had tried his best to keep the army
separate from civilian politics. When he became embroiled in conflict with
Evita's rise in political stature, Molina's own stature diminished and he lost
significant control over the military. This paved the way for Perón's eventual
politicization of the armed forces. "Every visit to a military installation, every
speech to a military audience, carried political overtones" (Potash 1980: 113).
Perón's rewards of "providing automobiles and cost-of-living benefits" as well
as rapid promotion to those who supported him, alienated those military officials
who did not receive Perón's assistance (ibid.: 110). Perón narrowed the boundaries between the commissioned and non-commissioned officers by making their
uniforms more similar. In the same way, he narrowed "the demarcation between
military and political careers" (ibid.: 115).

His mastery was his initial ability to embrace the diverse elements of Argentine society that would promote his ascendancy; his weakness was his eventual
politicization of the military by rewarding certain officers over others and integrating Perónist patronage into the military recruitment process. It was Perón's
questionable integration of diverse social classes into the military colleges and
the elevation of Evita that alienated many senior and retired officers.

Military style

Military, political, and personal style cannot be ignored during the Perón regime. The political style greatly affected the military style. Argentina was modeled in the British military tradition. It had its formal military academies that taught its soldiers to look and act like professionally Western-trained and well-uniformed soldiers. There was rank, discipline, and an *esprit de corps*.

Perón understood the military culture well, since he had achieved the rank of army colonel. However, he also knew that he had to connect with those who would secure his rise to power, namely the working class, the unions, and the *descamisados*. During the 1945 presidential campaign, Perón made it a ritual to take off his coat during working-class rallies. By doing this he was connecting with those who were not military men or part of the formal oligarchy. One Argentine citizen who lived through the Perón regime remembers that Perón wore his military uniform during official state ceremonies. But when appearing with Evita in a less formal civilian context, Perón wore civilian clothing (Argentine citizen interviewed by the author, Boston, MA, September 2007). Perón realized that Evita, by virtue of her common background, was able to connect with the citizenry and attract large crowds. She would remind the crowds of her impoverished background; yet once in power, she dressed with incredible style and fashion. In this manner, she was able to integrate her poverty-stricken background into her speeches while giving the less fortunate some hope to idealize or idolize a future in the person of Evita.

Style and charisma carried the day in Perón's Argentina. He and Evita were able to temper the more repressive aspects of the regime by demonstrating their love for one another and for the nation. The political and military rituals prior to Perón and Evita were based on "formal meetings," "magniloquent speeches," and strict military hierarchy and uniform designations among the officers and rank and file. Whenever Perón and Evita appeared in public, there was an "intense reaffirmation of love." As one foreign reporter wrote: "In Argentina today, it's love, love, love. Love makes the Peróns go 'round" (Fraser and Navarro 1980: 109–10).

When Perón and Evita appeared at the military base or school, they incorporated their theme of love into the union of the military, the Perónist movement, and the country as a whole. In one speech Perón affirmed: "the people of the nation trust and love their Army, Navy, and Air Forces because they see in them not only the instruments of their security but the effective causes of their happiness and greatness" (Potash 1980: 114). As already mentioned, Perón diminished the formal boundaries between the NCOs and the commissioned officers by making their uniforms more similar. Perón and Evita continued to play out these informal and formal styles and public rituals to connect with the military and the people.

Evita, for example, was known for her foundation work that financially affected only a tiny minority, but the publicity created a cult of adoration for her and the Perón regime. Evita would wear Dior dresses and stylish jewelry and distribute goods and money to select people in an effort to connect the regime to goodness and the hope of prosperity. Perón, by contrast, was the career military officer who would take off his coat to relate to the masses because he knew that "the labor movement in its rank and file was much less disciplined than the military" (Potash 1980: 11). Military style greatly affected the Perónist regime, which initially sought to diminish boundaries between the formalities of the army, the political elite, and the people.

The interpretation of military style in Argentina also reflects the foreshadowing of Perón's authoritarian regime and eventual discordance with the armed forces and the citizenry. Prior to Perón, the last general who served as president, Agustín Justo, downplayed his military ties. When Perón assumed the role of president, rather than take off his coat to identify with the masses as he had done during his presidential campaign, he wore military uniform that symbolized his military career and his control over the armed forces and the entire nation:

> General Perón stressed his military status, perhaps both as a warning to those at home and abroad who might still be disposed to obstruct his government and as a signal to his supporters that in the administration that was about to unfold, their role was to follow, his was to lead.
>
> (Potash 1980: 48)

Perón's 1945 election had been contested not only by Argentine political challengers, but by the United States during the Braden–*Blue Book* fiasco. Perón therefore made it a point to reaffirm his leadership symbolically with the military uniform. The theme of the "wearing the uniform" pervades other nations that have suffered from domestic military intervention, Pakistan being a case in point, with General Musharraf and his reluctance to agree to shed his uniform after he was reelected to the presidency (*The Economist* 2007b: 51).

While Perón choreographed his military and political style with his uniform and military presence, Evita also responded with her own international choreography during her European tour of 1947 – a move that would align with Perón's foreign policy. Even in her promotion on a world stage, Evita carefully reinforced Perón's identification with the *descamisados*:

> "I am going as a representative of the working-people of my dear *descamisados*. I leave my heart behind with them."... Evita, much like a director before a performance, assembled those who were with her and told them that they should be on their best behaviour because they were going to be carefully scrutinized by the world, press at home and the opposition.
>
> (Fraser and Navarro 1980: 90, 92)

Perón's decision to allow Evita her much publicized European tour played into his military and foreign policy goals. General Franco had initially extended the invitation to Perón, but he was in the process of consolidating his relationship with the army, acquiring better foreign-made weapons, and improving diplomatic relations with the USSR and the United States. A visit by him to Franco's Spain, which recalled far too many memories of World War II fascism, would have been a foreign policy disaster. Perón encouraged Evita to do a fuller European tour that included other countries such as France, Italy and Britain. Evita's trip, organized around ritual and regal appearance, was meant to solidify Perón's international standing as well as his domestic mandate. In addition to Perón's own choreographed military style, he shaped Evita's career as first lady into a series of events that would amplify his domestic authority and foreign policy influence.

Although concordance in Argentina did not rest on military style alone, the style indicator reflected the political genre as it relates to the role and function of the military. Perón's initial concordance with the citizenry and the military was symbolized by his intentional shirtsleeve approach that brought him closer to the people. He was far less inclined at this point to emphasize his military background. After assuming power, Perón transitioned to wearing military uniform to emphasize his positive alignment with the armed forces. Although had that been his only motive – to appear supportive of the military – he could have simply acknowledged his past career in the armed forces in public speeches. Maintaining concordance was not his motive. Rather, he wanted to reinforce his intent to rule authoritatively.

Summary

During Perón's rise to power and in the immediate aftermath there was agreement among the political elites, the military, and society. Perón was able to mobilize large segments of the population and the armed forces. Concordance theory offers the indicators to describe both institutionally and culturally the partnership that existed between Perón, the military, and the citizens in the early years of his regime. Concordance theory also reflects how the initial agreement among the four indicators evolved into discordance among the three partners. Although the Argentine military after Molina's tenure became politicized and contributed to Perón's eventual overthrow, separation theory does not sufficiently depict the critical relational, institutional, and cultural elements that contributed to Perón's demise and to Argentine discordance.

In the example of Argentina, we also see how the impact of foreign policy can play a vital role in the concordance equation and in the field of civil–military relations in general. The aggressive US stance Spruille Braden took toward Argentina during the *Blue Book* fiasco polarized the Argentine electorate and cemented Perón's early relationship with the military and the citizenry. Later, however, Perón had difficulty fixing a much-needed US relationship for the sake of his export economy and to renovate the Argentine military. The Marshall Plan, US preferential treatment toward nations that supported the Allies during World War II, and the unusual Argentine drought conditions severely impacted Argentina's agricultural economy and Perón's overall efforts to implement his five-year plan.

The economic threat conditions exacerbated by a mixed foreign policy relationship with the United States eventually had a detrimental affect on the Argentine political decision-making process and Perón's relationship with the officer corps – two key concordance indicators. Moreover, Perón's military style, in his decision to appear in military uniform once in office, gained the attention of the post-World War II US leadership which was trying to dissolve any symbols that harkened back to fascism and dictatorship (Potash 1980: 48). Perón's new military style also symbolically eroded his initial shirtsleeve connection to the *descamisados* and the broader Argentine citizenry. Concordance eventually dissolved as Perón gained autonomous decision-making power and the subsequent disaffection of both the citizens and officer corps.

7   Israel

Concordance in the "uncivil" state

I conducted the research and fieldwork for this chapter in Israel immediately prior to, during, and after the first Gulf War (1988–91). This chapter uses my fieldwork experience to explore concordance theory as it applies to Israel during the 1980s and early 1990s. In the summary of this chapter, I update the status of Israeli civil–military relations as presented here based on my conference presentation in Jerusalem entitled: "Civil–military relations in Israel: revisiting Israel as the 'uncivil' state" (Schiff 2006).

Scholarship on Israeli civil–military relations is strongly influenced by the US civil–military relations theory emphasizing the separation of civil and military institutions. Israel, according to one view, has not experienced domestic military intervention nor has it become a militaristic state. The predominance of civilian over military values in Israeli society and in the military – or the "civilianization of the military" – is the foundation of this viewpoint (Horowitz 1977). As Horowitz and others, such as Moshe Lissak and Yoram Peri, see it, valuing civilian needs over militaristic endeavors establishes the Israeli state as non-militaristic despite the high external threat level and looming presence of the military in almost every aspect of Israeli life (Peri 1983; Horowitz and Lissak 1989b).

However, these Israeli scholars note that there exists one crucial difference between the Israel Defense Forces (IDF) and most militaries in Western and developing nations: Israel's army is highly visible and active in both civilian life and the government. In *Trouble in Utopia*, Dan Horowitz and Moshe Lissak (1989b) described the societal prevalence of the Israeli army – a sharp contrast to other militaries in developing nations where lack of officer involvement in civilian government left government officials feeling threatened by their military counterparts. The IDF's presence and decision-making power within the government and its visible role in society have resulted in "permeable boundaries" between the military and society.

This permeability, however, is not coercive military intervention – a characteristic most commonly associated with militaristic regimes. The IDF has not threatened, blackmailed, or attempted anything as drastic as a coup against the government. In fact, it is a mutual and integrated relationship whose reality is not influenced by separate institutions but institutions characterized by overlapping boundaries. The government and the society provide the military with its required resources; in turn, the military takes an active role in security decision making without being perceived as intrusive (Horowitz and Lissak 1989b; Azarya and Kimmerling 1985–6). Despite this unique quality of the IDF, civil–military scholars use the US civil–military dichotomy in order to explain Israeli domestic military non-intervention. The question, and the crux of concordance theory, is whether or not the civil–military dichotomy is truly applicable to the Israeli case.

Despite touting "permeable boundaries," Horowitz has not completely abandoned dichotomous and Westernized approaches to the Israeli case. In response to an essay asserting that Israel was a Lasswellian garrison police state (al-Qazzaz 1973), Horowitz asked a simple question: Is Israel a garrison state (Horowitz 1977)? He eventually rejected the "garrison state" label primarily because of Israel's "civilianized military in a partially militarized society" (1982: 77). He also asserted the profound penetration of the military throughout Israeli society including the political, industrial, and economic spheres. Additionally, he sharpened the Lasswellian predicament that despite Israel's partial militarization, civilian standards still predominated in the IDF and the civilian democratic government maintained its control over the military (ibid.: 77–105). In spite of this seeming rejection of older approaches to Israel's civil–military status, Horowitz and Lissak (1989b) still asserted their main argument based on the assumption of the dichotomous separation theory – Israeli civilian values and the civilian government were crucial in preventing domestic military intervention:

> It can be argued that the partial involvement of the military in areas of national security officially under civilian control has, paradoxically, made it possible for Israel to preserve its democratic regime and its civilian way of life. The tendency of the civilian and military spheres to develop a resemblance to one another – through the partial militarization of civilian activities and the limited "civilianization" of the military – has prevented the military from becoming a separate caste which feels itself alienated from, and in conflict with, the values represented by the civilian elites. As a result, Israel's susceptibility to a military coup and to the ascendancy of the specialists in violence over the civilian sector has been low.
>
> (Horowitz and Lissak 1989b: 229)

Other major civil–military scholars such as Yoram Peri, Baruch Kimmerling, and Amos Perlmutter accepted the dichotomization portion of the Horowitz–Lissak argument. Peri, for example, summarized Horowitz's thesis by stating the following:

> there is no penetration of military values into other civil sub-systems. In fact the reverse is true because civil values penetrate into the armed forces. It is this dividing line between the two spheres, Horowitz sums up, that "enables Israel to function as a democratic society."
>
> (Peri 1983: 8)

The trend in Israel civil–military scholarship has been to accept the Western categories and the civil–military dichotomy in order to explain domestic military non-intervention. Although Horowitz and Lissak assert the permeability of boundaries, they also emphasize the distinction between civil and military spheres, which assumes the preponderance of the civilian institutions and values (1989b). Horowitz and Lissak question the idea of separation and dichotomy when they write about "permeable boundaries," the latter of which suggests a leaking of values in both the civilian and military directions. The "garrison state" argument rests on the image of dichotomization of civil and military, yielding a "good model" – the civil in control – and a "bad model" – the military dominating the civil. The image of permeable boundaries tends to override the image of dichotomy and actually alludes to the idea of concordance or agreement between the military, the political leadership, and the citizenry. However, Horowitz and Lissak backslide theoretically when they write about civilian values and government. They understand that Israel's unique citizen's army calls into question the traditional civil–military dichotomy, but they also insist on toeing the conventional theoretical line that weakens the "permeability" argument.

Thus the question still remains: is the civil–military dichotomy truly applicable to the Israeli case? It is suggested here that the current theory is inappropriate and that an alternative theoretical explanation is in order.

Concordance in Israel and the "uncivil" state

In 1992, I published an article in *Security Studies* entitled "Civil–military relations reconsidered: Israel as an 'Uncivil' State" (Schiff 1992). It was a response to the current theoretical literature in the field and specifically challenged Lasswell's garrison state hypothesis, Huntington's civil–military dichotomy, and the Israeli scholars who applied the dichotomy to the Israeli case. In this piece I argue the military's institutional and cultural influence over Israeli society is so great that the entire concept of "civil" is inappropriately applied to this nation. The case of Israel, in a regional environment of high external threat and having never suffered forms of domestic military intervention such as a *coup d'état*, undermines the premise of Lasswell's garrison state hypothesis and Huntington's separation theory or the need for civilian institutions to predominate over the military. Israel's "uncivil" status or lack of civilian influence over it institutionally and culturally points to partnership or concordance with the military and a condition of domestic non-intervention.

To depict Israel as an "uncivil" state requires an analysis of Israel's military and political institutions as well as its culture. A concordance or cooperative relationship between the military, the political establishment, and the citizens fosters Israel's uncivil status because there is long-standing agreement over the role and function of the military without reliance on civilian institutional control. The Israeli case study undermines Huntington's premise that strong civil institutions and civilian values, along with a sharp boundary between the professional soldiery and the civilians, are required to prevent domestic military intervention. Israel provides the opportunity for an alternative theory that focuses on concordance between the military, government, and society spheres instead of separate and exclusionary boundaries. In this chapter the four concordance indicators are applied to Israel as it existed during the late 1980s and early 1990s.

The social composition of the officer corps

A discussion of the Israel Defense Forces (IDF) officer corps requires the context of Israel's general security condition. The State of Israel was created in the aftermath of the Holocaust. That event convinced Jews and much of the world of the need for a Jewish political refuge. After gaining independence, Israel faced a serious national security issue, and it grew regionally as all the states surrounding Israel declared war on her. Since 1948, Israel has been involved in more wars than any other state. Its security situation extends beyond ground and air warfare to terrorist raids, border conflicts, and missile attacks.

The Israeli security condition integrates the memory of the Holocaust with the immediacy of war. The former, according to Amos Elon, "leaves an indelible mark on the national psychology, the tenor and content of public life ... [and] in the private rituals of people" (1972: 205). The latter gains its immediacy from the daily encounter with external threat. Both the memory of the Holocaust and the climate of war and conflict create a security condition that greatly shapes the relationship of the IDF with Israeli society.

In 1990, the population of Israel was over five million, and it is currently over seven million – the population increase coming largely from Russian Jewish immigration. While the Israeli government is reluctant to disclose the size of its military, according to GlobalSecurity.org (2007) its general numbers have not hugely fluctuated since the 1990s, although there are fewer reserve troops. There are now approximately 600,000 troops with about 370,000 in the reserves. In 1990, there were about 430,000 in the reserves, 170,000 regular forces, and 13,500 paramilitary forces. The trend since the 1990s is reduction of troop size and concentration on new technology such as better equipped battle tanks (ibid.).

There are three forms of military service in Israel: compulsory service (*sherut hova*), reserve service (*sherut miluimn*), and permanent service (*sherut keva*). All Israeli men and women (with notable deferments and exceptions) are inducted into compulsory service and the men into reserve service. In 1990, there were approximately 50,000 commissioned officers.

In Israel there exists an important group of officers who are responsible for military training, development, and war preparation. These officers have ranks that approximate their Western counterparts. However, at least two professional attributes advocated by both Huntington and Janowitz – insularity and conservative social values – are historically absent in the Israeli military. One major reason for this, as will be discussed at further length in the section on military style, is the pervasive informality of Israeli culture resulting from the original *kibbutz* lifestyle. While Huntington (1957) and Janowitz (1964) present a professional and exclusive officer corps with distinct standards and norms as found in post-World War II United States, the Israeli officer corps is not that different in manner and tradition from the rank and file that is composed of the average Israeli citizen.

Throughout this book, Britain has provided a consistent, contrasting, and influential military model because of its empire-building history with regard to the post-revolutionary US military, along with India, Pakistan, and now the Israeli military. For example, Stephen Cohen noted the significant molding of the Indian officer corps by the British military, which "systematized" the elite caste system within the Indian corps (Cohen 1971: 50–1). By contrast, the British Mandate period in Palestine (1917–48) was far shorter in time and political influence than in South Asia. Jewish soldiers had fought with and learned from the British army during World War II. Like George Washington, Israel's founder David Ben-Gurion attempted to model the newly established Israeli army on the British forces. And like the early US citizenry, the Israeli citizen's army would resist such influence; the militia-like nature of the corps was not conducive to the Western-influenced British structure and formality.

The British military was, until the late 1950s, officered by an upper-class elite comprising both members of the aristocracy and the "supporting class" of landowners and independent professionals (Otley 1968: 100). The British military, and especially its navy, eventually adopted the Prussian-influenced officer school by establishing the Royal Military College and the Royal Naval College in the early nineteenth century. These institutions were not solely schools for officers and aristocracy; they also recruited young British students from a variety of backgrounds who had completed secondary school education (Huntington 1957: 44).

In Israel, by contrast, all soldiers were inducted into the IDF in the same way and advance within the ranks according to their abilities. Since there was no separate officer recruitment, there were also no military academies established that gave preferential treatment to some soldiers over others. In his landmark book, *A Portrait of the Israeli Soldier*, former IDF Chief Psychologist Reuven Gal, distinguished the values of the Israeli officer from those of his British counterpart:

> Being a "gentleman," an academician or an aristocrat has never been a prerequisite. In fact most Israeli officers place little value on such behavioral, educational or social attributes ... being a gentleman or an aristocrat is, indeed, alien to the Israeli culture and unnecessary for its military.
>
> (Gal 1986: 128)

Most Israeli citizens, regardless of their social standing or socioeconomic background have gone through compulsory military service; all male citizens report to the reserves. The permanent officer corps (*sherut keva*) is a small group of officers who have proven themselves, usually in combat, and have chosen to remain in the military.

After four years of service, 90 percent of the officers decide not to become permanent soldiers but continue as officers in the reserves. The remaining 10 percent go on to staff school that includes officers from all branches of the military. After completion of staff school, officers, who usually hold the rank of colonel or above, are assigned to a unit, base, or region. Often they are assigned to the original specialty or brigade from which they started as conscripted soldiers (Gal 1986: 170).

Although a supposed objective selection of Israeli officers existed through the 1990s, the unbiased selection processes was called into question since the ethnic composition of the corps had been predominantly Eastern European. Traditionally, there appeared an absence of Asian and African-born officers in the IDF. Despite the fact that Asian and African Jews have constituted a significant minority (13.6 percent of the total population in 1949; 28.7 percent in 1964; 47.4 percent in 1972; and 42.1 percent in 1988), their representation in the permanent officer corps remained low. A 1983 survey showed that only about 13 percent of the officers from the rank of major and above were of Asian or African origin. It appeared that Eastern European officers dominated the corps throughout the early 1990s as well (Central Bureau of Statistics 1989: 83).

In some countries, such as Pakistan, where social and ethnic disparities exist, factions may occur in the military and thereby contribute to officer conflict, cliques, and domestic military intervention. Despite the disproportionate number of Eastern European as opposed to Asian or African Israelis in the permanent officer corps through the 1990s, Israel did not experience officer cliques that threatened the political fabric of society. The major reason for this was and still remains the high and early turnover rate of officers.

By their late forties or early fifties, most permanent officers seek second careers. Many go into politics or work for government or private organizations. Although the officers still remain in the reserves and can be called back to duty at any time, the permanent officer corps is frequently replenished so that new blood is allowed to maintain and further the direction of the IDF. Early officer retirement, along with the intimate and informal culture of Israeli society that permeates the corps, are important reasons why Israel has never experienced domestic military intervention by a small clique of officers (Smooha 1983–4: 17). These factors, along with the preponderance of labor-Zionist values from the state's founding through the 1990s, have also resulted in liberal values among the corps that contrasts with Huntington's assumption about an insular and conservative officer corps.

For the most part, there has always been a concordance or agreement based on shared values and objectives between the military establishment, the citizenry, and the political elites on the social composition of the officer corps. Yet there are at least two notable periods in Israeli history when the composition and military strategy used by the officer corps were questioned and publicly criticized: the Yom Kippur War (1973) and the Lebanon War (1982). Below is a brief summary of how the Lebanon War impacted the prestige of the officer corps.

The 1982 Israeli invasion of Southern Lebanon and subsequent occupation (1982–5) created one of the most polarizing experiences for the upper echelons of the IDF military establishment. National consensus had always been a key attribute of IDF military missions. The invasion of Lebanon was one of the few military operations that did not have full consensus, neither at the political nor social nor military levels. While dramatic changes did not occur within the structure of the officer corps, senior officers felt besieged in ways never before experienced. They were exposed to extreme public criticism in a nation where consensus over war aims was almost axiomatic. High-level officers resigned or were removed from their posts after the Sabra and Shatila massacre – a horrifying attack in September 1982 against Palestinian refugee camps carried out by Lebanese forces with the knowledge of the Israeli high command and political elites. In another incident, Colonel Eli Geva asked to be relieved from his command as his brigade was about to enter Beirut. During that time, the prestige of the permanent officer corps declined as many young officers decided not to remain due to "problems of conscience" and "burn out" experienced in Lebanon (Horowitz 1983: 96).

But issues of morality and burn out did not persist, and currently, the Israeli officer corps is comprised of an elite group of permanent officers responsible for IDF organization, administration, and training. Despite their pivotal role in the Israeli military, these officers do not possess the attributes of the "professional soldier" as espoused by Huntington and Janowitz. The Israeli officer corps is motivated less by rigid Western professional standards, such as spit and shine, polish and smart salutes, and more by an intimate and informal Israeli culture. The officer corps is not a separate and exclusive institution but a group of elite soldiers who sustain the citizen's army largely by maintaining the respect and trust of the citizen soldiers. When that respect and trust is breached, most notably during the Lebanon War, the officer corps suffers measurably. Despite this and other difficult periods, overall concordance on the makeup and structure of the Israeli permanent officer corps has been maintained. The officer corps may not be considered as distinguished and pristine as it was after the Six-Day War, but its overall integration into and support by the citizenry and the political establishment remains strong.

The political decision-making process

Unlike the Israeli officer corps that consciously merges the values and traditions of Israeli society into the military, the Israeli political establishment has always claimed to be a government represented by civilians, separate from the military. For example, government officials who have previously served in the army do not consider themselves to be military officials and do not don military uniforms in the Knesset (the Israeli parliament). Even with profuse military influence in Israeli society, nothing resembling an elite military dictatorship exists in Israel. However, this section argues that despite Israeli claims of a civilian government, the ambiguous nature of governmental responsibilities for defense, the interchangeability of official military and political functions such as prime minister, defense minister, and chief of staff, and the parachuting of military officers into politics result in the difficulty of isolating a distinct set of civilian political institutions.

More specifically, this section discusses the connection between political decision making and military security. It also discusses the ambiguity existing in military and political authority, most notably among the prime minister, defense minister, and chief of staff. Finally, this section reviews the functions of political and military elites who decide on military composition, budget, and materiel along with the decision-making process as it pertains to military budget and materiel, most notably the Israeli military–industrial complex.

Relationship between the political and military elites

Formally, defense issues in Israel are divided among the following institutions: the prime minister, the defense minister, the chief of staff, the cabinet, and the Knesset. Since Israel does not have a formal constitution, the functions of the ministers and institutions have varied throughout Israel's history. For example, the positions of prime minister and defense minister were held by one person for over 17 years. However, it is possible to delineate basic institutional functions and responsibilities pertaining to Israel's defense.

The prime minister of Israel is the elected head of state and assumes direct responsibility over the conduct of war and defense operations. Military operations cannot be carried out without the prime minister's consent. The prime minister is also in charge of the intelligence services as well as the science and research city of Dimona. The prime minister's cabinet assumes authority over the IDF and empowers the prime minister to maintain personal responsibility for war and defense.

While the prime minister possesses some sovereignty over military policy, the defense minister oversees military doctrine, training procedures, military appointments, and defense policy making. The defense minister also has authority over the defense industries and their purchases as well as the military intelligence services (Aman). In addition, the defense minister recommends the chief of staff to the cabinet and approves the appointments of generals.

Serving directly under the defense minister is the chief of staff who commands the operational plans and activities of the armed forces: land, air, and sea. In this capacity, they serve as administrative chief of the entire army and the general staff. They also command the army during wartime, supervise its training, and oversee deployment, strategy, and operations. In addition, the chief of staff recommends the appointment of generals to the defense minister and reports directly to the cabinet.

In some ways the chief of staff has the most influence over security matters. First, chiefs of staff are typically soldiers with backgrounds in military strategy and battlefield experience. As battle-tested soldiers, they are trusted by the government and the Israeli population to offer their best assessments and decisions for the security of the state. Moreover, they have a highly sophisticated system of military analysis and decision-making procedures. The IDF's staff and intelligence capabilities are far superior to any other institution concerned with security, including the Ministry of Defense (Ben-Meir 1986: 71). Nevertheless, the chief of staff usually works closely with the defense minister and is often called upon to report directly to the cabinet, since it is the cabinet that sanctions the prime minister and defense minister, and overall defense policy.

During the first 16 years of Israel's existence as a sovereign state, there was no clear legal definition of the cabinet's authority over the military. Israel, unlike other democracies, did not form under a constitution that delineated specific government and executive powers. During the establishment of the state, the religious parties opposed a constitution "claiming that the Torah was the only possible constitution" (Eisenstadt 1985: 164). In 1964, the Basic Laws of Israel were established to help define basic institutional state entities including the military, the prime minister, the parliament, and the judiciary. For example, the revised Basic Law of 1968 stated that security affairs should be entrusted to the cabinet, and the revised Basic Law of 1976 placed the IDF under the authority of the cabinet.

Thus, formally, the cabinet is the institutional mechanism that controls the army. Its major function is to approve the military budget and overall allocation of resources each year. In reality, however, the cabinet usually approves the budget recommendations offered by the prime minister and the defense minister without objections. Moreover, while the chief of staff is periodically called to report to the cabinet, the latter never exercises any real control over the daily responsibilities of the chief. For the most part, much of the cabinet's authority is formal in nature. While it is apprised of most major security concerns, its power of accountability is restricted.

Ambiguity and interchangeability of political and military authority

The institutional mechanisms for defining military and civilian roles in security matters were never implemented by the Knesset or by the cabinet. In the early years, Ben-Gurion (who served as both prime minister and defense minister) would "praise the efficacy of the state channel" when in fact the army was "mainly subordinate to him" (Peri 1983: 49). Peri claimed that the army was politicized by Ben-Gurion's Mapai party which effectively made the military "a partner in the political process." In short, what emerged in Israel was "not a civil-control pattern but a political military partnership" (ibid.: 51).

While the political tenor of the nation has dramatically changed since Ben-Gurion's day, there remains ambiguity among the powers of the prime minister, defense minister, and chief of staff. Often, rules are made to define the scope of military authority and then changed depending on the particular government cabinet. All this precludes the possibility for a distinct and well-regulated civilian authority to enable control of the military.

The lack of clarity of executive authority with respect to political decision making over security matters "has been subject to considerable fluctuations" (Horowitz and Lissak 1989a: 21). While this has not prompted domestic military intervention, it has led to negative political consequences. One of the most devastating outcomes of the ambiguous decision-making process was the Lebanon War. As discussed previously, this war left the political elites feeling alienated by military officials' unilateral decisions – decisions that both the political and military elites could legitimately make. At that time, General Ariel Sharon held the office of defense minister and General Rafael Eitan was chief of staff. Unclear boundaries of political and military decision making were manipulated and reminded the Israeli government and the citizens of the problems that can accrue as a result of the current system.

Despite the lack of parliamentary authority over the military and security matters in general, significant public criticism of the prime minister and defense minister, and the Lebanon War, there was no widespread distrust of the defense establishment by the parliament or by the Israeli citizenry during the 1980s and 1990s. Instatement of former military officers into the Knesset (parliament) prevented the onset of distrust and alienation between the defense establishment and parliament. There also existed an accepted interchangeability among high political and military positions. Former military men often filled posts that other countries reserve for "civilian" elites. But such an interchangeability of roles in a nation of citizen soldiers was not perceived as a conflict between military and civilian interests.

The career of Yitzhak Rabin is an excellent example of the interchangeability of military and political roles. Rabin was a war hero who fought in Israel's War of Independence and the Six-Day War. Rabin held numerous high military positions throughout his career including head of the Northern command, head of operations branch and general headquarters, deputy chief of staff, and chief of staff. Rabin's political career began as ambassador to the United States, and he later held the posts of minister of defense and prime minister after Golda Meir's resignation in 1974. During the Likud–Labor unity government of the late 1980s, Rabin served as the minister of defense. He was again elected prime minister during Israel's 1992 elections and also assumed the post of minister of defense. At no time during Rabin's career did a conflict-of-interest issue arise over his military past and his capacity to serve in the political arena. Rabin's career exemplifies the ease by which the military and civilian realms are traversed.

Military budget, materiel, and the military–industrial complex

Other important aspects of the decision-making process, as they existed during the 1980s and 1990s, are issues of military budget and materials. Economically, the military's huge consumption of the nation's GNP and the significant involvement of Israel's work in military industry foreshadowed high levels of industrial–military integration. The export of arms not only contributed to the Israeli economy but also enhanced the longstanding Israeli security strategy, i.e.

maintaining an indigenous weapons capacity during wartime and in the wake of international embargoes.

The military–industrial complex was laden with former military officers who offered advice and expertise and therefore contributed to the military–industrial relationship. Many of the scientists and technicians involved in weapons production have personally tested the weapons in battle:

> The fact that civilian scientists, engineers, technicians, and mechanics who produce Israeli's weapons are also soldiers who use them has proven to be a formidable advantage to Israel.
>
> (Harkabi and Neuman 1984: 195)

This integrative relationship between industry and the military fosters a basic concordance or agreement between the two spheres that centers on similar economic, strategic, and military goals.

The parachuting of officers into Israeli industries is critical to the discussion of the military–industrial complex because it reflects an interactive concordance between the industrial, political, and military elites. While in many countries such intense interaction was viewed with suspicion during the 1980s and 1990s, "public opinion in Israel generally views the activities of the complex with favor and support" (Mintz 1984: 109). A concordance within the military–industrial complex implies a deep interaction and agreement among the military, political elites, and industrial elites, as well as the active participation and consent of the Israeli citizenry.

The military's impact on the economy was also significant during this period. In the early 1950s, defense spending consumed only about 6 to 9 percent of the GNP and rose to 48 percent in 1975. By 1984, Israel had one of the largest per capita defense expenditures in the world. That year, Israel's fiscal-year defense expenditure was close to $8.5 billion, a figure that consumed 21.4 percent of the gross domestic product. By contrast, the United States spent $290 billion (a mere 6.4 percent of the US GNP) on its military outlays during 1984; in the Middle East, Israel's total defense expenditures were surpassed only by Saudi Arabia, Iraq, and Iran. Despite a reduction in Israel's defense outlays to $4 million by 1990, the military still consumed about half of the government's budget and a fourth of the nation's workforce during this time period (SIPRI 1991: 169, 170, 174, 175).

Israel was also a producer and exporter of military armaments. According to Israel Defense Forces statistics, during the late 1980s, of the total military production in Israel "about one-third supplies domestic needs and the remainder is exported" (Nathanson 1989: 4). Israel was considered a third-tier exporter of arms along with Spain, Brazil, and the Netherlands. In 1988, Israel supplied over $1 billion in arms to countries around the world, the vast majority going to developing nations. Israeli defense exports constituted approximately 25 percent of all Israeli exports and 75 percent of all its metals and electronic exports. During this time, Israel's "ratio of defense exports to total exports is the highest in the world" (Mintz 1984: 112).

Overall, Israel's political–military partnership points to a relationship of concordance between the military and the political establishment. Although the prime minister, the defense minister, and the chief of staff have particular functions related to defense, those functions have not always been clearly defined either in an official document or by a particular government body. The cabinet and the Knesset have some responsibility over Israeli defense, but we saw how those responsibilities are quite restricted and ambiguously defined. The ambiguity of responsibility, while it has caused significant political and military problems (such as in the aftermath of the first Lebanon War), still points to an overarching sense of concordance or agreement between the military, the political establishment, and the citizens.

Institutionally, to make the claim that Israel has a distinctly civil governmental sector is problematic. The impact of defense issues on the economy, the military–industrial complex, and in political decision making effectively integrates civilian and military activity with respect to control and productivity of the industrial establishments. Military integration into the various national sectors suggests the extent to which the military and society are in agreement and have achieved a concordance. While concordance may take on a different character and shape in other nations, in Israel concordance means a deep integration and mutual understanding between military and society. Thus, on the military, political, and industrial levels, the overlapping and often informal quality of functions and responsibilities is accepted and almost expected.

Recruitment method

The Israeli conscription method is persuasive and conditioned by the Israeli security situation and its citizen's army. Belonging to a community of citizens, in Western terms, often means being a "civilian," which can be defined as one who does not professionally belong to the military. Although most Israelis do not consider the military a permanent profession, the military is highly intrusive in the everyday lives of Israeli citizens. Security issues during the 1980s and 1990s penetrated the average Israeli's life to such an extent that the term "civilian" has problematic connotations in this nation of citizen soldiers.

In 2007 I participated in a conference on civil–military relations. On one of the panels that was honoring Israeli sociologist Moshe Lissak, I discussed my "uncivil" argument and how it had evolved during my time in Israel. From one Israeli scholar's viewpoint, the situation in Israel is now very different because only 70 percent of the population was being recruited instead of the 95 percent recruitment rate that occurred in the 1980s and 1990s. The US panelists, however, still found this statistic extremely high compared to the less than 1 percent of US citizens who currently serve in the US military.

Although persuasive, Israeli conscription is involuntary. Most Israeli citizens (with some notable exceptions) must serve. However, it is compulsion that on the whole meets with willing compliance. In a study conducted by the Israeli Institute for Military Studies in the spring of 1988, out of a total of 5,400 Israeli high school students, an average of 75 percent (both boys and girls) showed a strong desire to serve in the Israel Defense Forces (Mizlas *et al.* 1989: 53, 91). This strong desire to serve in the military is attributed to the Israeli security problem. Most Israelis perceive a threat to Israel's fundamental existence. This continuous burden has fostered a collective consciousness that values military service as a fundamental expression of citizenship (Gal 1986: 30).

Most Israeli men and women spend a significant part of their lives in the IDF. Israeli citizenship, or being part of the Israeli community of citizens, is dependent upon an activity traditionally considered non-civil – military participation. Full social and cultural acceptance by the collectivity hinges on military duty. For example, Israeli Jews (notably the ultra-orthodox population) and Israeli Arabs exempted from military duty are not considered complete Israeli citizens by the vast majority, although they may have formal rights of citizenship.

Most Israelis do not become professional soldiers, but participate in vital military duties on a part-time basis. Formally, most men engage in reserve duty until the age of 55; women can be called to duty until the age of 34 if they have no children. Israel cannot fully mobilize without its part-time soldiers who are often trained in very specialized military tasks that are scrupulously maintained during the off-duty period.

On a broader social level, most Israelis, including women, are groomed for war. This cultural fact contributes to the consent-based nature of conscription because military service is considered a natural part of Israeli life. For example, the hourly news broadcast is a daily ritual for Israelis since acts of terrorism could break out at any time and important military instructions are transmitted over the radio. Every parent is prepared to give their child over to the military and knows that a son or daughter could be killed, even during so-called peaceful times. Most young people prepare for the military by participating in youth movements and other activities, such as the IDF's youth corps Gadna, designed to prepare one to enter the military with a deep desire to defend the nation. Moreover, there is an entire military slang in the Hebrew language which young soldiers use among themselves, even after their tours of duty. The Israeli security condition fosters a deep concern for national defense that makes conscription involuntary yet persuasive.

Before young soldiers are inducted by the IDF, they have already experienced significant exposure to the values of the state that include the Jewish character of Israel and the importance of the military. The Israeli educational system is a major contributor of national values before military induction. Every child in Israel is given the option of attending a religious or state school, as both are funded by the Israeli government. Since most Israelis consider themselves (at least during the 1980s and 1990s) to be non-observant Jews, the majority study the state curriculum at non-religious schools. However, even in these schools children learn about the "historicity of the Jewish people and the renewal and coherence of the Jewish state" beginning as early as kindergarten (Shagmar-Handelman and Handelman 1989: 72). This includes traditions and celebrations of Jewish holidays such as Hanukkah and Passover as a way of exposing the child to both the "triumph of faith" and the "martial spirit" and the military significance of these holidays (ibid.: 82). The rest of the child's education is supplemented with Bible studies, the history of the Jewish people, and the political history of Zionism in addition to a conventional curriculum of science, math, and world history.

This picture of the intrusive nature of the IDF and military values on the political, social, and cultural levels of Israeli society reflects the difficulty in characterizing a distinctly civil or civilian realm separate from the military. There exists an interdependence between the IDF and Israel's political institutions and citizenry; and it is the relationship of concordance, rather than separation, that has resulted in Israel's uncivil status.

Military style

Military style refers mainly to the importance of clothing, military uniform, or military rituals and how they manifest authority among the ranks and in society. Bernard Cohn notes that "clothes literally *are* authority" (1989: 304, 308). The relationships between soldiers and citizens and the boundaries that they mark or elide are also conveyed through the military uniform.

In Western European history, for example, the Prussian uniform conveyed a distinct separation between citizen and soldier. The "shambled" looking peasant was contrasted with the "orderly" and "scrupulously clean" soldier who wore the "Emperor's uniform" (Dawson 1894: 29–30). In this regard, there existed a clear division between peasant and soldier. The aristocrat-dominated Prussian army wished to emphasize civilian–military division as it distinguished itself from the rest of society.

In Chapter 5, I described how the armies of India and Pakistan have allowed their soldiers to integrate indigenous cultural aspects into the uniform. This integration maintained a different type of authority relationship that was grounded in the British European military style while embracing elements of Indian culture that augmented a martial spirit. For example, Bernard Cohn describes late nineteenth-century British India where British rulers encouraged and formalized the turban worn only in the Sikh ranks. The British admired the Sikhs for their martial skills and encouraged their allegiance to the British–Indian military by having them wear the turban. The apparent eliding of boundaries between citizen Sikh and soldier Sikh, symbolized by the turban, represented a type of homage paid to indigenous colonial culture. Cohn emphasizes, however, that the British preference for the Sikh turban had less to do with respect for cultural distinctiveness and more with the authority and obedience the British wanted to maintain over their troops (Cohn 1989: 304, 308).

In Israel, the informal and intimate nature of Israeli society has penetrated the military ranks. In reality, however, the Israeli military and social ethos emerged contemporaneously rather than one giving rise to the other. The informal character of Israeli society was spearheaded by the kibbutz movement that not only emphasized the value of communal labor, but was critical in shaping early defense strategy. The concept of "citizen soldier" originated in the kibbutz that required all of its members to work the land and defend the settlements. The pre-state *Hashomer* (the watchman) group, according to Ze'ev Schiff, "stressed the bond that united settlement on the land and military training – a motif that was to continue through the formation of the Haganah in the 1930s, the Palmach in the 1940s, and the Nahal units of the Israel Defense Forces" (1985: 3).

The IDF, while considered a professional corps with uniforms and ranks, does not embody the symbols, signs, and bearing that are associated with the external imagery and possibly the inner mental states of professionalism in Western militaries, including the post-World War II US military. Reuven Gal (1986: 103) explains:

> Discipline is focused more on operational and performance accuracy than on ceremonial details. This requirement is more for a clean rifle than for spit-shined boots. Trainees are constantly disciplined to perform their duties within very tight time constraints; while a sharp uniform is not always essential, a sharp and timely performance is always demanded.

Therefore starched uniforms, smart salutes, ceremonial marches, strict obser-vance of rank, and meticulous quarters characteristic of Janowitz's "professional soldier," are not valued as much by the IDF as they are by other militaries.

A most conspicuous symbol of Israeli informality is the IDF uniform. The uniform's often sloppy and unkempt appearance reflects the easy interchange-ability from citizen to soldier, whereas in other countries, such as nineteenth-century Prussia, the uniform is the critical divider between civilian and soldier. In Israel, the uniform's appearance breaks down these traditional boundaries. It is a reflection of the general informality prevalent in Israeli society. This situ-ation is starkly contrasted to Pakistan where the citizenry called for President Pervez Musharraf to take off his general's uniform and thereby shed his distinct and formal ties to the military. In Israel, leaving informal street clothes and putting on an informal uniform is symbolic of the lack of distinction between civilian and soldier; it also parallels the lack of distinction between public and private demeanor.

An example of the easy interchangeability between citizen and soldier and public and private occurred one evening at an Israeli friend's home. My friend and I were reviewing some materials I had collected for my dissertation. She was helping me sort out the Hebrew data. It was very quiet, when all of a sudden my friend's husband, who was coming home from reserve duty, walked through the doorway dressed in his military uniform and carrying an M-16 rifle. I had already been in Israel over year, so the experience of soldiers walking into public and private places in full battle gear did not affect me anymore. Such scenes were so natural to me now that I could easily identify the difference between Uzi, M-16, and Galil rifles. This nonchalant reaction to an armed soldier entering a private home parallels the breakdown of public and private boundaries and casual demeanor in Israeli society. It is also indicative of the unceremonial style of the military and the public expectation of the informal manner and appearance.

The Israeli military not only supports the argument for concordance and the uncivil nature of Israeli society, it also calls us to consider the particular nature of military professionalism. Huntington and Janowitz argued for a separate, conservative, and formal professional army. Although the IDF is a citizen's army, it is considered to be a professional military with an officer corps, organized bureaucracy, and rank and file. However, Israeli military professionalism appears and interacts differently than the US and Western European models posed by Huntington. Informality reigns in Israel, in military and non-military life; and the informal Israeli style conditions military professionalism.

Summary

In this chapter, I used data from my experiences in Israel during the 1980s and 1990s to evaluate the applicability of separation theory, as well as present a new lens through which to evaluate Israel's civil–military relationship. As the Israeli political, social, and military landscape continues to evolve, a brief update is warranted. In particular, the prominence of what two Israeli scholars recently called the "Security Network" (Barak and scheffer 2006: 235) sheds additional light on the "uncivil" nature of Israel. The security network entails many of the qualities of officer and military influence on Israeli politics and culture mentioned above. Specifically it involves "prominent members of the state's large and varied defense establishment" from both the senior army officer ranks and the reserves. These members are integrated into "various political, socioeconomic, and cultural spheres" and they possess an informal relationship quality that "is not determined by formal agreements, and it is not hierarchical." In fact, the boundaries of the Network "continuously change ... they are blurred, significant overlapping is created ... movement between the DE [Defense Establishment] and each of these civilian spheres remains frequent, if not 'natural'" (ibid.: 235, 237–9).

Despite Israeli claims of a civilian government, the ambiguous nature of governmental responsibilities on defense, the interchangeability of official military and political functions such as prime minister, defense minister, and chief of staff, and the parachuting of military officers into politics results in the problematic of truly isolating a distinct set of separate civilian political institutions.

The discussion of the informal yet relevant Security Network fits nicely into the previous discussion of the Israeli officer corps and aspects of recruitment and the political decision-making process. Its informal quality also highlights the importance of military style. In this chapter, I have emphasized the symbolic importance of the Israeli uniform because its sloppy and unkempt appearance reinforces the informality of Israeli society. The informality is premised on the fluidity of boundaries, the lack of barriers between citizen and soldier. So too the Security Network, which influences Israeli policy, has that informal quality of boundary elision. While officers and retired security officials impact the political landscape, the peace process, and Israeli industry, the rapport of the soldier to these areas is comprised of informal networks and a web of close-knit relationships that are cultivated in military service. I agree with Yoram Peri's assertion that "clothing" is not what distinguishes the "two coalitions of military officers and civilian officials" because the two distinct coalitions alone simply don't exist (Peri 2006). As a result of Israel's complexity and intense overlapping boundaries, the clothing style among citizens and the military is in fact similar: informal and often interchangeable. Indeed, the style of the Security Network strengthens the argument of lack of distinctive civilian–military boundaries, and fosters the trend of Israel as the "uncivil" state.

8 Concordance and culture

From the military–industrial complex to corporate philanthropy

The importance of culture in evaluating outcomes has remained a dominant theme throughout this book. Previous chapters delineated the impact of culture on the civil–military relations of specific countries. They also provided a theory of concordance to account for such cultural and institutional influences. This chapter, however, hopes to solidify the importance of culture not as a theme specific to civil–military relations but as a theme that transcends disciplines, vocations, and organizational establishments. Corporate America is presented here as one such context in which culture vitally impacts its internal workings.

This chapter does not seek to prove concordance theory, nor does it try to transplant concordance theory and apply it to another context. Rather, culture's relationship to concordance and discordance is explored in a corporate environment – an environment both connected to and influenced by the military establishment (through the military–industrial complex), yet distinct in its forms of and motivations for concordance. While the military has considered the impact of indigenous cultures on foreign militaries, Corporate America has flattened its hierarchy and reorganized its corporate structure to adjust to the changing corporate culture of the time. For both, cultural changes and perspectives have to be embraced in order to successfully cope with their respective situations.

In the following sections, the dynamics of the military–industrial complex (MIC) is used to exemplify how easily the theme of concordance and culture can permeate very different organizational environments. Additionally, the idea of "corporate concordance" is introduced as one possible way in which organizations can account for culture and successfully achieve internal objectives. Corporate concordance, however, is not a predictive theory for determining overall company success, failure, or takeover; rather, it is a useful approach to creating teams and implementing objectives within a corporate environment, while paying attention to the partners involved and the uniqueness of corporate culture. *Corporate concordance is a framework for companies to consider in their quest for solidifying and implementing business objectives within their own corporate environment and beyond in our multicultural world.*

As a closing consideration, this chapter explores the current cultural context of Corporate America – a context which seems to be in the midst of changes that are culturally driven. Corporate America's relationship with the military through the military–industrial complex reached its height during the Cold War. Now, it is answering to more humanitarian callings through global philanthropy and social initiatives. As corporations adjust to a constituency that values the greater good, they are beginning to consider alternative ways to conduct business and how to affect worldwide social change beyond weapons production. Though this new role of Corporate America is yet unknown – we simply do not know what the future holds – considering corporate culture and the cultures of society at large will be an important factor in the future success of organizations, their corporate policies, and their philanthropic endeavors.

American's affinity for the greater good

While graduate students at the University of Chicago, my colleagues and I wanted to invite a distinguished scholar to present his work and dine with us following his presentation. I had always been an admirer of Stephen P. Cohen whose prolific scholarly contributions on India and Pakistan over the years influenced my study of those countries. I hoped to raise funds to host Professor Cohen at the University of Chicago campus. The money was not a substantial amount since he resided in Illinois, but I had no idea how to go about it. After all, I was a student of political science, and fundraising was far from the world of Heidegger, state building, and hermeneutics.

My advisor at the time was on sabbatical in India. It was suggested that I turn to Professor Charles Gray – husband of the then university president Hannah Holborn Gray, distinguished scholar, and high-ranking administrator in the Division of the Social Sciences. I remember thinking that this highly regarded scholar had much more important responsibilities than to help fund a small student-led dinner. I approached Professor Gray, presented our idea to host Professor Cohen, and requested funds for our guest's travel and post-talk dinner. Despite my apprehension, Professor Gray was polite, supportive, and knew how distinguished Professor Cohen was in the field, so he asked me to prepare a budget for the talk and the dinner. A few weeks later a check arrived at the Department of Political Science to cover the costs of the event. That was my first experience with fundraising in higher education and *definitely* my easiest.

Who knew that a decade later I would be sitting at CASE conferences (Council for the Advancement and Support of Education) gleaning the wisdom of speakers like Paul Schervish whose "enlightened philanthropy" often sounded like the political theory I had studied in graduate school. Philanthropy, according to Schervish, is not just about writing a check to your favorite charity. It is a social contract or relationship that implies community caring where "the donor must embody a higher level of moral sensitivity if a materially adequate philanthropic relationship is to exist" (Schervish *et al.* 1995: 5).

During one of those conferences I recalled the work of political observer and thinker Alexis de Tocqueville who wrote about the propensity for charity in nineteenth-century US culture. Indeed, the United States is the most philanthropic nation in the world. About 8 percent of the economy is used to fund nonprofit organizations. That is close to a trillion dollars. "Fifty-one percent of all hospital beds are funded by citizen generosity ... Citizen generosity funds a little more than 20 percent of all students in institutions of higher learning, 95 percent of all orchestras, and 60 percent of social service organizations" (Gaudiani 2004: 10). In a Tocquevillian way, Claire Gaudiani observes the following: "Generosity is not a luxury in this country. It is a cultural norm, a defining characteristic of our successful economy and our reasonably successful society" (ibid.:10). Scholarships, fellowships, awards, and prizes have become critical priorities for many university presidents and deans and important ways for alumni and friends to continue a meaningful legacy.

While authors in the field of philanthropy like Paul Schervish, Claire Gaudiani, and Charles Collier write brilliantly about the higher and enlightened reasons for charity, my own experience with fundraising has been an amalgam of individuals passing on meaningful legacies to loved ones, contributing to generations of scholars and practitioners, supporting organizations that further civil rights causes, acquiring immediate and long-term financial benefits, and receiving social recognition for giving. As the director of alumni giving at the Harvard School of Public Health, I came to know the alumni at Harvard University. They were grateful for the education they received and for the doors it opened for them professionally and socially. Most gave back to the university because they wanted to pass the torch of learning to future generations of public health professionals. Clearly, Harvard has the institutional infrastructure and fundraising expertise to encourage enlightened philanthropic activity such as this.

But enlightened philanthropy and altruism are not the only incentives that motivate people to donate. Charities understand this quite well and have created elaborate giving societies, naming opportunities, and other forms of recognition that motivate people to give in addition to promoting the organization's important cause, whether that is funding the student or curing the disease. With this approach, individuals receive recognition for their gifts while making a meaningful contribution that benefits the charity. University supporters could also participate in alternative forms of planned giving opportunities, thus providing the donor with social recognition as well as a significant stream of lifetime income from an endowment's overall performance – and still contribute to a meaningful philanthropic cause. This combination of long-term financial growth, charitable giving, and personal recognition often proved key in gaining the financial support of donors.

Some donors in fact are blatant about personal recognition. For example, I had a conversation with a donor to another charity who gave millions to his community for specific causes, but his niece was rather blunt about this amalgam of altruism and personal recognition: "My uncle cares very deeply about his community. But he also loves the naming opportunities. He loves to see his name in lights on a building." I have also attended receptions where hundreds of thousands of dollars were raised on the spot largely because one donor wanted to trump another donor and make certain everyone in the room witnessed it. These donors are dedicated to important causes but there is also an element of what I call "enlightened philanthropic one–up-manship" that people do not always talk about but admire and participate in if they can. It makes people feel good about themselves to be recognized for their charitable contributions, often in the company of others. This is not to say that people do not truly care about important causes and organizations. They have their social and political interests and favorite charities that support those interests, and Americans in particular enjoy giving back to society.

Business schools, and other schools where financial and professional gain is valued, pride themselves on having entire classes compete amongst each other during class reunions. University development staffs across the United States have elaborate strategies and fundraising events in place to encourage competitive giving. By contrast, alumni of public policy or public health programs often end up making less money than they did before they began their program. Public health is a truly altruistic calling. People do not enter this field unless they care more deeply about society than personal monetary gain. Preventing the further spread of AIDS in Africa, helping malnourished children in India, fighting obesity among children in the United States, preventing bird flu in Asia, maintaining effective smallpox and polio immunizations worldwide, understanding the effects of aging on baby boomers, creating a public health infrastructure for national emergencies – these are just some of the important causes public health servants research and support.

I found that public health alumni do not compete philanthropically amongst themselves in the same way business school alumni do. Perhaps differing motivations for entering the respective fields drive this distinction. For example, one of the most fascinating Harvard alums I met was a Boston-based physician who maintained a practice in the area. During our first visit, I anticipated a discussion on how she incorporated her public health education into her practice via research or alternative approaches to medicine – a scenario I heard many times before from other alumni. However, this alumna had worked previously as a tropical public health practitioner and had created a health care infrastructure among leper colonies in Tanzania. I remember thinking to myself, "How many people do you meet in a lifetime who have done *that* for a living?" As a result of this fascinating story and others, I took particular and deliberate approaches to fundraising that reflected a donor pool of public health alumni.

When I was the director of alumni giving at the Harvard School of Public Health, I concentrated on collective giving and individual donors who either had made money in non-public health fields or had inherited wealth. Some alumni, such as those in the nutrition, medicine, and health policy and management fields, did make significant contributions as a result of their public-health related incomes. But for the most part, reunion or class giving was simply not something I focused on.

Then one day, my colleagues at the Harvard Business School called me. Former Harvard President Larry Summers had formalized a creative and collaborative giving strategy: a cross-crediting system where Business School and other alumni from larger Harvard schools could give to "service-to-society"–oriented schools, like Public Health or the Kennedy School of Government, and receive reunion credit at their respective schools. Business school alums could compete amongst each other *and* find additional meaningful causes to invest in while still supporting the business school. They could affect research on AIDS, bird flu, malaria, and cervical cancer prevention. They could support future policies on aging, Medicare, and children's nutrition in the United States. The School of Public Health raised significant funds under this cross-crediting program from Harvard alumni who indeed wanted to give back to the global society and not sacrifice their immediate class-giving goals.

It is no coincidence that this cross-crediting program resonated quickly among Harvard Business School alumni. The broader synergy of philanthropic enlightenment and fulfilling immediate goals finds meaning in the business and corporate arenas. The Enron scandal ushered in a new era of corporate respons-ibility where financial transparency and profit-making intersected with commun-ity outreach and philanthropy. Even prior to the scandal, corporations and their foundations had given billions to local and international causes. They partnered with non-profit organizations and research institutions to assist in humanitarian projects and created new products to mitigate suffering and poverty. They manu-factured drugs to alleviate AIDS in South Asia and distributed mosquito nets to villages in Africa to combat malaria. One long-time senior vice president at PepsiCo confided to me that she was looking forward to retirement so as to pursue social causes. She would finally have the time to marshal her corporate and political contacts to assist with food delivery to malnourished children in Africa and Latin America.

More and more, corporate leaders not only carve out personal roles to assist humanitarian efforts but leverage their entire corporations for more charitable ends. As we will see in the following sections, this trend emerged from the mili-tary–industrial complex during the twentieth century. Additionally, it has placed Corporate America in strategic partnership with the civil–military realms through its still-developing role of corporation as social change agent.

The military–industrial complex

All the nations discussed in this book have experienced domestic military involvement in some form – coups, militarized civilians, tremendous civilian–military overlap, or significant tension among the political elites, the military, and the citizenry. In each case, concordance or agreement among the political elites, the military, and the citizenry was at best challenged by external threat conditions or at the worst exhibited severely impaired domestic relations to the point of *coup d'état*. As will be shown, the military–industrial complex has evolved from industrial supplementation of military endeavors through arms production, to integration into foreign policy decisions, and finally (with the influence of important corporate and defense figures such as Robert McNamara and others) to exchanges and mutual influences in institutional structures and civilian life.

Pre- and post-World War II military–industrial complex

The military–industrial complex as it relates to the evolution of civil–military relations theory is discussed in Chapter 2. Before and during World War II, the military–industrial complex underpinned the development of twentieth-century warfare with the creation of air power, tanks, ground-based antiaircraft artillery, and of course bombs that could destroy entire populations. These newer weapons required more specialized labor and a close collaboration between the military and private industry.

After the war, another phase of the military–industrial complex emerged that was mainly the result of the arms race between the United States and the Soviet Union. Some claimed the arms race was a form of militarism – a militarism that developed not for expansionist reasons as had happened during the Nazi period in Germany, but as a result of unavoidable national security concerns during the Cold War (Lasswell 1962: 54). Others argued that the United States merely utilized its highly organized military–industrial complex to maintain its "informal" empire in Europe, the Far East, and South America after 1945 (Berghahn 1982: 90). Still others, like C. Wright Mills, suggested that an elite militarism evolved since "the most important relations of corporation(s) to the state now rest on the coincidence between military and corporate interests" (1969: 28). Mills looked at domestic factors claiming that "the power elite in America" was based on the "big three": political, military, and economic institutions. In his 1961 farewell address, President Eisenhower also alerted the nation to the collusion between military and industrial interests:

> This conjunction of an immense military establishment and a large arms industry is new in the American experience. The total influence – economic, political, even spiritual – is felt in every city, every Statehouse, every office of the Federal government. We recognize the imperative need for this development. Yet we must not fail to comprehend its grave implications. Our toil, resources and livelihood are all involved; so is the very structure of our society.
>
> (Eisenhower Farewell Address, January 17, 1961)

As mentioned in Chapter 2, Paul Kennedy agrees with Eisenhower and Mills and argues that the arms industry in many nations, including democratic ones, was concentrated in a few gigantic firms enjoying a special relationship with their own governments' departments of defense. Kennedy also reinforced the predominance of a small circle of civilian and military elites while differentiating "elite" militarism from militarism in its traditional sense. He explained that it is the diversion of resources (and not dictatorial or militaristic repression) that can create a "top-heavy military establishment" in an elite militaristic conception (Kennedy 1987: 442, 445).

We see this distinction in the multitude of economic problems that result from uneven resource allocation. Manufacturing, service, and agricultural sectors could be negatively affected by large-scale military spending which diverts money and resources to specific military-related industries. In the United States during the 1980s, for example, several economic weaknesses resulted from huge defense spending: "the whole issue becomes one of balancing the short-term security afforded by large defense forces against the longer-term security of rising production and income" (Kennedy 1987: 445). It was during this time the United States experienced an agricultural crisis, a lower share of global manufacturing, and an international debtor status. These were just a few examples of critical domestic problems resulting from high defense expenditures rather than from dictatorial or militaristic repression. Pressures in these economic areas, influenced by diverse military needs rather than specialists in violence, pointed toward a democratic garrison state as initially envisioned by Lasswell.

Despite some authors' views of an elite militaristic state and Lasswell's view of a post-totalitarian garrison state, the United States remained a democracy. Even so, the United States (1948–91) maintained peacetime military mobilization resulting from the arms race with the Soviet Union. Whether the military–industrial complex is a form of military or civilian/corporate control and the status of post-World War II United States as "militaristic" have been fiercely debated. This debate highlights the complex integration of military and industry that makes the application of concordance theory relevant to both realms.

The geopolitical situation after World War II resulted in two realities: the United States' need to make better weapons than Russia and the US "mobilization of the civilian economy in the service of the state" (Roland 2001: 8). Government defense expenditures rose precipitously during the 1950s and 1960s, hovering between 6 and 14 percent of the total US gross domestic product. It was at this point that Corporate America willingly entered the defense field: "In 1958, 30 of the companies in the top 50 spots on the *Fortune 500* list of the largest industrial corporations also appeared on the list of the top 100 defense contractors" (ibid.: 9).

As mentioned above, President and former General Eisenhower first recognized the "delta of power" (Eisenhower Farewell Address, January 17, 1961) in the economic and political competition to win defense contracts. As a result, he willingly engaged in the complexity of legislative, corporate, and Department of Defense haggling over multi-million dollar defense projects. President Reagan revived the B-1 bomber to the tune of $280 million per plane – "more than ten times the projected price of the B-70 proposed to Eisenhower" (Roland 2001: 15). As the Cold War ended, the B-2 stealth bomber would cost $2 billion for each plane. Post-Cold War presidents would continue to secure costly military–corporate contracts, as Bill Clinton did for projects such as the Seawolf submarine (ibid.).

Again we see the highly reciprocal and interrelated infrastructures in which the military and US corporations existed. Those in charge of defense contracts often came from Corporate America. President Eisenhower appointed Neil McElroy, president of Proctor and Gamble, as secretary of defense. Perhaps the most notable secretary of defense, Robert McNamara, came along at the height of the Sputnik era and would further highlight the partnership between corporate and military interests through the corporate management style of the Pentagon.

Robert McNamara and the corporate–military intersect

Robert McNamara's tenure as secretary of defense escalated the level of civil–military integration to new heights. During and after World War II, the military merely depended on corporate arms production for the government's military goals. Now corporate interests could transform US foreign policy through sophisticated arms production. Additionally, corporations could send technology back to the civilian sectors for dual-use purposes such as personal computers and calculators. Robert McNamara came to symbolize this evolution in military–corporate interests and the structural and cultural similarities that shaped the growing partnership.

The TFX bomber project and sophisticated guided missile systems took companies like General Dynamics and Motorola to a new level in producing aircraft, weapons with pinpoint precision capability, and the associated computer technologies. The unintended but omnipresent consequence was the foreign/defense policy of mutual assured destruction (MAD) and preemptive first strike, which dangerously helped keep the superpowers at peace during the Cold War. Later, the large-scale IBM computers that shaped the sophisticated architecture for intercontinental air-defense systems would be repackaged and marketed in the 1970s and 1980s as civilian desktop computers. US citizens, for the most part, saw this dual-use technology as part of the natural evolution of modern comforts and conveniences, not as a by-product of a military foreign policy where multinational corporations played a critical role:

> Major corporations such as General Electric, Motorola, and IBM kept one foot in the military marketplace and one in the civilian, finding cross-fertilization that advanced technology in both. The Jeep, workhorse of World War II personal transportation, found itself transformed into a hot commercial product for upscale adventurers. By the end of the twentieth century, the military's global positioning satellite system was guiding everything from commercial ships and airliners to ... drivers of Cadillacs equipped with the company's "NorthStar" system.
>
> (Roland: 2001: 23)

Handheld calculators and computers were packaged and delivered to consumers in a similar way that the automobile was placed on the showroom floor. Robert McNamara, who came from Ford Motor Company to become secretary of defense, symbolized how the military–industrial complex would infiltrate the daily life of citizens through familiar consumer products.

McNamara himself was a product of the military–industrial complex as it took shape during World War II. Having served in the Army Reserve Officers

Training Corps and trained at Harvard Business School, McNamara was asked to make the transition to military service when called to consult for the Department of War on statistical analysis: "Although we were to start out as civilian consultants to the Department of War, there was a clear indication we would later be asked to accept commissions as army officers" (McNamara 1995: 9). Still in military uniform at the end of the war, McNamara and his colleagues, known as the Whiz Kids, were hired by Henry Ford to help turn his company around. At the time, quantitative "monitoring of progress" was considered "the bedrock principle of good management." McNamara and his group adopted this same "cerebral approach" to financial decision-making and management style that worked at Ford and sharply increased profits (McNamara 1995: 11). As a result, McNamara moved up the ranks to serve as president of the Ford Motor Company.

During his tenure at Ford, McNamara was tapped to become secretary of defense by President John F. Kennedy. McNamara quickly learned, however, that his financial decision-making and management approach at Ford was not effective during the Vietnam War – a regionally complex war with an emotionally charged social response. During a war with unclear battle lines and complex domestic struggles, body counts and prisoner tallies did not impress the US and international audiences. And unlike World War II, these realities of war appeared in almost every home with the advent of television (another by-product of the military–industrial complex). McNamara was operating in an environment quite opposite from that in which he developed the detached accounting algorithms of his corporate management style. The extreme social disaffection during the US anti-war riots of the 1960s and 1970s points to an emerging lack of concordance between the military, the political elites, and the citizens during the Vietnam War.

So why did McNamara fail to effectively manage the needs of these three key constituencies during the Vietnam War despite his prior success at Ford? *Ignorance of cultural context*. The "cerebral approach" that had worked so well for McNamara during a time of national and international stability fell short as the US and international cultural contexts shifted. McNamara even admits that the policy strategy and decision-making process were flawed, and the Pentagon and State Department both lacked the expertise in Southeast Asian and Chinese politics and culture:

> None of this made me anything close to an East Asian expert ... I had never visited Indochina, nor did I understand or appreciate it history, language, culture or values. The same must be said, to varying degrees, about President Kennedy, Secretary of State Dean Rusk, National Security Advisor McGeorge Bundy, military advisor Maxwell Taylor, and many others. When it came to Vietnam, we found ourselves setting policy for a region that was terra incognita. Worse, our government lacked the experts for us to consult to compensate for our ignorance.
>
> (McNamara 1995: 32)

The Vietnam debacle was indeed largely the result of top decision makers and advisors not having substantive insight into the region where they sent thousands of troops.

As mentioned in Chapter 3, abstract rational choice models (again becoming popular in political science circles) were dangerously used to support arguments for increased air strikes in North Vietnam. Had McNamara and other top advisors been more aware of the political and cultural situation in Vietnam, they might have entertained alternative interpretations of Ho Chi Minh's communist movement and quite possibly have saved over a million lives.

A similar cultural ignorance was manifest in the corporate world as well. The corporate management model of the 1960s was challenged in the 1970s largely on cultural grounds. Factors such as outdated hierarchies and management skills, lack of product innovation, and poor customer service played into a lack of concordance between Corporate America and the citizens/consumers at large. Ford Motor Company and other critical companies and industries began to suffer as foreign competitors who better understood the role of culture in corporate management surpassed the US market share. Peters and Waterman, authors of *In Search of Excellence*, understood how the hierarchical and rational US corporate model prevented innovation and top performance:

> We have observed few, if any, bold new company directions that have come from goal precision or rational analysis. While it is true the good companies have superb analytic skills, we believe that their major decisions are shaped more by their values than by their dexterity with numbers.
>
> (Peters and Waterman 1984: 51)

Soon *In Search of Excellence* became the management bible of the 1980s after Japanese automakers and computer companies began to eat away at the market share of Ford, Chrysler, and General Motors, as well as companies like IBM and Texas Instruments. The sophisticated and hierarchical management style – which produced guided weapons systems, field tanks, and bomber aircraft – gave way to more humane approaches based on Japanese concepts like *Kaizen*. This is a corporate process inspired by Toyota that fosters a humanized workplace within the context of a small group of workers. In English, *Kaizen* means continuous improvement that considers the complete work process not simple output or immediate results (Hammer and Champy 1994: 49). US companies began to realize that rational models of management had to become flatter and include a more employee-centered approach in order to achieve concordance with both employees and consumers.

Business organizations also began to encourage the "empowerment" of the workforce including the rank-and-file operational employees. Additional managerial approaches shunned "feudal" or hierarchical organizational thinking, opting instead for creative work environments that cope with business competition and corporate warfare (Belasco and Stayer 1993: 49–51, 56). Interestingly enough, Peters and Waterman used corporate and military examples interchangeably to show how successful examples of management styles and the connectivity between senior manager/officer and the line employee/rank and file could be utilized in both corporate and military contexts (1984: 255, 262, 263).

Finally, a true testament of military and industrial reciprocity and exchange was the revival of the classic book on warfare, *The Art of War*, in business circles. Its tenets of effective leadership and fostering an environment of harmony and cooperation among the rank and file continue to influence corporate strategy today. For Sun Tzu and his fellow masters and commentators, this was called "the Way" to share and embrace leadership goals.

> Harmony among people is the basis of the Way of military operations ... When the leadership is able, there will be good discipline ... If the leaders can be humane and just, sharing both the gains and the troubles of the people, then the troops will be loyal and naturally identify with the interests of the leadership.
>
> (Sun Tzu 2005: 3)

Indeed, on a corporate level, McDonald's has embraced "the Way" with the belief that "senior managers should be out in the field, paying attention to employees, training and execution" (Peters and Waterman 1984: 255). Similar to a persuasive military recruitment process, corporate concordance is achieved with a more "peripatetic management style" where upper management wanders around and is in constant contact with employees in the office, on the plant floor, or in the fast food restaurant. Management is persuasive in recruiting and retaining its employees, connecting with their goals, and celebrating their successes.

A more recent example of the transformations taking place in the military and civilian work environment was found in the State Department under former General Colin Powell. In his book *The World Is Flat*, Tom Friedman suggests that because of cells phones, Powell found that "no foreign minister can run and hide from him." His staff was also constantly reachable since he could text message his assistant around the clock. Friedman explains: "This is what happens when you move from a vertical (command and control) world to a much more horizontal (connect and collaborate) flat world. Your boss can do his job *and your job*. He is secretary of state and his own secretary" (2005: 212–13). With the onset of computers and cell phones, major players (military and civilian) began to take on roles that connected them more invasively with world leaders and support staff alike.

In the twenty-first century, business and military institutions have taken on a much closer manager–employee relationship because technology enables information to be transmitted in record time. The *Kaizen* or continuous improvement process, which is constantly being transformed by the integration of this sophisticated technology at work, can pierce the boundaries of the traditional workplace structures as we see in the Colin Powell example. The need for global yet flatter collaboration and sharpened strategic thinking among employees and customers is crucial to meet demand and competition; and the technology of cell phones and BlackBerrys (technology once exclusively part of the military domain) enhances the breakdown of the strict business hierarchies to support more flexible environments for business and military relationships.

The military–industrial complex has integrated two sectors traditionally seen as discrete and autonomous. This integration has resulted in the exchange of management structures and applications that eventually required the integration of culturally sensitive frameworks. While Robert McNamara fell short on the cultural sensitivity side of this corporate–military process, he did initially symbolize this confluence of military, corporate, and citizen interests by virtue of having participated extensively in each realm. His strategies in the corporate world, his experiences while secretary of defense, and the interchangeable application of both to military and corporate sectors provided a unique opportunity for theoretical application of theories (e.g., concordance theory) to both realms. In this spirit, the following section discusses a major theme of concordance theory – culture matters – within the context of Corporate America.

Concordance theory in a corporate context

After earning my PhD and developing concordance theory, I wanted to use my theoretical study of civil–military relations for a more practical, real-world discussion. An idea emerged that involved applying concordance theory to Corporate America and advising companies on how to create more harmonious work environments. Companies, like many nations, operate under high external threat conditions, and they can lag, fail, or become targets of hostile takeovers by other companies, especially in a hugely competitive multinational environment. The management books of the 1980s and 1990s had taken a close look at the internal structures and management styles of companies. They knew that the traditional and rational hierarchical structures that Robert McNamara had embraced were no longer effective in competing with foreign companies that began to dissolve strict hierarchies in favor of employee empowerment and team building.

These books often mentioned "productivity through people" or "being closer to the customer" – ideas considered critical to the success of many major companies. These ideas had an air of familiarity to me; corporations seemed to predict success by integrating all parties into their corporate strategy (even those traditionally ignored) much like civil–military concordance depended on agreement between all three key partners. And both had to consider culture in order to even attempt this "key player"-based approach. It appeared as though my civil–military framework and culture-based approach had practical relevance within Corporate America.

The parallel discussions of concordance theory in both civil–military relations and Corporate America evolved from their intertwining relationships within the US military–industrial complex. Large corporate conglomerates were often designed around the military requirements of a nation. Throughout the twentieth century, corporations manufactured the arms that nations used to engage in military efforts and produced products for civilian purposes as well. The arms industry grew at a rapid pace after World War II and became part of the civil–military relations equation. The partnership with civilian elites affected arms acquisition, military growth, budgets, and recruitment. The business community engaged in spirited negotiations resulting in military contracts that impacted the government and entire communities. These two establishments, the military and the corporate, were inseparably linked and depended on each other for arms and industry.

This linkage and dependency enabled other exchanges as well, namely managerial styles based on the separation of hierarchical spheres. For US civil–military relations this meant that while the military interacted with civilians in the corporate world, the latter devised distinctive weapons systems that enabled the military to remain institutionally and culturally separate from the rest of society. Corporations, in turn, adopted a strict hierarchy with little interaction between management and rank-and-file employees. Eventually, both corporations and the civil–military realms fell victim to cultural inattention. Corporations saw lack of concordance with its employees who often felt estranged in the workplace and with customers in dollars spent, and the military saw discord manifest through anti-war riots and opposition to the Vietnam War effort. Concordance theory, in the same way that it guides nations, could guide companies toward agreement on company mission and objectives by cultivating effective partnerships and focusing on cultural trends.

The military–industrial complex – through its industrial interdependency and subsequent exchanges in organizational structure – gives relevance to concordance theory in the corporate realm. As mentioned above, companies, like nations, operate under high external threat conditions. The automobile industry, during the 1970s and today, is an example of corporate insecurity in a competitive multinational business environment. Additionally, like nations with active militaries, a corporation first needs a framework that can assist with institutional change before alterations can be made. Corporate concordance thus borrows relevant partners, indicators, and themes from the civil–military relations world.

Under conditions of intense business competition, concordance between major company partners should be embraced. Nations have political elites and the officer corps that should be in agreement with the citizenry in order to prevent domestic military intervention. Likewise, corporations have a board of directors comparable to the political elites; CEOs and senior managers comparable to the military officer corps; and employees comparable to the citizenry of a nation. In other words, there exist counterparts in the corporate world for each of the three concordance theory partners, assisting in the application of concordance theory to the corporate realm.

Similar to concordance theory as applied to nations, the corporate concordance structure also provides four indicators over which the major company partners should be in agreement:

- strategic planning
- company decision-making process

- recruitment method
- company style.

These indicators reflect critical aspects of any major organization. They also provide a useful structural reference for companies that wish to undergo important changes without radically altering their present form, yet still embracing the importance of company culture.

Concordance theory, as it is applied to nations, is a model for institutional and cultural analysis in order to forecast domestic military intervention. As mentioned at the beginning of this chapter, corporate concordance does not predict company takeover or hostile employee intervention or profit failure; rather, it is a conceptual and practical tool to assist companies in achieving agreement between senior management and rank-and-file employees on issues of company mission and critical company objectives.

Corporate concordance reflects the similarities of the military and corporate realms and how the two institutions need to pay greater attentiveness to their respective cultures and the societies affected by them. It provides a useful guide for corporate endeavors based on the uniqueness of individual corporate cultures, the three crucial partners involved, and the corporate concordance indicators. Unlike concordance theory, corporate concordance is not a theory that predicts important outcomes such as *coups d'état* or company takeover. Corporate concordance allows companies to consider alternative ways for identifying and executing business objectives in a flatter and more culturally diverse world.

Presented below are two examples of strategic planning and team-building successes I achieved within the context of Corporate America. (The company types and the specific objectives have been changed to maintain corporate confidentiality.) Within the framework of corporate concordance, effective team building among all three partners is crucial to the achievement of a particular objective. Team building, therefore, will be the crux of the examples below. In addition to effective team building, several if not all levels of the company should participate in choosing the most appropriate objective. Finally, the objective should remain in-line with relevant concordance indicators throughout the problem-solving process.

The concordance team approach

Most company team programs and approaches are objective driven. They focus on how to achieve an objective, series of objectives, or specific company projects. While values may be developed or defined during the team process, rarely do we see an initial emphasis on and constant reinforcement of team values (Covey 1992). As cited earlier in this chapter, Peters and Waterman agree "while it is true the good companies have superb analytic skills, we believe that their major decisions are shaped more by their values than by their dexterity with numbers." Therefore, values provide the foundation or backbone of a team and the vehicle through which objectives remain in-line with concordance indicators.

Examples of values include trust, responsibility, effective communication, respect for individual opinions, and encouragement of professional skills. In her book *Confidence*, Rosabeth Moss Kanter borrows examples from successful sports teams to illustrate the importance of reinforcing in the business world "a list of core values" and routines that encourage "accountability, collaboration and initiative" (2004: 360). Additionally, values help shape corporate culture – the principles, ideas, and habits that inform a company's work environment. Teams that select values, and consistently reinforce them, are more likely to have higher morale and an ability to restore team motivation and determination in the face of setbacks. The ritual of reinforcing values is critical to team cohesion and ultimately the achievement of the team's objective.

Also critical to successful team building within the corporate concordance framework is the definition of one clear-cut objective. Having one and only one defined objective may appear simplistic and unsophisticated. Corporate cultures often encourage multiple objectives that incorporate complex terminology. However, the focus on multiple objectives often dilutes the purpose and clarity of the company's aims. The objective should be clear, precise, and easily understood so that anyone, including team visitors, could easily grasp it. In addition, it is more important for a team to successfully accomplish one objective than to tackle multiple, complex objectives and fail.

In defining the objective, team members should refer back to the concordance indicators: strategic planning, decision-making process, recruitment method, and company style. These provide a structure for defining the team's objective. Additionally, they may expose areas that require team solutions (Schiff 1997: 930). For example, the team may realize that one aspect of their company style needs improvement. The team proceeds to focus on one specific style objective (e.g., company-wide implementation of casual Fridays). Alternatively, the team may immediately define its objective (e.g., improve profit margin by reorganizing the customer feedback process). The team can place the objective into a company context by utilizing the most appropriate concordance indicators. As a result, the team may realize that the indicators of strategic planning and company decision-making process are affected by this proposed objective. Thus, the indicators provide a vision of concordance and a context for the team goal.

The construction firm

The concordance approach has assisted companies in achieving greater agreement among four critical indicators for business success. One such success was a major construction firm that hired me to create an effective upper management team. While "teams" existed at this company, they faced issues of low morale, lack of focus, and disconnect between upper management and the operational employees, including construction workers. It was clear to them that a different approach to team building was needed.

Since cohesive and agreed-upon values are what bind a team together creating a relationship of concordance, I engaged the team in discussion over the merits of different values such as trust, communication, and respect. The team members, however, were rather skeptical of the importance of values in team building and overall company success. It became apparent that in order to prepare the participants for high performance team building, preliminary exercises were required. The participants were given a week to reinforce one value of their choice during normal business activity, thus creating a connection between the concordance partners and indicators. Additionally, they were to think of creative ways to reinforce the selected value in a team environment.

The team went on to develop a company-wide objective within the context of the corporate concordance indicators: redefine the core competencies for specific job descriptions at the upper- and middle-management levels. Company decision-making process and recruitment method stood out as the key concordance indicators that affected the development and implementation of this core competency objective. The management team needed "buy in" from key company decision makers in order to implement the objective. The team developed a strategy for how to approach senior management for project support (i.e., choosing which senior managers to invite to specific team meetings); they also placed discussion of the objective on the company agenda prior to the discussion of other topics.

In addition to company buy in, defining company policy regarding job descriptions and tailoring them to the company's mission and profit-making strategy were central to the team's objective. Determining the best recruitment policy for the new jobs was also a highly detailed process that the team spent months developing. The team wanted to show how these new job descriptions would impact the level and caliber of employees, with specific skill sets, that the company now wanted to attract.

In implementing the team objective, this team placed importance on values from the beginning, which led to increased team morale and an understanding of the team's purpose. They also included key players in team meetings to ensure concordance was maintained among multiple employment levels. Finally, the team identified two of the four indicators (decision-making and recruitment process) as being critical to the success of their objective and referred back to these indicators throughout the process. By including not only key partners but also key concordance indicators in their objective-driven goal, this team took into account specific characteristics of their corporate culture and proved successful.

The service organization

Another success story involved a national service organization that was eager to create a high performance work team. These participants did not need to be convinced of the importance of values and defining one clear objective. The organization had a long history of promoting specific values to fulfill its service-to-society mission. The team participants took it upon themselves to find creative ways to reinforce their chosen group values. There were four team members, one from each level of the organization (upper management to clerical staff). They had chosen four specific values: trust, acknowledgment, communication among team members, and respecting the ideals of national headquarters. One team member offered the idea of creating headbands to be worn by each team member during every team session. Written on the headband was one of four values. At the beginning of each team meeting, the members would wear a different headband and briefly mention the value and its meaning to the team.

This team was also very successful in selecting one clear objective. Each team member had offered different possible objectives. In the end, the most ambitious objective was agreed upon – purchasing and installing state-of-the-art computer technology to implement more efficient accounting practices. The team knew that the objective was ambitious and could be easily rejected by the organization's board of directors, which preferred incremental changes and a lean budget over the most current technology. Thus, they utilized the concordance indicators to place the objective into an organizational context. This budget-related objective was relevant to strategic planning, company decision-making process, and company style.

This particular objective would affect the long-term strategy of the organization because the organization's accounting methods affected each employee and vendor. Therefore, the team needed to consider the organization's current accounting methods, employee participation, and future vendor relationships as they related to the strategic planning of the organization. The decision-making process was important to consider as well. The team would need the board of directors' approval for such an ambitious objective, and the board's approval would be required subsequently when the technology needed to be upgraded. Therefore, critically for its success, the team needed to determine the board's priorities and whether or not this was the best time to present this objective to them. Finally, this was a chapter of a very large organization. The style of the chapter was community-based and informal; but the organization as a whole was growing more sophisticated, and the team believed its accounting methods should be comparable to the method and style of the national office. Utilizing the concordance indicators as a reference point for discussion gave the team a better understanding of how their goal might benefit the entire organization.

In addition to consulting the concordance indicators in establishing the objective, this team consisted of different organizational levels: senior management, mid-level managers, and clerical employees. This equitable mix of upper and lower management encouraged greater concordance at each level of the organization, and the team tried its best to inform all levels of management and the board of its intended objective.

Team members had successfully outlined three phases for implementing the goal, a specific time frame for each phase, and each team member's cross-disciplinary responsibility. After several months of discussion with the board of directors, the ambitious objective was voted down. The board decided that the organization's business style and strategic planning, especially regarding budget allocations for improved software, did not warrant expensive computer technology. The team decided to submit a less ambitious objective that would alter the chapter's accounting procedures incrementally; the board quickly approved this objective.

Throughout the entire process, the team found it useful to discuss the proposed objective within the context of the concordance indicator framework among team members and board members. When the two objectives came up for board approval, the concordance indicators provided a context for the team and the board to discuss the merits and challenges of each objective.

Both organizational examples reflect the effectiveness of defining one objective within the corporate concordance framework while reinforcing team values. In addition to my work with these organizations, I created high performance teams for several coffee divisions of one of the largest international food companies. The concordance indicators assisted in providing an organizational context for their long-term team objectives. Corporate concordance indicators gave these teams a vision and supported their development of fundamental team-building skills.

The concordance approach to strategic planning and team building provides companies with a vision for achieving greater internal agreement among four indicators for business success. The indicators of strategic planning, company decision-making process, recruitment method, and company style reflect vital aspects of any company attempting to prevail in a highly competitive business environment. The concordance vision can be achieved in high performance team settings that are both value and objective driven. The two company examples reflect how these team-building skills may affect different company levels, empower employees to overcome obstacles, and move the entire organization toward greater concordance or agreement on specific objectives.

While the value of corporate concordance is to provide a practical framework to guide team-driven objectives, its purpose here is also to reflect on the structural similarities of military and business as initially found in the military–industrial complex. Corporate concordance also points to the cultural context of both military and industry: it does not predict the rise and fall of companies, but it borrows from concordance theory to provide a framework for understanding key corporate indicators for building strategy and objectives. Corporate concordance, like concordance theory, embraces both the structural and cultural elements of a corporation and the partners that should determine collaboratively the company mission and key objectives. Corporate concordance is a framework that guides companies by understanding that the CEO, management, and line employee must synergize and determine together the best path for company success.

The best-aligned militaries, as we saw in chapters 4, 5, and 7, were those sensitive to all levels of their armed forces from the officer corps to the rank and file. In India, for example, we saw greater democratization among the ranks and the loosening of social barriers such as the caste system. Unlike Pakistan, the Indian military was closely synergized with a government that took great pains to be inclusive of its population even within the context of a caste culture and other social barriers. The military's close partnership with the government also provided the much-needed "aid to the civil" – disaster relief, medical emergency response, and alleviation of acute distress in poverty-stricken areas. Corporations could begin to play a similar role within their own corporate structures. Greater synergy between the top corporate elites and the rest of the corporate hierarchy in this regard could once again show the dual applicability of concordance theory to both civil–military relations and corporate environments.

Additionally, the corporate concordance approach provides an opportunity for companies to impact communities as social change agents. As many companies move away from building military armaments and move toward more humanitarian and philanthropic projects, corporate concordance may assist in shaping and defining these global efforts.

Concordance theory, corporate philanthropy, and beyond

While the field of civil–military relations begins to question the validity of exporting the US civil–military dichotomy abroad, Corporate America also considers alternative ways of conducting business and how to affect social change beyond weapons production. During the 1960s and 1970s, both realms embraced the concept of social responsibility: civil–military relations by considering or at least being affected by the impact of indigenous culture on foreign militaries (Vietnam) and Corporate America by considering the changing corporate cultures and thus eventually flattening its hierarchy. Currently, Corporate America is taking new strides to adjust to another dominant cultural trend of the time: to fulfill a humanitarian call through philanthropic and social responsibility efforts.

If corporate concordance can help companies align their objectives with the unique structure of the company, then corporate concordance might also become a viable tool for militaries and civilian elites (including corporate leaders) to achieve healthier civil–military relations. In essence, corporate concordance has the potential to move outside the walls of corporations and define and achieve goals relevant to the corporate, military, and civilian relationships. Specifically, the role of corporations could transform from solely internal profit-driven motivations to external humanitarian partnerships with the military, governmental elites, and citizens. Already, many corporations (while still participating in the military–industrial complex) are playing a larger role than ever before in executing objectives that are in-line with the needs and goals of all three partners. These emerging objectives primarily involve humanitarian and philanthropic efforts.

Corporations and philanthropic efforts

As de Tocqueville witnessed 170 year ago, US citizens in particular enjoy giving back to society (1901: 798). We have seen this enthusiasm escalate into grander schemes of targeted philanthropic efforts by corporations, many of which participate in the high-profit partnership of the military–industrial complex.

Companies such as Verizon and Citigroup Inc. are collaborating with organizations and programs, such as the Clinton Global Initiative, that support economic relief efforts in several regions of the world. Some important initiatives are micro-financing and micro-entrepreneurship. These are small loans given to individuals in poverty-stricken villages throughout the developing world. One individual with a trade such as shoe making will take a $500 loan and create a small business that often impacts an entire village. The loans are paid back and village and town businesses often flourish and promote real local and regional economic growth. The Citigroup Foundation has "contributed nearly $40 million to more than 200 micro-financing organizations over the past seven years" (Citigroup Foundation 2007). In 2006 alone, Citigroup Foundation contributed $137 million for philanthropic efforts, $30 million of which went to alleviating natural disasters worldwide. The funding was a combination of corporate foundation grants and employee giving.

Similarly, The Coca-Cola Company has bridged local micro-financing with corporate branding and profit. In Vietnam, for example, Coca-Cola has affected the economy by providing "pushcarts, kiosks and mini-tables" to entrepreneurs who are mainly "disadvantaged women" and interested in becoming the company's "business partner." As it states on Coca-Cola's corporate responsibility website, "these women not only receive their own pushcarts to sell Coca-Cola products but also are provided with initial product and sales training. At the end of 2005, more than 4,000 women in Vietnam owned small pushcarts" (Coca-Cola Company 2007). The program in Vietnam to establish small local businesses while increasing Coca-Cola market share and branding has been replicated in Thailand, Indonesia, Ghana, and Egypt.

More recently, companies like Verizon rapidly dispatched employees armed with cell phones to New Orleans during the 2005 hurricane disaster. Food, sanitation, and temporary housing were delivered through an emergency partnership between the National Guard, Corporate America, and the local civil authorities. Coca-Cola also partnered with "local governments and international relief and development agencies ... on-site to provide immediate aid." The company "mobilized [their] trucks and employees, who worked around the clock to distribute water to affected communities. [They] also provided other emergency supplies, such as food, medicine, blankets and tents, according to local need" (www.thecoca-colacompany.com/citizenship/disaster_relief.html).

It is obvious that corporate philanthropy has played a progressively larger and almost expected role in US life since the days of de Tocqueville. Currently, philanthropic efforts have escalated to more than just isolated relief efforts. Corporations are now becoming key players in nation building and other humanitarian efforts as social change agents, a role once held solely by the governments and militaries.

Corporations as social change agents

In previous chapters, we have seen nations attempt to align military goals with those of existing governments and the citizenry at large. Similarly, corporations (while not straying from profit-making motives) are also trying to align themselves with a new mandate for corporations as social change agents. The four corporate concordance indicators allow for cross-functional teams to place their objectives into a company-wide context by consistently reviewing what is of critical importance to the company and how the objective will further the corporate mission. Once the upper-level management is synergized with the other company levels and employees, the company will be better prepared to act as corporate change agent. It will help alleviate the problem of "matching lower-level actions to top management commitment in the realm of social policy" (Frederick 2006: 32). Corporate concordance assists upper management and operational employees to think and act collaboratively within a company context and move toward the meaningful impact corporations can make outside of the company and outside of traditional philanthropic efforts. In other words, internal alignment of corporate goals with corporate culture makes possible the achievement of external goals.

As mentioned in the chapters on India and Israel, the military has often played a role in nation building without incidence of domestic military intervention such as coup. For example, during the 1950s and 1960s the Israeli Defense Forces assisted with immigration issues, administering food and medicine, and providing housing. In India, as mentioned in Chapter 5, "aid to the civil" was frequent and often involved cooperating with government authorities in road repair, flood control, disaster relief, and the distribution of food and medicine in times of famine or epidemic. In these countries, the military assisted in building a social infrastructure through public housing and public health and medical care without concern that the army would coercively usurp government power. With targeted strategies in-line with concordance theory, corporations could begin to play a similar role in nation building and social relief efforts as governments and militaries have in the past.

Henry and Edsel Ford personified this changing role of corporations from profit-making entities and military-equipment manufacturers with targeted philanthropic goals to entities that furthered the most prolific humanitarian causes. Seventy years ago, the father–son team created the Ford Foundation to be used "all for the public welfare." They never imagined their initial $25,000 investment would one day grow large enough to promote programs such as "new approaches and solutions to inequality in school systems in Argentina, Chile, Peru and Colombia" (Ford Foundation 2006: 102). While the automobile company no longer controls the foundation, the philanthropic efforts are spirited by the initial dream of a corporate entrepreneur who wanted to affect greater humanity. It is no secret and it should not be understated that Henry Ford had unconscionable personal shortcomings regarding his attitudes toward and writings about world Jewry. Nevertheless, he and subsequent Ford family members were social change agents, and the Ford Foundation now spans the crevices of the globe supporting projects that advocate on behalf of democratic values, the elimination of poverty and injustice, and the advancement of human achievement.

Thus, the very company that created tanks and weapons during World War II and critical technology during the height of the military–industrial complex also had the vision to turn the instruments of corporate and military success into a force for social and economic change. While the automobile assembly line has been criticized for augmenting alienation in the human condition, the process of creating industrial infrastructure and automation spawned the emergence of practical technology and employment – a social benefit for the masses in itself. Ford prospered, and many of the proceeds were eventually redirected to a family and corporate-inspired entity that would assist in alleviating tragic global conditions the average American knew little about. The study and alleviation of poverty, disease, and illiteracy would become the hallmark of additional family and corporate-inspired foundations – Hewlett, Rockefeller, Mellon, Gates to name a few – that indeed further the mission of the social change agent.

Most recently, corporations and foundations have assumed their role as social change agents through efforts to alleviate disease and poverty. Throughout the Bill and Melinda Gates Foundation website, for instance, there are examples of grants and partnered initiatives to eradicate polio, poverty, and Guinea worm disease, and to create vaccines and drugs to assist with preventing malaria and AIDS (www.gatesfoundation.org). Foundations such as Gates and Rockefeller are often no longer satisfied with funding research without impact. That is not to say that they don't fund important scholarships, fellowships, conferences, and research to analyze and discuss critical topics. But the trend and fundamental missions of many of these foundations is to eliminate the suffering in the world that appears to have solutions, if not through vaccines, then with preventative measures or educational tools that can be made available to communities in distress. Along with social change comes a dynamic corporate and foundational paradigm shift that measures grant-making success through problem eradication.

As social change agents, corporations and their foundations also impact our values and culture – "they have become our value centers, where important sociocultural values are formulated" (Frederick 2006: 24). Through mass media, including the Internet, corporations affect our consumption habits, product selection, and social values. While Coca-Cola may push its products in Vietnamese villages by training women to open kiosks, US corporate culture is also affecting social and political values in the workplace and ultimately at home.

In the twentieth century, the partnership between the military and Corporate America during World War II augmented the suffragist movement. Women were called to serve their country by leaving the kitchen and working in ammunitions factories to build weapons in defense of the nation. "Rosie the Riveter" became a symbol and a government-initiated movement during World War II that inspired women to support the war effort. The number of working women in the United States rose dramatically during World War II. The appearance of women in factories and on the work front in general dropped precipitously after the war. Nevertheless, Corporate America (and specifically the military–industrial complex during World War II) opened the door to women's social and political rights and eventually the feminist movement, both of which brought women back to work en masse during the 1970s.

Within the US military institution, the attack on Pearl Harbor and the support from Eleanor Roosevelt created the first Women's Army Auxiliary Corps and military training center. By 1944, there were 100,000 women in uniform, many of whom lived in tents and served as nurses in the foxholes of the European War theater. During the war in Vietnam, each of the US armed forces – Army, Navy, Air Force, and Marines – benefited from the dedication of over 120,000 women in service from nursing to intelligence to evacuation flights in South East Asia.

More recently, corporate efforts to promote equality at the workplace have bolstered the gay civil rights movement. In this situation, corporations (though not the military) have come to understand that lesbian, gay, bisexual, and trans-gendered people are productive employees and consumers just like everyone else. In turn, business motives have translated into broadening the human rights struggle in multiple contexts. Employees take home their common workplace interactions with gay and transgendered colleagues to discuss over the dinner table with their families. Television shows such as *Will and Grace* and *Ellen*, owned by multi-billion dollar conglomerates, only serve to reinforce the values of equality at home and at the office water cooler. While the corporate social-change agent influence may not be purely altruistic or philosophical, many cor-porations try very hard to align themselves with quantitative value indicators of fairness and equality provided by organizations like the Human Rights Cam-paign.

In an ideal world, the partnering between government and corporation would involve the government determining goals and priorities by setting the national agenda with the citizenry. The role of businesses would be the implementation of "social programs, carried out under the policy umbrella of government." This partnership "moves away from dependence upon self-initiated corporate action in the field of social problem solving." The more comprehensive partnership also would move away from "corporate philanthropy" and into the realm of "marshaling national resources and the assessment of how they should be used within the context of national goals" (Frederick 2006: 33–4). Indeed, this could become a partnership or concordance between the government, the corporation, and society that best determines top national priorities and how corporations may assist in their implementation. In turn, such a partnership crystallizes the role of corporation as profit-making entity, philanthropic decision maker, and social change agent.

Summary

The military–industrial complex represents the overlap and exchange present in current military, governmental, and corporate relationships. Each institution influences not only the other's success but also its goals and overall organi-zational structure. Accordingly, the concordance theory framework that predicts domestic military interventions finds its place in corporate concordance issues, as demonstrated by the examples of this chapter. Just as important, corporate concordance encourages critical corporate partners to come together and think strategically about their relationships to one another, to the company, and to society as a whole.

While corporate concordance can provide guidance to improve employee synergies and strategic planning within the corporation, corporate philanthropy has provided a natural nexus between the military–industrial complex and the momentum toward corporations becoming truer social change agents outside of the organization. Historically, corporations (and now the military–industrial complex) have greatly encouraged cooperation between military and corporate interests. Former Ford Motor Company president and US secretary of defense, Robert McNamara, symbolizes this attempt to solidify corporate and military interests for the sake of national security and achieving a more peaceful world; although McNamara showed that a corporate executive may not necessarily be the best person to run a war.

Similar to attempts to align military goals with those of existing governments and the citizenry at large, companies are trying to align themselves with a new mandate for corporations as social change agents. But, for all of the corporate "reengineering" that took place during the 1980s and 1990s and current observations and prescriptions of a "flatter" corporate world, the corporate hierarchy still prevents the full institutionalization of initiatives that would truly impact social justice. Upper management must continue to synergize with all levels of the company to fully understand its company culture. With targeted strategies that are aligned with corporate concordance, corporations could begin to move outside their company, beyond corporate philanthropy, and into more humanitarian roles typically reserved for governments and militaries.

The overlapping boundaries of civil–military relations, the military–industrial complex, corporate sustainability, and corporate social agency reflect the importance of a prominent theme throughout this book: culture matters, multidisciplinary approaches are needed, and connections must be made among interrelated scholarly and practical fields to further the most pressing humanitarian needs. The prevention of domestic military interventions through more cooperative relationships between the government, the military, and the citizenry, the influence of corporate development on weapons proliferation and arms control, and the alleviation of social problems through corporate philanthropy and social change agency all point to this – institutions and culture are inextricably connected and theories and practical frameworks that embrace these synergistic relationships need to be developed and embraced. Concordance theory and corporate concordance are two alternative and interrelated approaches for achieving this vital synergy.

9 Conclusion

I have been going to the same chiropractor for several years now. She knew that I was writing this book and for the past 12 months has asked me about its progress. At one of my appointments, I reported to her my latest book-related feelings of angst and anxiety. Then we quickly moved to a more common and less stressful topic – Whole Foods, a favorite mutual shopping stop. Our 30-minute appointment turned into a critique of different Whole Foods locations in the area and covered such critical topics as produce and cheese selections, salad bar offerings, and of course the new gelato bar at the Newton venue.

Feeling relaxed and de-stressed as I left my appointment and stepped into my car, I thought what a luxury it was for us to spend part of a work-week chatting about such minutiae. But I was soon transported to a more international reality as NPR's lead story blared on my car radio – the former prime minister of Pakistan Benazir Bhutto had been assassinated a couple of weeks ago and the report was covering the latest round of political issues facing Pakistan. Pakistanis, for the most part, do not have the luxury of wondering at which high-end gourmet supermarket they prefer to shop. The people of Pakistan are busy with more fundamental hopes and aspirations wondering each day if they will participate in free elections and have less military influence in their lives. They look forward to the day when their nation's leadership will shed its military uniform and allow for true participatory politics. How different indeed are the Pakistani military and civilian realities from those here at home. Then a totally random and not particularly scholarly thought entered my mind: I couldn't remember the last time I saw a uniformed US soldier shopping at Whole Foods.

On my way back to work I decided to stop at a deli to pick up a sandwich. As I waited for my sandwich I scanned the counter for flyers and brochures. There was a local newspaper, a menu, and a wide assortment of local business information. Tucked away in the corner, I noticed a few US Army brochures. Had the sandwich not been delayed, I would have never noticed those brochures. I picked one up and started leafing through it: a basic information piece on military recruitment probably aimed at high school students in the area. On the back of the brochure was the army recruiter's business card. I thought to myself, I wonder what he thinks about civil–military relations? I had been intellectually traversing through several countries around the world applying my theory of concordance to foreign or historical civil–military scenarios. I knew that discussions of civil–military relations and concordance theory were part of the military academic curriculum at places like West Point and the Naval Postgraduate School, and scholarly debates on the subject continue to rage at military and other academic institutions. But what did the typical military recruitment officer from this middle- to working-class American region think about civil–military relations here and abroad? I decided to call him and find out.

The process of speaking with the local Army recruiter was quite easy and interesting, and reminded me of my time in Israel during the 1990s when I was interviewing Israeli army officers. The army in Israel tried its best to put on a very positive public face and was pleasant to work with as I set up interviews with high-ranking officers in charge of military education and recruitment matters. In Israel, however, they were a bit more cautious about clearing the specific questions I intended to ask each officer. My contact there was "Major Orna" – I never knew her last name, I never met her personally, and I did not know exactly where she worked. But when I asked a question that was inappropriate for security reasons, Major Orna, who spoke perfect English, would gently let me know and help me rephrase the question. I often interviewed officers in Hebrew, and Major Orna was happy to correct my grammar. Every interview and every military publication I acquired went through Major Orna. When I left Israel, she wished me luck on my project and I never heard from her again.

Major Orna reminded me of the security staff at the Israeli El Al Airlines – very congenial but would not let you proceed without due diligence on the security front. Major Orna had a purpose in every conversational exchange, and she wasn't going to let me near a high-level IDF officer without proper clearance. Overall, however, the IDF security clearance process was not terribly burdensome and was very educational.

So here I was with my own military at home, setting up a final interview. I had to go through a few channels before being connected to my interviewee, and my conversations with Army staff were congenial yet deliberate. The military suggested I speak to a high-ranking officer instead of a first sergeant responsible for day-to-day recruitment. But I insisted on speaking with someone who was working with soldiers on a daily basis. I really wanted a candid interview not an "official line" – although in the end I spoke with two non-commissioned officers, selected by the military, who had served in the Army for many years. I also spoke briefly with the commander in charge of the first sergeant prior to setting up the interview. This was as close as I would get to a candid yet still official interview with someone dealing with US Army recruits and soldiers on a daily basis. I was secretly excited that the US Army approved of my work and would help me conclude it. I also knew what a luxury it was to live in a country where I could personally speak with a military the average American does not fear – a situation most US citizens take for granted. One day I could be discussing the finer points of Whole Foods with my chiropractor, then listening about the tragic Pakistani situation on the radio, and the next day I could call a local Amy recruiting station to set up an interview without fearing the institution, as a civilian.

The US military, with the exception of the "Don't Ask Don't Tell" policy, is an institution that protects American interests. The military, however, should respect and honor its gay and lesbian soldiers and allow them to publicly be who they are. Many of us find it shameful that it does not and we wait for that moment of courage in US military history and government policy to come when this discriminatory policy is ended.

For the most part, however, American citizens do not consider military matters that closely or frequently and do not find the institution threatening. Is this the result of a highly successful separation theory having been implemented in the United States, or is it a result of concordance theory? In my opinion, it is the result of both. Again we see how the separation of civilian and military institutions works in the United States and is based on the agreement or concordance between the civilians, the political elites, and the military. I was surprised to discover in this interview that both military personnel saw more overlap between the military and civilian sectors than I had anticipated. In fact First Sergeant Antonio Correa, one of my interviewees, spoke twice of the progressive co-mingling of the military with Corporate America without any prompting.

While partnership and not separation, especially on the industrial–military level, does indeed flourish in the US, (as discussed in Chapter 8), case studies such as Israel and eighteenth-century America reflect a far more significant level of co-mingling military and citizen spheres (as discussed in chapters 4 and 7). While many US citizens today prefer that our military not remain in Iraq and have deep convictions on this matter, for the most part, on a day-to-day level US citizens prefer less domestic co-mingling with the military. This allows us to live out our gourmet lives at Whole Foods without having to think too much about the grizzlier side of national defense. But when we need the military, either abroad for defense matters or to seek out that final set of quotes for the conclusion of a book, the armed forces are there to serve and protect our lives as US citizens. Americans agree to this relationship between the military and the citizenry, and we expect our civilian politicians to reinforce it and abide by it as well. This is how our institutions work, and this is an important part of current US culture.

Concordance theory explains the military and civilian separations that exist in the US, but concordance allows us to understand how what appears to be culturally ordinary and commonplace in the US, also becomes a revealing snapshot of the unique relationship between military and society – and how sharply it is contrasted to countries like Pakistan and Argentina as discussed in chapters 5 and 6. Concordance theory embraces this unique perspective because of its focus on culture. This is similar to the movie *Bobby* described in the beginning of this book, which gave us important societal snapshots that led to the telling portrait of the brutal Bobby Kennedy assassination within the context of the United States during the 1960s. The snapshots of the Kennedy campaign workers during the peace movement, Perón's deliberate style of dress (sometimes military, sometimes civilian) during his Argentine rule, and the eighteenth-century American agrarian distaste for military professionalism and a constabulary force all provide pointillistic brushstrokes that create larger portraits of magnificent eras in history. Each of these historical eras encompasses, in its own unique way, a vibrant relationship between the military, the political elites, and the citizenry as we saw while applying concordance theory to the American post-revolutionary period, India, Pakistan, Argentina, and Israel.

In the American post-revolutionary period a partnership existed between the citizens and the political elites, both of whom had fought in the War of Independence. Despite President Washington's preference for a more professional and separate British-inspired military, a preference often based on real national security threats, the citizenry favored the less efficient militia forces that were culturally more similar to the agrarian post-revolutionary era. This partnership between the citizens and many political elites, despite high external threat conditions, prevented domestic military intervention and political disintegration during this early American period.

Culture as well as institutional traditions mattered in India where their post-independence civil–military relations transition became an amalgam of British-inspired government and Indian-inspired multiethnic integration. Domestic military intervention was averted in India because the political elites were very careful to maintain not only a separation between military and civil institutions but a level military recruitment field (both officers and rank and file) among all segments of Indian society. This is contrasted to Pakistan where the generals have ruled for too long at the expense of political institutional development and the recruitment of broad social segments into the Pakistani military. Decades of political insecurity and the alienation of large sectors of Pakistan society have contributed to several incidents of coup.

Argentina, during the first Perón period, appeared to initially achieve partnership among the political elites, the military, and the citizenry; but Juan Perón, in the midst of economic and political challenges, preferred dictatorship over partnership. Perón eventually alienated his initially supportive *descamisados* and many important military figures – the result being the overthrow of Perón and the demise of his regime.

Finally, there is Israel where generals often become prime ministers and occasionally defense ministers at the same time; but the country appears coup-proof. The high external threat conditions result in the vast majority of the country participating in the military, which makes the military a cultural norm rather than a focal point for citizen alienation. This case-study completely debunks separation theory as a method that explains why domestic military intervention or anything approximating *coup d'état* is averted here.

Applied to each of these case studies, concordance theory, with its emphasis on institutional and cultural analysis, explains why domestic military intervention occurred in Pakistan and Argentina and not in early America, India, and Israel. Concordance theory, and not separation theory, is the model that grasps the pulse of a nation by focusing on the four critical concordance indicators: social composition of the officer corps; recruitment method; political decision-making process; and military style. These indicators provide institutional and cultural perspective to a nation and the role of its armed forces, and demonstrate the evolution of partnership, concordance, or discordance, among the military, the political elites, and the citizenry. Separation theory and its rational choice variations remain static 1950s perceptions of what civil–military relations should be in the US and around the world. Whereas concordance theory is in step with the dynamic and ever changing post-Cold War environment filled with multiethnic and multicultural synergies, social evolutions, and national realities.

As I conclude this book, I realize in all the discussion and case studies of foreign nations or situations long-since past, I have reflected the least so far on the military which I am closest to yet farthest from. As a US citizen whose daily contact with the military exists only through television news and radio programs, it seems particularly relevant to conclude with the words of someone who lives with and affects US civil–military relations each day.

I stated in the introduction of this book that the relationship between the military and society is really about people with unique stories who are part of the ongoing civil–military relations drama. The study of civil–military relations should not be isolated from or dwarf the cultural reality that exists in each individual community. It should not ignore the people living and participating in that cultural space. It should expose particular elements of history and individual experience that are often ignored in favor of grand propositions. In this spirit, the following excerpts come from an interview with United States Army First Sergeant Antonio Correa, who also asked United States Army Sergeant First Class Justine M. Beaulieu to sit in on the interview. She was visiting this Massachusetts recruitment office for the day from her post in Maine, and at times supplemented the interview. Together we explored their perception of US civil–military relations, the recruitment process as they experience it in their daily interactions with soldier recruitment, thoughts on civil–military relations, concordance and separation theories as it applies to the US and around the world. It is these dedicated and thoughtful US military personnel who will have the final word in this book, reflecting on the ever-important and unfolding drama of the relationship between military and society.

Question: What is your professional role in the US Army?
Answer: Antonio Correa, First Sergeant, United States Army:
"I am a company First Sergeant for a recruiting company ... a supervisor in civilian terms a manager ... we operate all over Northern Massachusetts, that is our area of operations ... the Commander and I oversee the operations of seven recruiting stations ... along the way we teach, coach, and mentor soldiers ... it's a lot more than recruiting ... there are a lot of things that we do on a daily basis."

Answer: Justine M. Beaulieu, Sergeant First Class, United States Army:
"Basically, I am a company trainer. I am a trainer for the State of Maine as well as I help overlook seven recruiting stations. I go from station to station and help the soldiers there, whether it be administration, computers, helping them learn better techniques to improve the civilian sector, anything that my First Sergeant who runs the company needs help with."

Question: Civil–military relations is an important academic field that often integrates political science and sociology. As US Army personnel what is your understanding of civil–military relations?

Answer: Antonio Correa, First Sergeant, United States Army:

"First of all, we are not commissioned officers ... My commander she is a captain, she is an officer. She handles logistics, personnel. Non-commissioned officers pretty much handle day-to-day operations on the ground. We deal directly with the soldiers, more so than the actual commanders. The caliber of soldier that we have now is incredible. Before we enlist anyone into our ranks they go through a series of tests ... physical tests, aptitude exams ... the caliber of soldier that we are dealing with now ... well it is very competitive to get in ... a lot of folks think well I am going to join the Army ... well that is not the case if you cannot do all of these benchmarks, i.e. pass the armed forces vocation aptitude battery test, be in great physical condition, be able to operate some of the equipment that we have ... you won't make it in. We have less folks now because the technology is there. Many years ago we had an Army that was twice the size of the Army today, but we are steadily decreasing in our numbers basically because technology has taken over ... and that is due to soldiers on the ground being able to maintain this equipment.

"From day one we teach them Army values. A lot of applicants that join the ranks, some have great values, some have different values ... you know we are different cultures, we are brought up differently. In the Army we have one set of values and they are called Army values. It is leadership, duty, loyalty, respect, integrity ... these are things that we live by from day one in basic training. As you develop as a soldier it stays with you. I think this is one of our core competencies. These soldiers are being developed from day one all the way through the ranks. I have been in the army 21 years. I still live and breathe those army values."

Question: Current civil–military relations appears to be a relationship of separation between civil and military institutions and culture. Is this an accurate portrayal of civil–military relations, and does it work effectively in this country?

Answer: Antonio Correa, First Sergeant, United States Army:

"There is definitely a separation of course because you are talking military and you are talking civilian, but there is definitely a common ground in between ... what I mean is a lot of Corporate America is conducting business the same way we are conducting business nowadays. They have a rank structure which of course is everywhere ... they use some of the techniques and tools that we use. Again there is a separation because of the different lifestyles, but overall there is definitely a big common ground there, and as we evolve I think that we are getting close to blending both together. I have been in the service twenty-one years, before it was 'military' and 'civilian,' now it is closer ... maybe it is because we are growing closer because of the war ... things that are happening ... it is all over the news ... maybe more media attention and us being in the spotlight ... I see banners down the street here ... that 'we support our troops.'"

Question: Do you feel that the average US citizen feels disconnected from the armed forces? Whatever the relationship is how is this affecting the quality of the armed forces?

Answer: Antonio Correa, First Sergeant, United States Army:

"I would not say disconnected. I would say there are a lot of people that we touch and they cannot be part of the ranks ... but I think 'disconnected' is a strong word. I talk to parents of young applicants and they tell me that at one time I tried to do this, but I couldn't because of this or that ... but they [the parents] are fully aware of it ... so I would not say disconnected. The media, however, capitalizes on anything. Any little blemish, they will take it to the next level, i.e. we are doing ninety-nine great things but that one time that something pops up or something goes wrong they capitalize on that, so it takes away from the ninety-nine other good things that are happening. We are rebuilding a country, we are building schools in Iraq, we have done a great deal of work there, but then the minute a bullet goes here or something goes wrong, that is in the media, that is what is happening."

Answer: Justine M. Beaulieu, Sergeant First Class, United States Army:

"I agree. In the recruiting command and that is what I have to refer to ... in everyday life, for example First Sergeant Correa and I were on a plane to Virginia and people said thank you for serving, want to shake your hand, want to buy you a cup of coffee etcetera because of recognition of the war. On the other hand, when a soldier dies or gets injured obviously that is all the news and people focus on that a lot more. I think that being in a recruiting command when you are out here and they don't see an army base ... they say 'What is that person doing in that uniform, where are they stationed?' ... the recruiting command is making very good headway to be in the civilian sector so that they can see us more and see how we walk, how we talk, what we do, because typically most people have never been on a military base before and they have no idea what happens on base ... I think we are incorporating ourselves in the civilian sector a lot better actually."

Question: With the recruitment process, what are some of the key issues that you face, positive and negative issues?

Answer: Antonio Correa, First Sergeant, United States Army:

"Positive, we are definitely doing great things. We made our mission last year and we are on track to make our mission this year. The army nationally made its mission, a little over 80,000 and a little over 26,500 for the reserves. Because we recruit for two components: the active army and the army reserves ... we are doing great there ... we are doing good things thus far so we are on track according to our benchmarks to make our final mission in September. I would say that some of the positives things are that we deal with the schools and the community, a lot of support there ... we do have some pockets of resistance ... some schools let's say just don't want to release the list ... but it is not just the Army, they do not want any of the military branches there ... because they feel that it may be taking away from their institution or they feel that their students should go here instead of there ... whatever the case may be that is their prerogative ... but there are pockets of resistance ... but overall just when you see these applicants ... and you do their paperwork and you talk to mom and dad and they come back a couple of months later, they are clean-cut they are a little bit more disciplined they're happy now their life is going into a different direction ... I think that is what keeps us recruiters going. The same feeling I had when I first came through, I see in these kids' eyes. And I have family members in the military, I have two nephews who are enlisted ... again I definitely think that the pros outweigh the cons."

Answer: Justine M. Beaulieu, Sergeant First Class, United States Army:
The younger generation needs a lot of coaxing and someone to guide them and that is what recruiters do ... and mom and dad are begging us to put the kids in sometimes."

Question: What do you know about civil–military relations or the relationship between military and society in other countries?
Answer: Antonio Correa, First Sergeant, United States Army:
"We conduct a lot of operations with different countries. We have special commands like Special Forces Command ... they are the liaisons ... if there is any conflict they deal directly with the community. We also have a Civil Affairs Department that also deals directly with the community. From our perspective in the Recruiting Department it is a little bit different. Again our goal is to find qualified young men and women to fill the ranks – that is what we do. Yes we deal with the community, my commander does ... she talks to the Chamber of Commerce, she talks to the high school principals, and colleges, and makes them aware that we are here, this is what we offer, and if the students need this kind of service, we are here to help them out."

Question: If you wanted the average American citizens to know something about the US Army, what would that be?
Answer: Antonio Correa, First Sergeant, United States Army:
"In general the community is not aware about how we operate or what we are all about. You think Army, you think tanks, you think war – but that is just part of what we do. I've had some people ask me – 'Do you guys get a paycheck? Do you guys get screamed at all the time? Do you guys work 24/7?' There is a lot of misunderstanding. Unless you actually serve then you know that the Army is like a job ... we are just like you are. A firefighter puts on his gear every day to go to work; a policeman puts on his gear ... we put on our gear which is this uniform. It is very similar to the civilian sector. We get a paycheck. We have a rank structure and everything else like every other organization ... but I think that the general public maybe feels that hey you are in the Army ... they own you for life ... you are their property. Believe me, I am nobody's property. A lot of it is stereotyping from way back. It is demanding. It is a tough job. We are on

call. They could call me today to serve my country and I have got to pack up and go and kiss the wife and kids goodbye. But I am aware of that because when I signed, I signed to defend the Constitution of the United States. That is part of our oath of enlistment. So what I would say is that [they] really do not know exactly what the Army is all about. We have cooks, we have mechanics, we are a self-contained organization. Every job in the civilian sector, we have in the Army ... lawyers, doctors ... so it is not just tanks ... it is not just helicopters ... but a lot of folks don't know that ... they think 'What kind of a tank do you drive?' – I have never driven a tank. I think that it is just the lack of knowledge that the community may have in regards to our organization and what we do and what we are able to do from within."

Answer: Justine M. Beaulieu, Sergeant First Class, United States Army:
"The dedication that you have to put in every single day to live the Army values ... that is something that is instilled in you and you carry out ... no questions asked. You don't get out of bed every morning and say 'Oh I am just here to get paid.' You do it for other reasons."

Question: As I mentioned to you before, this book is really about the role of domestic military interventions or the darker side of militaries in specific nations. Countries like Pakistan and Argentina suffered from *coup d'état* or military supplantment or coercion of the civilian government by the military. In your opinion, why has the US never experienced domestic military intervention?

Answer: Antonio Correa, First Sergeant, United States Army:
"I would bring it back to the caliber of the soldier, just basically back to the beginning of time. I was deployed to Haiti when they had an intervention going on. I think my Commander has been to Bosnia. We have been deployed to several areas where there is exactly what you are talking about. My opinion is that it is just the way you have been developed from day one. Our rank structure is something that is very precious to us. What I mean is that I am fortunate that I have made it all the way to this level. Soldiers understand that what I am wearing on my chest is highly respected, because to get here you have got to earn it. So we don't just give away this or give away that. I'm not sure how other countries operate it, if that is the case – today I am a general tomorrow I am the biggest guy here ... maybe that affects it. It is just the caliber of soldier we have or the way we have been developed and trained through the ranks through the years, I think that plays a big role. Plus we are an all-volunteer force. These kids here, we are not twisting their arm, we are not telling them that they gotta do this. This is you coming to us saying I am ready to do this which is the key to the whole question. It is an all-volunteer force. Now we are, in the past it wasn't."

Question: But in the past, even when it wasn't an all-volunteer force there still was no incident of coup or domestic military intervention. Is there

something else at work here that is happening in the US that makes it almost coup-proof?

Answer: Antonio Correa, First Sergeant, United States Army:

"It may be just the culture, the upbringing of the American citizen. You are absolutely correct, in the Vietnam era there was a draft, and folks were told hey you have to go and you have to serve and a lot of folks weren't happy. I have an uncle who came back, and he didn't come back wrapped too tight ... but hey it was just a different army back then ... but again we didn't have any type of coup or any type of issues. I think that if you peel that onion back, I think it is just being American in general. You know we look at history, Benedict Arnold and these names stick out as people that betrayed or did this. Again to me it is just the culture. It is just us being who we are that makes us night and day from the other organizations."

Question: This book offers an alternative perspective and theory of civil–military relations, and it is an alternative to this concept of separation: separation between civilian institutions and culture and military institutions and culture, which prevails in the scholarly world as a model which helps explain why coup or domestic military intervention does not happen here in the US. What I have offered up in this book is concordance theory. The concordance theory is really about agreement or partnership, not about separation. But agreement or partnership between the military, the political elites, and the citizenry over the role and the function of the armed forces. It is a partnership over the role and the function of the armed forces both on institutional and on cultural levels. To be a little bit more specific, the agreement or the partnership, basically what I argue with respect to these five countries is that agreement or partnership should take place among these three actors, the military, the political elites, and the citizenry at large, over four indicators: one is military recruitment method; the second is the social composition of the officer corps; the third is the political decision-making process, the process which goes into defining what the military should be and do; and finally military style, how you look as an institution, this could be the uniforms you wear as opposed to civilian uniforms and generally the military culture. So the argument here is that if there is agreement or concordance among these three actors over these four indicators the likelihood of domestic military intervention or coup happening in any country is less likely to happen. What is your opinion about the model of civil–military relations based on agreement or partnership between the military, the political elites, and the citizenry from an institutional and cultural level? Does this make sense or should we go back to this idea of separation – separate civil and military institutions?

Answer: Antonio Correa, First Sergeant, United States Army:

"No, I will tell you, as you were posing the question, a lot of things came to mind. Right now we have systems in place where believe it or not a lot of our institutions train in the civilian sectors, sniper school, we have people from the law enforcement departments, Homeland Security, so we are integrating a lot more with the civilian sector. Along the same lines, even right now with the recruiting command, we have partnerships with Fortune 500 companies, where we get a young applicant who enlists in the Army, let's just say to be a mechanic, he signs an agreement that after his four years are over he will work with General Motors. So there are partnerships between the civilian sector and the military that kind of give us that melting-pot that you are talking about. So these corporations understand that they are getting a young man who is not only trained on the equipment, is disciplined, is drug-free, is healthy ... again there is a lot more interaction between the civilian sector and the military sector. Now this program called the PAYS program was incorporated a couple of years back ... and we started maybe with a handful of companies and right now it is just taking it to the next level where we have law enforcement departments, general construction equipment, corporations ... just everybody saying 'Hey when are you guys coming out of the service, so we can hire them to work for our company?' So I think that correlates directly to what you were asking – how we are blending along the same line. Another thing we are doing is ... you know the soldiers are precious. We are in a time of war ... that is obvious. So we need troops on the ground to deploy ... we have a huge civilian force that support the military, i.e. DOD [Department of Defense] civilians. These DOD civilians are folks that have served in the past, or might not have served in the past, and they directly do some of the same jobs that the soldiers are doing, but we can't deploy civilians of course ... they are doing it locally here within the States ... that way we can free up the soldiers to deploy in theater and take care of what we have to do over there. And that program if you would like you go on the Internet and go onto our website which is www.goarmy.com. I'll give you my business card, I believe it is at the bottom. Great partnerships between the civilian industry and the military. I'm not sure if the other branches have this, I think the US Army is the only branch right now offering the PAYS program – but it has been a breakthrough ever since it has been developed, and it is great now. You have a young man who has served his country for four years, he is getting out and guess what, he has a good job lined up for him, so it is no longer the time when that man gets out and he has to look around or he is unemployed. No you served your country, you are skilled, you are trained, now we are going to help you out to do bigger and better things. It's a big plus."

Answer: Justine M. Beaulieu, Sergeant First Class, United States Army:
"Especially to the civilian sector. Everybody has a piece of the pie, each of these factors must understand each other in order to function in our culture. Each entity of the four concordance indicators must contribute a certain influence to systematically function so that we may produce an impressionable character to avoid intervention of any sort."

References

Allen, C. (1977) *Raj: A Scrapbook of British India 1877–1947*, New York: St. Martin's Press.

Anderson, J. (1998) *Civil–Military Relations and Concordance Theory: A Case Study of Argentina*, Monterey, CA: Naval Postgraduate School.

Asian Development Bank (2001) "India GDP growth to slow to 5.6% in 2001." Online, available at: www.adb.org/Documents/News/2001/nr2001152.asp (accessed November 9, 2001).

—— (2007) "ADB upgrades developing Asia's 2007 growth forecast to 8.3%." Online, available at: www.adb.org/Media/Articles/2007/12156-asian-developments-outlooks/default.asp (accessed November 17, 2007).

Azarya, V. and Kimmerling, B. (1985–6) "Cognitive permeability of civil–military boundaries: draftee expectations from military service in Israel," *Studies in Comparative International Development*, 20: 42–63.

Bacevich, A.J. (2005) *The New American Militarism*, Oxford: Oxford University Press.

Bailyn, B. (1967) *The Ideological Origins of the American Revolution*, Cambridge, MA: The Belknap Press of Harvard University Press.

Barak, O. and Scheffer, G. (2006) "Israel's 'Security Network' and its impact: an exploration of a new approach," *International Journal of Middle Eastern Studies*, 38: 235–61.

Barua, P.P. (1992) "Ethnic conflict in the military of developing nations: a comparative analysis of India and Nigeria," *Armed Forces and Society*, 19: 123–37.

BBC (British Broadcasting Corporation) (2007) "Bush talks on India nuclear deal," *BBC News*, May 8, 2007. Online, available at: http://news.bbc.co.uk/2/hi/south_asia/6633733.stm

Beach, E.L. (1986) *The United States Navy*, Boston: Houghton Mifflin Company.

Belasco, J.A. and Stayer, R.C. (1993) *Flight of the Buffalo*, New York: Warner Books.

Benedict, R. (1934) *Patterns of Culture*, Boston: Houghton Mifflin Company.

Ben-Meir, Y. (1986) *National Security Decision-Making: The Israeli Case*, Tel Aviv: The Jaffee Center for Strategic Studies.

Berghahn, V. (1982) *Militarism*, New York: St. Martin's Press.

Betts, R. (1991) *Soldiers, Statesmen, and the Cold War Crisis*, New York: Columbia University Press.

Bland, D.L. (1999) "A unified theory of civil–military relations," *Armed Forces and Society*, 26: 7–26.

—— (2000) "Who decides what? Civil–military relations in Canada and the United States," *Canadian-American Public Policy*, 41: 1–22.

Cannadine, D. (2002) *Ornamentalism: How the British Saw Their Empire*, Oxford: Oxford University Press.

Central Bureau of Statistics (1989) *Statistical Abstract of Israel*, Israel: Central Bureau of Statistics.

Chambers, J.W. II (ed.) (1999) *American Military History*, Oxford: Oxford University Press.

Citigroup Inc. (2007) "Citi Foundation and *Financial Times* announce launch of Microentrepreneurship Awareness Campaign," press release, April 18, 2007.

Clausewitz, C. von (1950) *On War*, trans. O.J. Matthijs Jolles, Washington, DC: Infantry Journal Press.

The Coca–Cola Company (2007) "Economic impact." Online, available at: www.thecoca-colacompany.com/citizenship/economic_impact.html (accessed January 7, 2008).

Cohen, E.A. (2002) *Supreme Command: Soldiers, Statesmen, and Leadership in Wartime*, New York: Anchor Books.

Cohen, S.P. (1971) *The Indian Army*, Berkeley, CA: University of California Press.

—— (1984) *The Pakistan Army*, Berkeley, CA: University of California Press.

—— (1992) "The military in India and Pakistan: contrasting cases," paper presented at South Asia–Middle East Seminar, University of Chicago, February 1992.

—— (2001) *India: Emerging Power*, Washington, DC: Brookings Institution Press.

—— (2002) *The Indian Army*, Oxford: Oxford University Press.

—— (2004) *The Idea of Pakistan*, Washington, DC: Brookings Institution Press.

Cohn, B.S. (1989) "Cloth, clothes and colonialism," in A.B. Weiner and J. Schneider (eds) *Cloth and Human Experience*, Washington, DC: Smithsonian Institution Press.

Copeland, P.F. (1976) *American Military Uniforms*, New York: Dover Publications, Inc.

Covey, S. (1992) *Principled Centered Leadership*, New York: Simon and Schuster Fireside.

Dawson, W.H. (1894) *Germany and the Germans*, vol. 2, London: Chapman and Hall.

Desch, M. (1999) *Civilian Control of The Military*, Baltimore: The Johns Hopkins University Press.

The Economist (2007a) "Showdown at the mosque," *The Economist*, July 14–20, 2007.

—— (2007b) "Musharraf's messy victory," *The Economist*, October 6, 2007.

—— (2007c) "Lest old acquaintance be forgot," *The Economist*, December 1, 2007.

Eisenhower, D.D. (1961) *Farewell Address to the Nation*, Washington, DC, January 17, 1961.

Eisenstadt, S.N. (1985) *The Transformation of Israeli Society*, Boulder, CO: Westview Press.

Elia, T. de and Queiroz, J.P. (1997) *Evita: An Intimate Portrait of Eva Perón*, New York: Rizzoli International.

Elkins, S. and McKitrick, E. (1995) *The Age of Federalism: The Early American Republic, 1788–1800*, New York: Oxford University Press.

Elon, A. (1972) *The Israelis: Founders and Sons*, London: Sphere Books.

Faber, D. and Faber, H. (1989) *The Birth of a Nation*, New York: Charles Scribner's Sons.

Farcau, D.W. (1994) *The Coup: Tactics in the Seizure of Power*, Westport, CT: Praeger.

Farwell, B. (1991) *Armies of the Raj: From the Great Indian Mutiny to Independence 1858–1947*, New York: W.W. Norton & Company.

Feaver, P. (2003) *Armed Servants*, Cambridge, MA: Harvard University Press.

Feit, E. (1973) *The Armed Bureaucrats*, Boston: Houghton Mifflin.

Finer, S. (1975) "State and nation-building in Europe: the role of the military," in C. Tilly (ed.) *The Formation of National States in Western Europe*, Princeton, NJ: Princeton University Press.

—— (1988) *The Man on Horseback*, 2nd edn, Boulder, CO: Westview Press.

Ford Foundation (2006) *Annual Report*, New York: Ford Foundation.

Francis, M.J. (1977) *The Limits of Hegemony: United States Relations With Argentina and Chile During World War II*, Notre Dame, IN: University of Notre Dame Press.

Fraser, N. and Navarro, M. (1980) *Evita: The Real Life of Eva Perón*, New York: W.W. Norton & Company.

Frederick, W. (2006) *Corporation Be Good! The Story of Corporate Social Responsibility*, Indianapolis: Dogdear Publishing.

Friedman, T.L. (2005) *The World Is Flat: A Brief History of the Twenty-First Century*, New York: Farrar, Straus and Giroux.

Gal, R. (1986) *A Portrait of the Israeli Soldier*, New York: Greenwood Press.

Gall, C. (2007) "US official in Pakistan for talks," *International Herald Tribune*. Online, available at: www.iht.com/articles/2007/09/13/asia/13pakistan.php (accessed September 12, 2007).

Ganguly, S. (1991) "From the defense of nation to aid to the civil: the army in contemporary India," *Journal of Asian and African Studies*, 26: 11–26.

Gaudiani, C. (2004) *The Greater Good: How Philanthropy Drives the American Economy and Can Save Capitalism*, New York: Henry Holt and Company.

Geertz, C. (1983) *Local Knowledge: Further Essays in Interpretive Anthropology*, New York: Basic Books.

GlobalSecurity.org. (2007) "Israel–Army." Online, available at: www.globalsecurity.org/military/world/Israel/army.htm.

Green, D. and Shapiro, I. (1994) *Pathologies of Rational Choice Theory: A Critique of Applications in Political Science*, New Haven, CT: Yale University Press.

Greenstone, J.D. (1984) "Pluralism, hegemony, and dissensus in American political culture: Lincoln on liberty and union," unpublished manuscript, Department of Political Science, University of Chicago.

Hammer, M. and Champy, J. (1994) *Reengineering the Corporation*, New York: Harper Business.

Haqqani, H. (2005) *Pakistan: Between Mosque and Military*, Washington, DC: Carnegie Endowment for International Peace.

Harkabi, R. and Neuman, S. (1984) "Israel," in J.E. Katz (ed.) *Armed Production in Developing Countries: An Analysis of Decision-Making*, Lanham, MD: Lexington Books.

Hitchens, C. (2004) "To the shores of Tripoli," *Time*, July 5, 2004.

Horowitz, D. (1977) "Is Israel a garrison state?" *Jerusalem Quarterly*, 4: 58–65.

—— (1982) "The Israeli defense forces: a civilianized military in a partially militarized society," in R. Kolkowicz and A. Korbonski (eds) *Soldiers, Peasants and Bureaucrats*, London: G. Allen.

—— (1983) "Israel's war in Lebanon: new patterns of strategic thinking and civilian–military relations," *Journal of Strategic Studies*, 6: 83–102.

Horowitz, D. and Lissak, M. (1989a) "Democracy and national security in a protracted conflict," *Jerusalem Quarterly*, 51: 3–40.

—— (1989b) *Trouble in Utopia*, Albany, NY: State University of New York Press.

Huntington, S.P. (1957) *Soldier and the State*, Cambridge, MA: Harvard University Press.

—— (1968) *Political Order in Changing Societies*, New Haven, CT: Yale University Press.

Jacob, J. (1857) *Tracts on the Native Army of India: Its Organization and Discipline*, London: Smith Elder.

Janowitz, M. (1960) *The Professional Soldier, a Social and Political Portrait*, Glencoe: The Free Press.

—— (1964) *The Military in the Political Development of New Nations*, Chicago: University of Chicago Press.

Kamdar, M. (2007) *Planet India*, New York: Scribner.

Kanter, R.M. (2004) *Confidence*, New York: Crown Business.

Kaplan, F. (2005) "All pain, no gain: Nobel laureate Thomas Schelling's little-known role in the Vietnam War," *Slate*, October 11, 2005.

Kennedy, P. (1987) *The Rise and Fall of Great Powers*, New York: Random House.

Khalidi, O. (2001) "Ethnic group recruitment in the Indian army: the contrasting cases of Sikhs, Muslims, Gurkhas and others," *Pacific Affairs*, 74: 529–52.

Kimmerling, B. (1983) "Making conflict routine: cumulative effects of the Arab–Jewish conflict upon Israeli society," *Journal of Strategic Studies*, 6: 13–45.

Kipp, J., Grau, L., Prinslow, K., and Smith, D. (2006) "The human terrain system: ACORDS for the 21st century," *Military Review*, September–October: 8–15.

Knotel, R., Knotel, H., and Sieg, H. (1980) *Uniforms of the World*, New York: Exeter Books.

Kodikara, S.U. (1993) "Bangladesh," in S.U. Kodikara (ed.) *External Compulsions of South Asian Politics*, New Delhi: Sage.

Kohli, A. (1990) "State–society relations in India's changing democracy," in A. Kohli (ed.) *India's Democracy*, Princeton, NJ: Princeton University Press.

Kolko, G. (1985) *Anatomy of a War*, New York: Pantheon Books.

Labott, E. (2007) "US, India reach deal on nuclear technology." Online, available at: www.cnn.com/2007/WORLD/asiapcf/07/27/us.india.nuclear/index.html?iref=newssearch (accessed July 27, 2007).

Larkin, J. (1989) *The Reshaping of Everyday Life 1790–1840*, New York: Harper Perennial.

Lasswell, H. (1952) "The threat to privacy," in R.M. MacIver (ed.) *Conflict of Loyalties*, New York: Institute for Religious and Social Studies.

—— (1954) "The world revolutionary situation," in C. Friedrich (ed.) *Totalitarianism*, Cambridge, MA: Harvard University Press.

—— (1962) "The garrison state hypothesis today," in S. Huntington (ed.) *Changing Patterns of Military Politics*, New York: The Free Press of Glencoe.

Lebow, R.N. (2006) "Reason divorced from reality: Thomas Schelling and strategic bargaining," *International Politics*, 43: 429–52.

Lewis, D.K. (2003) *The History of Argentina*, New York: Palgrave Macmillan.

Lewis, P.H. (1990) *The Crisis of Argentine Capitalism*, Chapel Hill, NC: University of North Carolina Press.

—— (2006) *Authoritarian Regimes in Latin America: Dictators, Despots and Tyrants*, Lanham, MD: Rowman & Littlefield Publishers.

Lipset, S.M. (1981) *Political Man*, Baltimore: Johns Hopkins University Press.

Llanos, M. (2002) *Privatization and Democracy in Argentina: An Analysis of President–Congress Relations*, New York: Palgrave.

Long, G. (1998) *Macarthur as Military Commander*, Conshohocken, PA: Combined Publishing.

Lowe, C. (2007) "Army taking dragon skin case to Hill." Online, available at: www.military.com/NewsContent/0,13319,136557,00.html (accessed May 22, 2007).

Luttwak, E. (1979) *Coup d'état*, Cambridge, MA: Harvard University Press.

Luxemburg, R. (2003) *The Accumulations of Capital*, London: Routledge.

MacDonald, C.A. (1990) "The Braden campaign and Anglo-American relations," in G. di Tella and C. Watt (eds) *Argentina Between the Great Powers 1939–46*, Pittsburgh: University of Pittsburgh Press.

McDonald, F. (1974) *The Presidency of George Washington*, Lawrence, KS: University of Kansas Press.

McNamara, R.S. (1995) *In Retrospect: The Tragedy and Lessons of Vietnam*, New York: Times Books.

Madgoff, H. (1970) "Militarism and imperialism," *American Economic Review*, 60: 337–42.

Madison, J., Hamilton, A., and Jay, J. (1961) *The Federalist Papers*, New York: New American Library.

Mares, D.R. (1988) "Middle powers under regional hegemony: to challenge or acquiesce in hegemonic enforcement," *International Studies Quarterly*, 32: 453–71.

Miller, D. W. (2001) "Storming the palace in political science," *Chronicle of Higher Education*, September 21, 2001.

Millet, A.R. and Maslowski, P. (1984) *For the Common Defense: A Military History of the United States of America*, New York: Free Press.

Mills, C.W. (1969) *The Power Elite*, New York: Oxford University Press.

Mintz, A. (1984) "The military industrial complex: the Israeli Case," in M. Lissak (ed.) *Israeli Society and its Defence Establishment*, London: Routledge.

—— (1985) "Military–industrial linkages in Israel," *Armed Forces and Society*, 12: 9–27.

Mizlas, E., Gal, R., and Peshof, E. (1989) "World outlook and attitudes of high school students with regard to the military and defense," *Zicharon Ya'acov*, Israeli Institute For Military Studies (Hebrew).

Mokkarawut, S. (2007) "Prime time protest," *Asia Media News Daily*, June 17, 2007.

Monroe, K.R. (ed.) (2005) *Perestroika!: The Raucous Rebellion in Political Science*, New Haven, CT: Yale University Press.

Moran, M. and Goodlander, M. (2007) "Musharraf and his labyrinth," *Council on Foreign Relations, Daily Analysis*, July 19, 2007.

Morgenthau, H.J. (1973) *Politics Among Nations*, New York: Alfred A. Knopf, Inc.

Moskos, C. (2007) Interview with National Public Radio's *Morning Edition*, July 10, 2007.

Musselman, F.K. (1980) *The Federal Period*, Encino, CA: Glencoe Publishing Co.

Nathanson, R. (1989) "Israel, the arms race and international competition," *Israel Defense Force*, 18: 3–7.

National Association for the Practice of Anthropology (2007) "Job posting for social scientist (cultural anthropologist)." Online, available at: www.practicinganthropology.org/employment/?jobid=1270&action=view (accessed November 7, 2007).

Nordlinger, E. (1970) "Soldiers in mufti: the impact of military rule on economic and social change in non-Western states," *American Political Science Review*, 66: 1131–48.

Omissi, D. (1991) "Martial races: ethnicity and security in colonial India, 1858–1939," *War and Society*, 9: 1–27.

Otley, C.B. (1968) "Militarism and the social affiliations of the British army elite," in J. van Doorn (ed.) *Armed Forces and Society*, The Hague: Mouton.

Pan, E. (2006) "The US–India Nuclear Deal," *Council on Foreign Relations Backgrounder*. Online, available at: www.cfr.org/publication/9663/ (accessed January 26, 2006).

Pauker, G. (1959) "South East Asia as a problem area in the next decade," *World Politics*, 11: 325–45.

Peri, Y. (1983) *Between Battles and Ballots, Israeli Military in Politics*, Cambridge: Cambridge University Press.

—— (2006) "Generals in the cabinet room: how the military shapes Israel's policy," paper presented at the Van Leer Institute Conference: An Army that Has a State?, Jerusalem, Israel, June 5–6, 2006.

Perlmutter, Amos (1970) *Anatomy of Political Institutionalization: The Case of Israel and Some Comparative Analysis*, Cambridge, MA: Harvard University Press.

Peters, T.J. and Waterman, R.H. (1984) *In Search of Excellence: Lessons from America's Best Run Companies*, New York: Warner Books.

Pion-Berlin, D. (1997) *Through the Corridors of Power: Institutions and Civil–Military Relations in Argentina*, University Park, PA: Pennsylvania State University Press.

Potash, R.A. (1980) *The Army and Politics in Argentina 1945–1962*, Palo Alto, CA: Stanford University Press.

Pye, L. (1968) "Armies in the process of political modernization," in J.J. Johnson (ed.) *The Role of the Military in Underdeveloped Countries*, Princeton, NJ: Princeton University Press.

al-Qazzaz, A. (1973) "Army and society in Israel," *Pacific Sociological Review*, 16: 143–65.

Raphael, R. (2001) *A People's History of the American Revolution*, New York: New York Press.

Rock, D. (1987) *Argentina 1515–1987*, Berkeley, CA: University of California Press.

Roland, A. (2001) *The Military Industrial Complex*, Washington, DC: American Historical Society.

Rudolph, L.I. and Rudolph, S.H. (1972) *The Modernity of Tradition: Political Development in India*, Chicago: University of Chicago Press.

—— (1987) *In Pursuit of Lakshmi: The Political Economy of the Indian State*, Chicago: University of Chicago Press.

—— (2007) Conversation with Lloyd and Susanne Rudolph, Barnard, VT, June 17, 2007.

Ryan, A. (1970) *The Philosophy of the Social Sciences*, New York: Pantheon Books.

Sarkesian, S., Williams, J.A., and Cimbala, S. (2002) *US National Security: Policy Makers, Processes, and Politics*, Boulder, CO: Lynne Reinner.

Schervish, P.G., Hodgkinson, V.A., and Margaret Gates and Associates. (1995) *Care and Community in Modern Society*, San Francisco: Jossey–Bass.

Schiff, R.L. (1992) "Civil–military relations reconsidered: Israel as an 'uncivil' state," *Security Studies*, 1: 636–58.

—— (1995) "Civil–military relations reconsidered: a theory of concordance," *Armed Forces and Society*, 22: 7–24.

—— (1996) "Concordance theory: a response to recent criticism," *Armed Forces and Society*, 23: 277–83.

—— (1997) "The concordance approach to team-building," paper presented at American Society for Quality Annual Quality Congress, Orlando, FL, May 1997.

—— (1998) "Concordance theory: the cases of India and Pakistan," in D. Mares (ed.) *Civil–Military Relations*, Boulder, CO: Westview Press.

—— (2006) "Civil–military relations in Israel: revisiting Israel as the 'uncivil' state," paper presented at the Van Leer Institute Conference: An Army That Has a State?, Jerusalem, Israel, June 5–6, 2006.

Schiff, Z. (1985) *History of the Israeli Military*, New York: Macmillan.

Shagmar-Handelman, L. and Handelman, D. (1989) "Holiday celebrations in Israeli kindergartens: relationships between representations of collectivity and family in the nation-state," in M. Arnoff (ed.) *The Frailty of Authority*, New Brunswick, NJ: Transaction Books.

Shanker, T. and Cloud, D.S. (2007) "US generals seek patience in judging Iraq," *New York Times*, July 20, 2007.

Shils, E. (1962) "The military in the political development of new states," in J.J. Johnson (ed.) *The Role of the Military in Underdeveloped Countries*, Princeton, NJ: Princeton University Press.

Siddiqa, A. (2007) *Military Inc.: Inside Pakistan's Military Economy*, London: Pluto Press.

Skelton, W.B. (1992) *An American Profession of Arms: The Army Officer Corps, 1784–1861*, Lawrence, KS: University Press of Kansas.

Slaughter, T.P. (1986) *The Whiskey Rebellion*, New York: Oxford University Press.

Smooha, S. (1983–4) "Ethnicity and the military in Israel: theses for discussion and research," *State, Government, and International Relations*, 22: 5–32 (Hebrew).

SIPRI (Stockholm International Peace Research Institute) (1991) *Yearbook 1991*, Oxford: Oxford University Press.

—— (2006) *Yearbook 2006: Armaments, Disarmaments and International Security*, London: Oxford University Press.

Stuart, S.A. (2003) "The revolution from within," *University of Chicago Magazine.* Online, available at: http://magazine.uchicago.edu/0306/features/index.shtml (accessed June 2003).

Sun Tzu (2005) *The Art of War*, Boston: Shambhala.

Tocqueville, A. de (1901) *Democracy in America*, vol. 2, trans. H. Reeve, New York: D. Appleton and Company.

Urwin, G.J.W. (2000) *The United States Infantry 1775–1918*, Norman, OK: University of Oklahoma Press.

Vagts, A. (1959) *A History of Militarism*, New York: Meridian Books.

Weigley, R.F. (1973) *The American Way of War*, New York: Macmillan.

Welch, C.E. (1992) "Military disengagement from politics: paradigms, processes, or random events," *Armed Forces and Society*, 18: 337–8.

Wells, R.S. (1996) "The theory of concordance in civil/military relations: a commentary," *Armed Forces and Society*, 23: 269–75.

Williams, J.A. (1995) "The international image of the military professional," *African Security Review*, 4: 24–7.

Williams, R. (2007) "Military, civilians follow different callings," American Forces Press Service, US Department of Defense, November 25, 2007.

Wright, R.K. (1983) *The Continental Army*, Washington, DC: Center of Military History United States Army.

Index

62–3, 153; economic conditions 52–3; external/internal threat conditions 3, 51–5, 60, 63, 153; Federalists vs Republicans 51, 56–8; military style 50, 54–5, 60–2, 68–9; militia system 15, 50–1, 54–61, 62, 68–9; modernity of tradition 68–9; nation building 49; political decision-making process 57–59, 62; recruitment method 59–60, 62; social composition of the officer corps 55–7, 62; *see also* Jay Treaty; militaries: British model
University of Chicago 8, 9, 10, 15, 16; *see also* Chicago theoretical approach

Vietnam War 4, 18, 23–4, 34–5, 134–5, 159

war *see* military conflicts
War on Terror 5, 18
Washington, George 3, 38, 50, 51, 53–5, 56, 57, 58, 59, 61, 62, 68, 113, 153
Western citizens: military realities 5, 18–19, 34–5, 151, 152, 154–60; views on nation building 49
Westerners *see* Western citizens
Whiskey Rebellion 51, 53–5, 56, 57–8, 61–2, 69
World War II 4–5, 20, 28, 29, 38, 93, 147

Yom Kippur War 114

Zia-ul-Haq, Muhammad 84